The Contexts
of Juvenile Justice
Decision Making

The Contexts
of Juvenile Justice Decision Making

When Race Matters

Michael J. Leiber

State University of New York Press

Published by
State University of New York Press, Albany

For information, address State University of New York Press,
90 State Street, Suite 700, Albany, NY 12207

Production by Michael Haggett
Marketing by Jennifer Giovani

Library of Congress Cataloging-in-Publication Data

Leiber, Michael J.
    The contexts of juvenile justice decision making : when race matters /
Michael J. Leiber.
        p. cm.
    Includes bibliographical references and index.
    ISBN 0-7914-5767-2 (alk. paper)—ISBN 0-7914-5768-0 (pbk. : alk.
paper)
        1. Juvenile justice, Administration of—Iowa.   2. Discrimination in
juvenile justice administration—Iowa.   3. Discrimination in criminal
justice administration—Iowa.   4. Juvenile delinquents—Iowa.
5. Minority youth—Iowa.   6. Prison sentences—Iowa.   7. Juvenile
corrections—Iowa.   I. Title.

HV9105.I8L45 2003
364.36'089'009777—dc22
                                                                2003057272

10 9 8 7 6 5 4 3 2 1

Contents

Foreword

The Contexts of Juvenile Justice Decision Making: When Race Matters by Dr. Michael J. Leiber is a welcome addition to the discourse regarding the impact of race on juvenile justice processing. One of the more pressing issues within both the adult and juvenile justice systems is the extent to which race influences processing decisions, thus differentially impacting minorities, principally those of color. Simply put, the question is, Are minorities more at risk than their white counterparts and thus disadvantaged within the justice system? More than four decades of research has attempted to address this question with mixed results. Some research finds evidence of race/ethnic bias while other research does not. Thus, the central question is, When does race and/or ethnic status make a difference? This book addresses this question in a most thorough and concise manner.

I have been involved in research focusing on race and adult and juvenile processing for almost three decades. For the past fifteen years my research agenda has tended to focus on race/ethnicity and the juvenile justice system and I am quite familiar with almost all of the research in this area, particularly Leiber's prior work on race and juvenile processing that has always been theoretical, reasoned, and analytically sound. This book focuses on the implementation of the federal initiative dealing with Disproportionate Minority Confinement (DMC) in the state of Iowa. I was fortunate to be part of a technical assistance team that dealt with DMC in the five pilot states (discussed in this text) which included Iowa. Therefore, I have more than a passing familiarity with the four county analysis and policy initiatives of the Iowa DMC project as well as with Leiber's involvement with this project.

In my opinion, *The Contexts of Juvenile Justice Decision Making* represents an important contribution to the field of juvenile justice and reflects groundbreaking work. The book should be of interest to students, researchers, and practitioners alike. Chapter 1 presents a very clear discussion of the history and focus of the federal DMC initiative that also provides a frame of reference for the remainder of the book. This is followed by an excellent discussion of the research focus of DMC and an elaboration of various theoretical orientations toward understanding DMC (e.g., consensus, labeling, and conflict theory).

Leiber concludes that a contextual approach (which I agree with) is the most appropriate technique for understanding race and juvenile justice decision making, thus providing the foundation for the analysis to follow.

Without going into detail let me make a few statements regarding what I think are some of the other major strengths of this book. One major strength is that the author utilizes both a quantitative and qualitative approach in understanding the context of race and decision making in Iowa. Quantitative analysis of DMC processing data most often relies on logistic regression. Leiber's use of multivariate techniques and logistic regression is most appropriate, very straightforward, and relatively easy to comprehend even for those not well versed in these techniques. The results of the analyses support the conclusions drawn in the book as well as the stated policy implications.

The qualitative component involves semistructured interviews with juvenile court personnel in the four counties. At the outset, the technical assistance team strongly recommended a qualitative application for DMC research in the five pilot states. Leiber obviously followed this recommendation. Qualitative approaches, such as the use of interviews and observations, often provide rich and valuable information that may inform data analysis. Such is the case in this book. The commentary provided by juvenile justice respondents provide meaningful insights that aid the reader in understanding how they view the operation of the system and, moreover, the rationale behind decision making. More specifically, the qualitative data illustrate how views regarding delinquency, the family, and cooperation with the proceedings are often tied to racial stereotyping and fostered by historical, structural, and organizational factors associated with the community and the juvenile court. These contexts, individually and sometimes in combination, influence decision making and have implications for the treatment of youth, especially nonwhites.

Another strength of the book is the analysis of Iowa's juvenile justice system as a series of interrelated processing stages at which decisions are made regarding youthful offenders. This provides a systemic view of the system and is not limited, as in some prior research, to discreet decision points. The analysis follows youth through (1) release/adjustment versus further court processing, (2) release versus adjustment/further court processing, (3) petition, (4) initial appearance, and (5) adjudication, and judicial disposition. The first two decision points separate out variations of the release decision and possible diversion and further processing thus giving a more accurate picture of what actually happens to youth at that stage of the proceedings. This approach provides one with a comprehensive picture of juvenile processing within the four Iowa counties.

Rather than aggregating juvenile justice decision making across the entire state or limiting the analysis to one specific county, Leiber examines juvenile justice processing in four counties with some common and discreet characteristics. Juvenile justice is not a monolithic entity in that there are variations across jurisdictions and localities. Simply put, what happens in one jurisdiction may not be the same as what happens in another. Thus, it is important to examine juvenile justice processing in more than one locality. The author accomplishes this by analyzing DMC effects across four Iowa counties. The variations noted are important in that DMC and juvenile processing not only varies by decision point but also by county. The analysis undertaken in this book not only underscores the importance of race and contexts but legal characteristics such as prior referrals, number of current charges, and crime severity. While legal factors were found to explain decision-making outcomes, past contentions are confirmed that such factors may be racially tainted (i.e., prior record) and raise questions concerning the extent they should produce the differences in outcomes they produce for nonwhites relative to whites.

In sum, the book is an excellent example of DMC research. It will serve as a valuable text and reference guide for those interested in the question of how race manifests itself in juvenile justice decision making, under what conditions, and its implications.

Carl E. Pope
University of Wisconsin, Milwaukee

Preface

In the last thirty-five years or so, there has been a tremendous amount of inquiry into the relationship between race and social control. Much of this activity has been spurred on by minority overrepresentation in the front end of the juvenile and criminal justice systems in terms of arrests and in the back end in terms of the placement of both juveniles and adults in secure facilities. For example, on an average day one out of three African American men age 20 to 29 will either be in jail or prison or on probation or parole. Furthermore, over 75 percent of African-American males will be arrested and confined at least once before they reach the age of 36 (Mauer, 1995; Sentencing Project, 2000). Theoretical, methodological, and empirical advances in the academic arena also have contributed to the increased attention paid to the study of the influence of race on case processing and outcomes. Finally, the 1988 reauthorization of the Juvenile Justice and Delinquency Prevention (JJDP) Act of 1974 and the act's Disproportionate Minority Confinement (DMC) amendment stimulated additional research, including the present study.

Beginning with fiscal year 1994 funds, states participating in the Federal Formula Grants Program were to develop a comprehensive strategy to address DMC that included the identification of the existence and extent of overrepresentation, an examination of the causes of DMC, the implementation of solutions to reduce it, and a monitoring component. As of December 2000, all but Wyoming and South Dakota participated in the Formula Grants Program.

In 1991, the Office of Juvenile Justice and Delinquency Prevention (OJJDP) issued a Request for Proposals seeking the participation of states that would analyze disproportionate minority confinement and develop model programs to address its causes. OJJDP awarded funding to five pilot states, one of which was Iowa. The strategies undertaken by these five pilot states were to be used by OJJDP to move the DMC initiative beyond rhetoric into workable courses of action that could guide other states addressing minority youth confinement.

The objective of this book is to provide a detailed examination of the contextual nature of decision making and the causes of DMC in four relatively homogenous juvenile courts in Iowa. In the early 1990s, minority youth and adults were overrepresented in both the juvenile and adult systems in Iowa and still are today (Division of Criminal and Juvenile Justice Planning and Statistical Analysis, 2000). For example, at least 1 in 12 African American Iowans is in prison, on parole, or on probation, while the similar ratio for whites is 1 in 110. The incarceration rate for African Americans in Iowa tops the national average (Des Moines Register, 2000).

The present study attempts to overcome limitations of previous research on race and juvenile and criminal justice decision making by more thoroughly assessing the subjective social psychological processes of juvenile court officers and the contexts that shape those processes and give them meaning. While the foregoing discusses historical (e.g., segregation and migration); cultural (e.g., prejudice and religion), and structural (e.g., community race composition and urbanism) contingencies of decision making, greater emphasis is given to the mediating social psychological processes involved at the organizational level, the individual level, and the interplay between the two.

The focus of the inquiry is on the relationships between adherence to correctional orientations (e.g., retribution and rehabilitation) and decision makers' views concerning race, crime, family, and respect for authority with decision making and differential outcomes for youth. These relationships are examined by the use of quantitative and qualitative methodologies. The use of both of these analytic strategies allows for a direct test and closer inspection of decision makers' perceived role(s) of the court for dealing with juvenile delinquency and racial stereotypes of minorities. The study assesses how these perceptions may interact with a wide range of historical, cultural, community, and court characteristics; impact the case processing and outcomes of whites, African Americans, and Native Americans; and vary by jurisdiction. The contextual framework represents a refinement conceptually and in application.

The findings reveal that two jurisdictions scoring highest on economic and racial inequality exert the greatest amount of social control over minority youth and youth generally. African American youth, however, are still subjected to relatively greater social control in the other two jurisdictions. In fact, the racial gap—the difference in the amount of social control exercised over minority versus nonminority youth—is greater in these two jurisdictions than in the jurisdiction evidencing structural and racial disadvantage. In all four jurisdictions, legal and extralegal factors alone do not account for these differences.

The results also indicate that decision making by court personnel in each jurisdiction is tied to legally justifiable criteria and to a complex set of relationships that exist between beliefs about the purpose of corrections, racial stereotyping, and overt bias that are fostered at times by historical, cultural, structural, and organizational contingencies. For example, the court ideology of one jurisdiction revolves around offender accountability, intervention in the lives of offenders, and rehabilitation that accounts, in part, for the willingness to exercise social control. The source of this ideology appears to be the court's history; a certain influential judge's view of juvenile justice; beliefs among decision makers concerning single-parent families; and particular community characteristics, including relatively high rates of poverty, racial inequality, babies born to unwed teens, and crime rates, as well as a strong African American presence. African American youth are seen as more likely to come from single-parent homes and to adhere to subcultural values that include favorable definitions of delinquency and are passed on from one generation to the next and hence are subject to greater social control than whites.

Conversely, the correctional orientations of the juvenile court in another jurisdiction emphasizes *parens patriae* and the "protection of society"; it also tries to divert young offenders from formal court involvement. This court's ideology is also driven by history and by a strong commitment to middle-class values. With increased minority immigration into the community and increased concern over a "moral decline" in society, the abidance to middle-class standards appear to have taken on greater importance. Generally, decision makers believe that minorities are in greater need of rehabilitation, since they are allegedly more likely to be involved in gangs, commit crime, listen to rap music, and dress and act "inappropriately." Decision making in this jurisdiction is also guided by an organizational policy that diverts young Native American offenders to an outside agency that deals specifically with this minority group. Underlying the policy is the belief that Native Americans can be best handled by "their own kind." Similar types of processes influence decision making in the remaining two jurisdictions.

The overall findings lend support for the use and continued development of contextual frameworks to understand juvenile justice decision making. Broad conceptualizations of the social contexts involved, including the social psychological processes operating at the individual level can provide greater insight into the complexities of the relationships between race and decision making. A fruitful line of inquiry in this area would be the further exploration into how the need to intervene into the life of youth and in particular, African American youth, is socially constructed by decision makers and fueled by stereotyping and concerns of morality, accountability, rehabilitation, and safety (e.g., Bridges and Steen, 1998). The use of both quantitative and qualitative strategies can also open doors into how these processes may or may not be associated with historical, cultural, structural, and organizational contingencies; impact the case processing of youth; and vary by minority group, juvenile court processing stage, and individual juvenile court.

ORGANIZATION OF THE BOOK

Chapter 1 outlines the requirements of the federal DMC mandate and the factors leading to its focus on the equitable treatment of minority youth in the juvenile justice system. The extent of DMC in Iowa, followed by a review of my earlier research on the causes of DMC and research on the contexts of decision

making in general, are presented in chapter 2. Chapter 2 also provides justification for the adoption of a refined contextual framework in order to study race
and decision making and for the need to further study the causes of DMC in
Iowa. The contextual framework focuses on the relationships between adherence to correctional orientations and decision makers' views concerning race,
crime, family, and respect for authority with decision making.

Chapter 3 elaborates upon the need to expand conceptually the social psychological processes involved in decision making at the level of the decision-
maker. Studies are reviewed that reveal support among the general public and
among juvenile justice personnel for a number of correctional philosophies that
include punishment and rehabilitation. Also highlighted are the disproportionate involvement of African Americans in crime, their greater likelihood of living in homes headed by a single female, and their greater likelihood of viewing
the criminal justice system in a negative light. Next, an argument is presented
that emphasizes the racial stereotyping of African Americans across these domains. The chapter concludes with a discussion for the need to directly measure
and capture the attitudes of decision-makers and the sources of those attitudes
through the use of both quantitative and qualitative methodologies.

Chapter 4 is devoted to a description of the samples, methodology, variables, and analysis procedures. In chapter 5, cross-tabulations are used to determine if jurisdictional differences exist in the case processing and outcomes of
youth and, in particular, African Americans and, when applicable, Native
Americans. The results reveal that the concept of social control is more complex than argued by previous contextual approaches and lend support for a
broader inquiry into the contextual nature of race and decision making. Chapter 6 presents results from regression analyses to determine the extent the patterns in decision making and outcomes observed in chapter 5 hold once legal
(e.g., crime severity) and extralegal factors (e.g., age) are taken into account.
Race effects are evident in all four jurisdictions and the effects vary by stage and
racial group. Information derived from interviews with juvenile court decision-
makers in each jurisdiction provide further insights into the contexts of decision making and are cited in chapters seven through 10. A summary and the
implications for theory, future research, and policy for reducing the overrepresentation of minority youth in the juvenile justice system are discussed in
chapter 11.

Acknowledgments

Partial funding for the research was from the Division of Criminal and Juvenile Justice Planning, Des Moines, Iowa, in conjunction with the Office of Juvenile Justice and Delinquency Prevention (OJJDP). The Graduate College and The Center for Adolescence at the University of Northern Iowa and in particular, Bill Downs, provided support that included moneys for supplies from Project Grants, a paid Development Leave, and feedback on empirical questions and concerns. The department staff and the chair, Keith Crew, at the University of Northern Iowa and Kris Mack must also be acknowledged for their support.

Earlier versions of some of the material in the book have been published in *Justice Quarterly* (1994) 11(2): 257; *Journal of Quantitative Criminology* (1995) 11:363; *Journal of Crime & Justice* (1995)18: 79; *Criminology* (1995) 33: 431; Michael Lynch and E. Britt Patterson, eds., *Justice with Prejudice: Race and Criminal Justice*, 2d ed. (New York: Harrow & Heston), Pg. 121; *Journal of Research in Crime and Delinquency* (1999) 36 (1): 56; *Crime & Delinquency* 48 (1): 3; *Journal of Research in Crime and Delinquency* (2003) 40: 34–70.

This project would have not been possible if it were not for the encouragement I received from a number of agencies and individuals over the last twelve years. I would like to thank the Division of Criminal and Juvenile Justice and Planning group in Iowa, especially Dave Kuker. The chief juvenile court officers and staff at each of the counties included in the study also need to be acknowledged for their cooperation and patience. I would also like to thank OJJDP, especially Heidi Hsia and Gail Olezene, for providing me with the opportunity to act as a consultant on issues pertinent to DMC. Reggie Morton was extremely instrumental in getting me involved at the national level. He, along with Donna Hamparian, taught me quite a bit about DMC and issues related to juvenile justice.

The individuals who worked on the DMC project are too numerous to be acknowledged here; I have thanked these individuals elsewhere (Leiber, 1992a, 1992b, 1993). However, I would like to recognize the special contributions of Michelle (Roudebush) Staley, Tad Cline, Mary Wacker, David Atwood, Anita Norwood, Cher Carney, Carrie Barritt, Laticia Valdes, Molly

(Cargin) Brown, and Jeff Spears. Kurt Roth, Kimberly Schwarze, Jenny Wiedherholt, Chia-Chi Kuo, and Susan Frommelt also deserve a thank-you for their help in the preparation of this book.

A special thank-you must also be given to Clem Bartollas for his encouragement to undertake and complete the book (I finished it before you retired!). Sean Anderson, Margaret Farnworth, and Lisa Kelly-Wilson provided substantive and editorial suggestions. I'm particularly grateful to Lisa who read it numerous times and gave extensive commentary. The opinions, views, and findings contained in the book, however, are mine and in no way represent the position of any of the aforementioned agencies, entities, or individuals.

I would have not been able to undertake such a project without the love and support of Anne, Kevin, and Ray. The book is dedicated to the memory of my father—Marvin James Leiber.

Chapter 1

Disproportionate Minority Confinement (DMC)

This book is based on the view that the effects of race on justice system decision making are variable—dependent on time, macrosocial factors (e.g., racial composition of communities), the characteristics of the court in question (e.g., degree of bureaucratization), and the presence and extent of racial stereotyping. The few quantitative contextual studies of juvenile justice decision making have emphasized the relationship between the characteristics of the community and the court, beliefs in punitive correctional responses to delinquency, and decision makers' perceptions of minorities as drug offenders with increased social control.

The research presented in these pages not only pursues this train of analytic thought but expands the inquiry beyond the rather narrow confines of punitiveness and racial stereotyping of African Americans as drug offenders.[1] The interrelationships between decision makers' adherence to varied correctional orientations (e.g., rehabilitation and accountability) and racial stereotyping involving crime, family, and respect for authority with the case processing and outcomes of youth are examined. A quantitative and qualitative examination of the social psychological processes involved in decision making—processes that may be influenced by historical, structural, and/or organizational factors—is conducted to better understand the presence of race effects in four relatively homogenous juvenile court settings in Iowa. The initial impetus for this research was the federal initiative that requires states to address the issue of disproportionate minority confinement or DMC.

THE DMC REQUIREMENT

The first iteration of the Juvenile Justice and Delinquency Prevention (JJDP) Act of 1974 contained three mandates: the deinstitutionalization of status

1

offenders, the removal of juveniles in adult jails, and the separation of juveniles from adults in institutions. The DMC requirement was included when the JJDP act was reauthorized in 1988, requiring states to study the extent minority youths are confined in secure detention facilities, secure correctional facilities, jails, and lockups, and at other points in the juvenile justice system (JJDP Act of 1974, as amended [Public Law 93-415], section 223[a][23]).

In 1992, Congress reauthorized the JJDP act and made DMC a "mandate" or a "core requirement." Consequently, states participating in the Formula Grants Program have since been required to determine whether disproportionate minority confinement exists to identify the causes, and to develop and implement corrective strategies (Federal Register, 1991:22969).[2] States failing to make progress or at least to show a good-faith effort toward this endeavor risk losing one fourth of their Formula Grant funds for that year, with the remaining three fourths to be directed exclusively toward achieving compliance.

The Office of Juvenile Justice and Delinquency Prevention (OJJDP) recognized that the extent of DMC and possible cause(s) vary by state and that there is variability in the availability of resources and the data needed to understand and address DMC. Therefore, officials at OJJDP believed it would be more beneficial for individual states to design their own approaches to meet the DMC mandate (Coalition for Juvenile Justice, 1993: 12; Leiber, 2002). In this regard, the DMC mandate differs significantly from the other three mandates: the number of juveniles in adult jails, the number of status offenders confined, and the number of juveniles in sight or sound of adult incarcerated offenders can be easily counted. Should the number of youth in any of those circumstances exceed the maximum limit dictated by regulation, legislative and public policy changes can be used to correct the situation, and progress can be measured by returning to the facilities and taking count again. The DMC initiative is much more complex than the first three mandates (Church, 1994; Feyerherm, 1995).

Although states are allowed considerable freedom in addressing DMC, they must indicate in their application for formula grants funds how they are progressing on this issue within the context of three interrelated phases or stages: the identification phase, the assessment phase, and the intervention phase (DMC Technical Assistance Manual, 1990, 2000; Hamparian and Leiber, 1997). While not formal "phases," evaluation and monitoring are also considered essential components of the DMC initiative (DMC Technical Assistance Manual, 2000). The identification phase is descriptive and involves ascertaining the number and proportion of minority youth in secure detention facilities, secure correctional facilities, jails, and lockups.[3]

If the identification phase determines that disproportionate minority representation exists, the state must conduct an assessment that investigates the specific reasons or causes for the situation. Assessments should, at a minimum, identify and explain differences between whites and minorities in arrest, diversion, adjudication, court disposition, admission to detention and correctional facilities, and waiver to adult court. In essence, the assessment phase requires an examination of minority youth involvement at justice system stages beyond incarceration and a search for why overrepresentation exists. The assessments should include information for each county in which minority youth represent 1 percent or more of the population.[4]

The third phase entails selecting and implementing the specific interventions to reduce minority overrepresentation. Depending upon the location(s) and causes of DMC that were identified in the earlier phases, appropriate intervention activities may include developing or revising policies and procedures, decision-making criteria, and/or legislation; establishing services and programs; providing training and staffing; and improving information systems. OJJDP views evaluation of the intervention strategies as a central component of a state's DMC efforts.

States are also encouraged to develop methods to monitor DMC. The underlying premise driving the concern for monitoring is that minority overrepresentation is an ongoing issue and requires continuous and systematic tracking over time. Ideally, DMC monitoring is coordinated with monitoring for other initiatives, such as the deinstitutionalization of status offenders, the separation of youth from adults in institutions, and the removal of youth from adult jails and lockups.[5]

In short, states are to develop a comprehensive approach that includes the identification of the existence and extent of DMC, a determination of its causes, and the development and implementation of solutions to reduce it. Progress toward compliance with the requirements of section 223(a)(23) is reported by each state and territory in their Comprehensive JJDP Three-Year Plans and annual Plan Updates that are reviewed by OJJDP to determine the status of compliance.

Because of its focus on differences in outcomes between minority and white youth, the DMC effort is an initiative that focuses on decision making within the juvenile justice system. A number of events and factors influenced and shaped this systems-oriented approach to DMC.

EQUITABLE USE OF CONFINEMENT

Minority youth are overrepresented in terms of both arrests and their presence in the juvenile justice system (Miller, 1996; Bilchik, 1999). Although differential offending could be one explanation for these occurrences (e.g., Hindelang, 1978; McNeely and Pope, 1978; Hindelang et al., 1981; Mann, 1993; Farrington et al., 1996; Sampson and Lauritsen, 1997; Hawkins et al., 1998; Pope and Snyder, 2003), for a number of reasons, those involved in bringing attention to minority youth overrepresentation in the system focused on selection bias or on the equitable usage of confinement for whites and minorities. That is, the focus of the DMC initiative is on decision making by juvenile justice and law enforcement personnel.

A number of legislative, organizational, and individual actors, including Congress, the Coalition for Juvenile Justice, the National Council of Juvenile and Family Court Judges, Ira Schwartz of the Center for the Study of Youth Policy, and Barry Krisberg of the National Council on Crime and Delinquency set the stage for a systems focus and pushed the issue of disproportionate minority youth confinement as both a national and a state issue (Feyerherm, 1995). For example, at a hearing before the House Subcommittee on Human Resources, a member of Congress stated that "minority juveniles are disproportionately incarcerated and we need to determine if a dual juvenile justice system is emerging" (Tauke, 1987: 3).

In their third and fourth annual reports, *An Act of Empowerment* (1987) and *The Delicate Balance* (1989), as well as at their 1988 spring conference, the Coalition for Juvenile Justice (CJJ) addressed issues concerned with minority youth in confinement and the differential processing of children of color. The theme of selection bias is also found in the title of the coalition's ninth annual report, *Pursuing the Promise* (1993) and in the text of the report, "Consistent with the mandates of the Juvenile Justice and Delinquency Prevention Act, the Coalition is primarily concerned with problems directly related to the juvenile justice system itself and, in this case, its potential for 'selection bias'" (CJJ, 1993:9).

The adoption of a systems perspective also grew out information provided by the Children in Custody (CIC) census of juvenile detention, correctional, and shelter facilities (Krisberg et al., 1987; see also, Snyder et al., 1995). CIC data revealed not only the presence of minority youth overrepresentation but that it had been increasing since the late 1970s. Barry Krisberg and his colleagues, for example, were among the first to show that the proportion of minority youth in public correctional facilities increased by 26 percent from 1979 to 1982 even though the number of minority youth arrested declined during these same years. They also found that African American males were almost four times more likely than white males to be incarcerated in detention centers and training schools during this time (1987: 184).

Furthermore, between 1985 and 1989, there were pronounced increases in minority overrepresentation in delinquency referrals to juvenile court, petitioned cases, adjudicated delinquency cases, and delinquency cases placed outside of the home (e.g., McGarrell, 1993). During this period, the proportion of African American and Hispanic youth detained increased by 9 percent and 4 percent respectively, while the proportion of white youth detained *declined* by 13 percent (Krisberg et al., 1992:2).

The increase in minority overrepresentation in the system continued into the mid-1990s. African American youth represented 41 percent of those held in detention, 46 percent of those placed in public long-term facilities, and 52 percent waived to adult court (Snyder and Sickmund, 1995:91). In 1995, minorities made up 68 percent of the detention population compared to 65 percent in 1991 and 53 percent in 1983 (Sickmund et al., 1997:42). The minority population in public long-term facilities (i.e., training schools) in 1995 was 68 percent compared to 69 percent in 1991 and 56 percent in 1983 (Sickmund et al., 1997:42). Minority youth outnumber white youth in public facilities by more than 2 to 1. In private facilities, however, white youth slightly outnumber minority youth (42). Keep in mind that minority youth make up 30 percent of the general juvenile population age 10 to 17, with African Americans representing 15 percent, Hispanics 12 percent, Native Americans 1.2 percent, and Asians 3.3 percent.

Recent data indicate a decline in African American youth overrepresentation at most decision points in the juvenile justice system (Snyder and Sickmund, 1999). However, African Americans are still disproportionately represented in the system. Figure 1.1 presents a breakdown of African American overrepresentation within the juvenile justice system for the years 1990–1991 and 1996–1997.

The work of David Huizinga and Delbert Elliott (1987) and Carl Pope and William Feyerherm (1990a,b, 1992) were influential in shaping the direction of the DMC mandate. Huizinga and Elliott used six waves of data from the National Youth Survey covering the years 1976 to 1983 and information from arrest records to assess the relationship between race, offending patterns, and the likelihood of arrest.

In an earlier study (Elliott and Ageton, 1980) involving the first year (1976) of the data, African Americans were found to be disproportionately represented among the high-frequency offenders. With the exception of that year, Huizinga and Elliott found few consistent differences between delinquency involvement and racial groups for the years 1977 to 1980. Furthermore, African Americans were apprehended and charged with more serious offenses than whites involved in the same kinds of offenses. In their conclusion, the authors state:

> . . . a summary of the findings would suggest that differences in incarceration rates among racial groups cannot be explained by differences in offense behavior. . . . The assertion that differential incarceration rates stem directly from differences in delinquency involvement is not supported by these analyses. There is some indication of differential arrest rates for serious crimes among the racial groups, but further investigation of the relationship of race to arrest and juvenile justice system processing is required if reasons underlying the differences in incarceration rates are to be more fully understood (1987:221).

FIG. 1.1.
African American Overrepresentation in the Juvenile Justice System,
Comparison between 1990–1991 and 1996–1997

U.S. population
ages 10–17 _____ 15%

		1990–1991	*1996–1997*	*% change*
Delinquency referrals to juvenile court	_____	32%	30%	−2
Detained delinquency cases	_____	41	45	+4
Petitioned delinquency cases	_____	37	33	−4
Adjudicated delinquency cases	_____	36	32	−4
Delinquency case out-of-home placements	_____	43	36	−7
Juveniles in public long-term institutions	_____	46	40	−6
Cases judicially waived to criminal court	_____	52	46	−6

Source: Adapted from Snyder and Sickmund (1999:192). Juvenile Offenders and Victims: A National Report. Washington, DC: Office of Juvenile Justice and Delinquency Prevention.

These findings were referred to by both Ira Schwartz (1986) and Barry Krisberg (1988) in their testimony before Congress prior to the passage of the DMC mandate in 1988.

In 1988, Carl Pope and William Feyerherm received funding from OJJDP to conduct a literature review of research on the influence of race on case processing and outcomes within juvenile courts. For the years 1970 through 1988, Pope and Feyerherm (1990, 1992) found that roughly two-thirds of the studies reported that minority youth, primarily African Americans, received the more severe outcomes relative to white youth. They found evidence in the more sophisticated research of both direct and indirect race effects. There was also evidence that minor racial differences can accumulate and become more pronounced as minority youth penetrate further into the system. The influence of race on decision making was not always present across the entire system or more or less pronounced at one particular stage in the juvenile justice system. However, a substantial body of research showed that the greatest disparity between racial groups occurred at intake and detention.

The Children in Custody Data and the research by Elliott and colleagues and by Pope and Feyerherm set the stage and agenda for addressing DMC within the context of the equitable usage of secure confinement for minority youth. Although the DMC mandate centers on secure confinement, the intent of the mandate is to focus on decision making at *all* stages in the system (Feyerherm, 1995). The emphasis on fairness in case processing and outcomes for minority youth decreased the concern as to why minority youth get to the system and therefore, made the issue of minority criminality an unnecessary controversy (Feyerherm, 1996).

THE EXTENT OF DMC IN IOWA

In the early 1990s, minority youth overrepresentation existed in Iowa's secure facilities (Moore and Kuker, 1993). Minority youth comprised 37 percent of juveniles held in jail/lockups, 32 percent of those placed in detention, and 28 percent of the admissions to the State Training School (Moore and Kuker, 1993). African Americans were the most overrepresented minority group in the system. For example, they accounted for 21 percent of the State Training School population (Kuker, 1991). Minority youth and especially African Americans also spent on average longer periods in both jail/lockup and detention than whites (Moore and Kuker, 1993). Minority youth comprised 4.8 percent of the total population of Iowa, and up to 10 percent or more of some cities (Bureau of the Census, 1990). In the city of Waterloo, located in Black Hawk County in the northern part of Iowa, African American youth made up just over 19 percent of all youth.

Minority overrepresentation was also present in the adult corrections system in the early 1990s, and research yielded evidence of racial bias (Equality in the Courts Task Force, 1993). As noted earlier in the preface, minority overrepresentation still exists in both Iowa's adult and juvenile corrections systems (Division of Criminal and Juvenile Justice Planning and Statistical Analysis, 2000). In fact, a study by the Sentencing Project (2000) indicates that Iowa's proportion of African Americans incarcerated is the highest in the nation.

As previously discussed in the identification phase of the DMC initiative, documentation is required that indicates the extent minority youth are disproportionately arrested, confined in secure detention or correctional facilities, jails and lockups, and transfers to criminal court. States calculate an index value of disproportionality to assess the extent of over-/under-representation for each of these outcomes (DMC Technical Assistance Manual, 1900, 2000; Hamparian and Leiber, 1997). The index value is arrived at by dividing the percentage of minority juveniles represented at each point by the percentage of minority juveniles in the state's total juvenile population at risk for secure confinement. An index value over 1.00 indicates that minorities are overrepresented. For example, an index value of 2.00 would mean that minority youth are represented at a rate twice their representation in the total at-risk population (usually defined as age 10 to 17, but some states, such as Iowa, use ages 0 to 18).

The greater the index number, the greater the amount of disproportionate representation. Conversely, an index under 1.00 indicates that minorities are underrepresented. Data could not be located representing youth minority overrepresentation in Iowa in the form of the index values for the early 1990s. Instead, index values are used for the first half of 2000 and are presented in table 1.1.

As can be seen in table 1.1, minority youth are disproportionately arrested and confined in secure detention, secure correctional facilities, and adult jails

TABLE 1.1.
Identification of Youth Minority Overrepresentation in Iowa (January to July 2000)

	Total Number of All Youth	Total Number of Minority Youth	Percent Minority	Index Value[1]
Population at risk (ages 0 through 18)	5,968	39,389	7	N/A
Juveniles arrested[2]	24,670	3,273	13	1.86
Juveniles confined in secure juvenile detention facilities	5,243	1,625	31	4.43
Juveniles confined in secure juvenile correctional facilities	299	123	41	5.86
Juveniles confined in adult jails[3]	330	131	43	6.14
Juvenile confined in adult lockups	41	18	44	6.29
Total	5,888	1,897	32	4.57

Source: Division of Criminal and Juvenile Justice Planning and Statistical Analysis (2000).

1. The index value is arrived at by dividing the percentage of minority juveniles represented at each point by the percentage of minority juveniles in the state's total juvenile population at risk for secure confinement. An index value over 1.00 indicates that minorities are overrepresented.

2. Hispanic ethnicity was not factored into these figures.

3. Race/ethnicity was only reported on 305 youth.

and lockups. The index values for lockups, jails, and secure correctional facilities are most disturbing. Minority youth are represented at a rate three times their representation in the total at-risk population. Minority youth overrepresentation is no better, if not worse, than it was in the early 1990s (Moore and Kuker, 1993). The extent of the overrepresentation of minority youth in secure facilities also parallels nationwide findings (Hamparian and Leiber, 1997; Leiber, 2002).[6]

SUMMARY

The DMC requirement asks states to examine the extent of minority overrepresentation at all juvenile justice decision points, to assess its causes, and to develop and implement strategies to reduce it. The primary focus of the initiative is on the equitable usage of confinement for youth, instead of the causes of delinquent behavior and solutions to reduce delinquency (Pope and Leiber, 2003).

In 1991, OJJDP issued a Request for Proposals seeking the participation of states to analyze disproportionate minority confinement and to develop model programs to address its causes (Roscoe and Morton, 1994). OJJDP awarded funding to five states on a competitive basis to see how these states would implement the phases as stipulated by the *Disproportionate Minority Technical Assistance Manual* (1990). The five pilot states were Arizona, Florida, North Carolina, Oregon, and Iowa (Pope and Feyerherm, 1993). The purpose of this book is to provide a detailed examination of the causes of DMC in Iowa by assessing the contexts of decision making, especially the relationship between the correctional philosophy of the court and, at the individual level, racial stereotyping.[7]

Chapter 2

Understanding DMC

The following pages present a review of two initial assessment studies and additional research conducted by the author to determine the causes of disproportionate minority confinement (DMC) in Iowa. The more recent research relied upon a contextual framework that emphasized the structural characteristics of communities and, to a lesser extent, the organizational features of courts. This information is presented to illustrate the inability of this contextual analysis and, in particular, Robert Sampson and John Laub's (1993) macrostructural approach to account for decision making and for the presence of race differences in communities and courts that are more homogenous than varied in terms of structural and organizational attributes. A review of prior research reveals evidence of similar inconsistent findings and lack of thoroughness in understanding when and under what conditions race matters. The chapter concludes with a discussion of the need for a contextual approach that broadens (1) the focus of inquiry beyond the relationship between punishment and the racial stereotyping of African Americans as drug offenders and (2) the methods employed to capture the intricacies involved.

A SEARCH FOR THE CAUSES OF DMC

The Initial Assessment Studies

In the early 1990s, the author conducted two separate assessment studies to discover the causes of DMC in Iowa. The first study examined case files to assess whether race influenced juvenile court processing and outcomes in the four jurisdictions with the largest minority youth populations in Iowa (Leiber, 1992a,b). The second study employed qualitative analysis in the form of self-report surveys and interviews with juvenile court personnel from each of the four jurisdictions (Leiber, 1993). The findings from both of these studies showed the presence of race effects. The race effects varied by the racial group, the decision-making stage, and the juvenile court. In some instances, minority youth received more lenient outcomes; in other instances, more severe outcomes. The qualitative information from the interviews with the juvenile justice personnel placed the race effects within the context of the court's correctional orientations, racial stereotyping, and overt bias. The two assessment studies confirm that race influenced decision making and accounted to some degree for the overrepresentation of minority youth in Iowa's juvenile justice system.

Expanding the Inquiry to Include the Contexts of Decision Making

Traditional approaches used to guide research on race and criminal and juvenile justice processing usually draw on one or more perspectives based on consensus theory or labeling or conflict theory (Hagan, 1974; Myers, 1979; Tittle and Curran, 1988; Engen et al., 2002). According to the Durkheimian tradition, law, punishment, and treatment derive from a broad consensus of societal norms and values (Durkheim, 1964). State intervention into people's lives and the incarceration of individuals result primarily from criminal behavior and from its severity. Social structure has an indirect effect on social control by creating and sustaining inequality in the distribution of resources, which is conducive to criminality (Merton, 1957; Blumstein, 1982; Langan, 1985). Racial bias is seen as a random occurrence, since legally relevant criteria constrain the discretion of decision-makers and promote objective and egalitarian decisions (e.g., Wilbanks, 1987). Differences between whites and nonwhites in case processing and outcomes are attributed to differential involvement in crime (Hindelang, 1978).

Labeling and conflict theories, on the other hand, presume a lack of consensus. Majority groups are able to serve and protect their own interests by manipulating the law, law enforcement practices, and the courts. Both perspectives contend that crime is a *political concept*, a label imposed by those in positions of power. Consequently, labeling theory and conflict theory argue that social structure has a direct impact on social control, since those in power are more likely to label as deviant the powerless, most notably the poor and minorities (Becker, 1963: 156-161; Liska, 1994). Being poor and/or minority also increases the probability of being sanctioned and the severity of the sanction (Quinney, 1970; Chambliss and Seidman, 1971).

Relative to conflict theory, labeling theory traditionally stresses stereotyping, status or personal resources, and disadvantaged groups' skills in offsetting or resisting efforts of state control (e.g., Farnworth et al., 1991). The emphasis of labeling theory has been primarily at the individual level and on middle-level agents of social control. In comparison, conflict theory places greater emphasis on macroprocesses, most notably the use and structure of power in society with a focus on the relationship between economic and political power and punishment (Liska, 1994; Lynch and Groves, 1989). The traditional interpretation of conflict theory revolves around the premise that the powerless represent a threat to the ruling elite, and therefore these groups must be subjected to social control (Turk, 1969). Following this line of thought, the criminal and juvenile justice systems are seen as biased against the poor and/or minorities. The belief that the "system" systematically operates to the disadvantage of minorities has generated much debate in terms of the "no discrimination thesis/discrimination thesis" (see Wilbanks, 1987; MacLean and Milovanovic, 1990).

The first point of contention involves differences of opinion concerning what constitutes systemic discrimination. The issue centers on the concepts of overt and subtle racism and the extent to which these forms of discrimination should be incorporated into the concept of institutionalized racism. William Wilbanks's book, *The Myth of a Racist Criminal Justice System* (1987), and a series of articles (Wilbanks, 1990a,b) set the framework for the consensus position that discrimination toward minorities perpetrated by the criminal justice system is not widespread and that the concept of institutional racism should be abandoned. He argues that we should define racism only in terms of conscious, intentional acts resulting from psychological attitudes. Wilbanks also contends that we need to first establish that disparities in formal outcomes exist and then attempt to discover through statistical analyses if the differences are the result of prejudicial attitudes.

Many have critiqued Wilbanks's view on his prerequisites that institutionalized discrimination be reduced to malicious intent, that quantitative research methods be employed to discover institutionalized racism, and that the sole focus of attention be formal decision-making outcomes (i.e., arrest, bail, and sentencing) (e.g., Hagan, 1987; Lynch, 1990; Zatz, 1990). The latter two points are first discussed.

Criticisms of Wilbanks's position on the study of formal decision-making outcomes, center on the failure to consider informal behaviors and practices that are discriminatory, such as insults; rough or brutal treatment; unnecessary stops, frisks, and searches by the police; and the acceptance of lesser standards of evidence to convict minorities by juries and courts (Georges-Abeyie, 1990). The experience of being pulled over by police for no other apparent reason than one is black, for example, would not fall under Wilbanks's emphasis on formal outcomes (Harris, 1997; Crawford, 2000). Wilbanks's position on quantitative methods has been criticized for being overly reliant on positivism and failing to recognize the value that multiple research methodologies that include observational, ethnographic, and other qualitative techniques can bring beyond a "variable orientation" to the study of race and social control (e.g., Georges-Abeyie, 1990; Crew, 1991; Conley, 1994).

Most definitions of institutionalized racism move the argument beyond intent to a focus on result and indirect forms of discrimination (Georges-Abeyie, 1990). Institutionalized discrimination is often the legacy of codified laws, practices, and criteria that were once overtly racist. Institutionalized racism can also include the more subtle forms of discrimination—unintentional acts or procedures that have become part of the criminal justice system. Marjorie Zatz (1987a), for example, defines overt discrimination in statistical terms as a main race effect (i.e., statistically significant effects that remain after other relevant factors are statistically controlled). Subtle forms of discrimination are evidenced by statistically significant indirect and interaction effects that operate through other variables and that are closely associated with race. According to this view, laws, procedures, and legal criteria may appear racially neutral but can enhance race disparities in arrests and incarceration. Inquiries into the neutrality of laws and procedures have examined, for example, determinate sentencing schemes, sentencing guidelines, crack-cocaine sentencing laws, and criteria to determine success on parole (Miethe and Moore, 1985; Zatz, 1987a; DeKeseredy and MacLean, 1990; McGarrell, 1993; Chambliss, 1995; Tonry, 1995; Chiricosi, 1996; Miller, 1996; Beckett and Sasson, 2000; Ziedenberg, 2001).

In many instances racial disparities have developed "because the system adopted procedures without analyzing their possible effects on different racial groups" (Petersilia, 1983: 112). The legal criterion that has been the focus of the most discussion has been prior record. Some have argued that prior record is a racially tainted legal factor (i.e., the result of differential police deployment patterns, and false arrests) that operates to the disadvantage of African Americans (e.g., Hagan, 1974; Farrell and Swigert, 1978; Farnworth and Horan, 1980; Welch et al., 1985; Zatz, 1987a; Anderson, 1990).[2] For others, proof of a discriminatory system does not come in the form of indirect, subtle effects but only in the form of overt statistically significant effects (Wilbanks, 1987; Sampson and Lauritsen, 1997: 347).

A related aspect of this debate has focused on the pervasiveness and the magnitude of racial discrimination that must exist to support the view that the system is discriminatory. For some, proof of a discriminatory system is evident when the poor and minorities receive more severe outcomes; such effects are present at every stage in the proceedings, in all jurisdictions, and under all circumstances (Wilbanks, 1987). Furthermore, the direct effects of race must be stronger than legally relevant variables in predicting case processing and outcomes (e.g., Akers, 1994: 26-27; Tittle, 1980). Conflict theory does not make many of these explicit claims.

Conflict theorists, for example, argue that "the probability that criminal sanctions will be applied varies according to the extent to which the behaviors of the powerless conflict with the interests of the power segments" (Quinney, 1970: 18). Daniel Georges-Abeyie (1990), Zatz (1990), and others (e.g., Hagan et al., 1979) also point out that the criminal justice system is not really a unified "system" but a series set of interrelated processes that are loosely tied together by the people moving from one stage to the next. The juvenile justice system has also been described as loosely coupled (Leiber and Jamieson, 1995; Sampson and Lauritsen, 1997). Thus, it is highly unlikely to expect race effects to be present at all stages, especially in the juvenile justice system where there can be anywhere from three to five stages or more. On the matter of race effects being the most influential predictor, Raymond Paternoster and LeAnn Iovanni (1989: 365–368) contend that only *some* statistically significant effect is sufficient to provide support for the theory.

Perhaps the most controversial aspect of the debate, and most damaging to labeling and conflict theory, is research that fails to find evidence of racial discrimination (e.g., Hagan, 1974; Cohen and Kluegel, 1978, 1979; Hagan and Bumiller, 1983; Aday, 1986; Wilbanks, 1987; DeLisi and Regoli, 1999; Gorton and Boies, 1999). Other findings point to contradictory outcomes involving both harshness and leniency or just leniency for African Americans compared to whites (Kleck, 1981; Dannefer and Schutt, 1982; Peterson and Hagan, 1984; Humphrey and Fogarty, 1987; Myers and Talarico, 1987; Leiber, 1994).[3] For some, these anomalous findings cast doubt on the assumption that the system systematically discriminates against minorities (Petersilia, 1985; Myers and Talarico, 1987; Langan, 1994) and on the validity of labeling theory and conflict theory as explanations for understanding race and social control (Tittle and Curran, 1988). For others, these criticisms are misdirected and perhaps premature (see Zatz, 1987a, 1990; Mann, 1993).[4]

Debate concerning the no discrimination thesis/discrimination thesis and related research paved the way for the development of contextual approaches to understanding race and social control (e.g., Hagan and Bumiller, 1983; Myers and Talarico, 1986a; Zatz, 1987a; Chiricos and Crawford, 1995). In addition, conventional interpretations of consensus theory versus traditional labeling and conflict perspectives appear to be inadequate to conceptualize the complexities of the structural and interactional processes that shape the relationships between race and decision making (Peterson and Hagan, 1984; Bridges et al., 1987; Hawkins, 1987; Tittle, 1994; Sampson and Lauritsen, 1997). For example, consensus theorists are naive to not accept evidence that structural factors and other contingencies affect race and punishment some of the time and in some places beyond a random occurrence (Peterson and Hagan, 1984; Bridges et al., 1987; Sampson and Lauritsen, 1997). Similarly, the elements of both labeling theory and conflict theory have not been developed fully and are too simplistic to allow for a complete understanding of race and social control (Hawkins, 1987).

Although labeling theory implies structure by focusing on who is more likely to be labeled, the perspective is indifferent to how social structure creates labels and how power operates to sustain labels (Liazos, 1972:115; Taylor et al., 1973: 166-170; Melossi, 1985). Alternatively, while conflict theory does take these factors into account, it does not adequately explain the determinants of social reactions and the role and use of stereotypical images to guide decision making and social control (Bell and Lang, 1985; Tittle and Curran, 1988; Leiber and Stairs, 1999). More importantly, the conflict perspective treats race as a proxy for class (Hawkins, 1987:722–724; see also Daly and Tonry, 1997). In simplistic terms, underlying conflict theory's emphasis on economic conditions is the belief that African Americans are more likely to be involved in the system because they make up a larger portion of the poor and are more criminal either due to impoverishment or powerlessness (cf. Blalock, 1967). Consequently, a structural analysis that emphasizes economic contingencies is unable to make predictions regarding differences in the treatment of the African American poor relative to the Native-American poor, the Hispanic poor, and other low-status groups, including poor whites.

It is proposed here that, rather than viewing the effects of race on social control as constant under all circumstances, the effects should be expected to be variable. An analysis is needed that is guided by conceptualizations sensitive to contexts that heighten or negate the influence of race on decision making. Myers and Talarico make a case for a contextual approach to studying racial differences in outcomes in the criminal justice system:

> The most recent research . . . underscores the need to change our focus of attention, and move away from an assessment of the relative importance of race and legally relevant factors toward an examination of *the structural contexts* where discrimination is likely to occur. In short, the question to pursue is not whether race affects treatment, but under what social and economic conditions and for which types of offenders and outcomes race makes a *significant difference*. (1987: 4) (emphases added)

Similarly, Dale Dannefer and Russell Schutt, suggest such an approach in order to analyze decision making in the juvenile justice system:

> . . . [F]uture research in this area should concentrate on comparative studies in which social environments are sampled and on direct measures of characteristics of social environments. The theoretically important question is not whether there is bias in the juvenile justice system, but, rather, *under what conditions* it is more likely or less likely to occur. An answer to this question has been suggested . . . in terms of

basic features of the social environment, . . . and of an interaction between the two. (1982: 1130) (emphase added)

Leiber and colleagues (1994, 1995, 1999) attempted to improve upon the assessments of the overrepresentation of minority youth in secure confinement in Iowa (Leiber, 1992a,b; 1993) by examining the contexts of juvenile justice decision making. The first study examined the effects of being white, African American, or Native American on case processing and outcomes and the role that stereotyping and organizational policy play in this process. The second and third studies attempted to discover the contexts of decision making through the refinement and application of Sampson and Laub's (1993) macrolevel structural contextual perspective. This background information is presented because the findings from those prior studies led to, and justify, the strategy used in this book.

As I will discuss, conflict-oriented theories, such as Robert Sampson and John Laub's perspective, pay too much attention to the influences of social structure on decision making and rely too much on quantitative strategies. Consequently, the social psychological processes involved at the level of the decision-maker, especially racial stereotyping, have not been developed and examined fully. The present research attempts to overcome these limitations. The forthcoming discussion examines the initial research conducted to understand DMC in Iowa.

DIFFERENTIATING AMONG MINORITY GROUPS

Many studies fail to assess how outcomes may differ for whites and African Americans compared to other racial groups. In their review of research covering the years 1969 through 1988, Carl Pope and William Feyerherm found only seven studies that focused on Hispanics, one on Native Americans, and one on Asians (1990:34). Although Pope and his colleagues' (2001) more recent review of studies conducted during the period of 1989 to 1999 revealed somewhat of a greater awareness for the need to differentiate among minority groups, the overall pattern of indifference is still the same. Researchers either ignore non-African minority groups (e.g., Bishop and Frazier, 1988) or fail to distinguish among ethnic populations and describe the sample simply as "minority" or "other" (e.g., Brown et al., 1980). Research that has been sensitive to this issue has found racial and ethnic differences in case outcomes and processing in both the juvenile justice (Fisher and Doyle-Martin, 1981) and the criminal justice systems (Zatz, 1984, 1987a; LaFree, 1985; Farnworth et al., 1991; Steffensmeier and Demuth, 2001). The first study by Leiber (1994) attempted to address this shortcoming.

Utilizing an interpretation of Weber's (1969) theory of decision making and formal rationality, Leiber examined two hypotheses: (1) Native American and African American youth would receive more severe outcomes than white youth with similar backgrounds and legal histories, and (2) Native Americans would be at a greater disadvantage in general than African Americans. Leiber used data from one jurisdiction in Iowa and found mixed support for the hypotheses. Youth of both minority groups received different outcomes from white youth. However, Native Americans received less severe outcomes than African Americans and whites, and the race effects differed by the stage in the proceedings. Interviews with decision-makers pointed to cultural and organizational contexts to help explain the results. The cultural and organizational contingencies will be elaborated upon in later chapters.

A Refinement and Application
of a Structural Theory

In this section, Sampson and Laub's (1993) macrostructural perspective is described. Next, the discussion focuses on the application of the perspective to explain DMC in Iowa, followed by a summary of the results and a critique of the conflict-oriented theory.

Sampson and Laub's Perspective
A modified version of Sampson and Laub's (1993) integrated theory of macrostructural contexts was used in two additional studies to provide further insights into race and case processing and outcomes in general (Leiber and Jamieson, 1995) and in the use of intake diversion (Leiber and Stairs, 1999). Sampson and Laub (1993) refine the concept of minority group threat as proposed by Tittle and Curran (1988) by emphasizing decision-makers' use of stereotyping within a larger context symbolized by the "war on drugs" and characteristics of the social structure. Tittle and Curran (1988), and later Tittle (1994), focus on the contexts of crime and official perceptions and the conditions under which the perceived threats result into social control.

Tittle and Curran contend that rather than perceiving youth as directly undermining their position of dominance and authority because of power or powerlessness, decision makers instead feel a psychological discomfort or uneasiness as a consequence of specific behaviors and characteristics displayed by youth. Tittle and Curran hypothesize that "nonwhites and youth symbolize to white adults resentment-provoking or fear-provoking qualities like aggressiveness, sexuality, and absence of personal discipline" (1988: 53). These stereotypical perceptions of youth are assumed to be "threatening" because justice officials are unable to identify with African Americans or cannot, as adults, experience the lifestyle of youth. Specific forms of behavior may also make decision-makers fearful of youth, especially minority youth. The primary emphasis, however, is on the perception and stereotyping of youth and categories of youth as well as on their specific behavior.

Overall, the perceived threat is more symbolic than real. Class and race differentials in sanctioning practices are conditioned by decision-makers' perceptions of, and reactions to, stereotypical notions and behaviors concerning the poor and minority youth. According to Tittle (1994: 41), the less decision-makers identify with and the more they fear youth—particularly minority youth—the more likely social control will occur.[5]

Sampson and Laub (1993) incorporate Tittle and Curran's (1988) notion of the symbolic threat thesis within their perspective by arguing that the portrayal of minorities and the poor as drug users and delinquents augments existing perceptions of these groups as potential or actual threats to middle-class standards. This position is in contrast to the traditional conflict proposition that minorities represent threats to the power base of the dominant group. According to Sampson and Laub (1993:293), the poor and African Americans are subject to greater control if they reside in counties characterized by racial inequality and by the presence of a large underclass and if it is believed that they have participated in drug offenses.

Sampson and Laub examined case outcomes for two hundred U.S. counties to test these hypotheses, and they found support for understanding juvenile court variations across structural contexts. Macrolevel factors such as racial inequality and poverty levels and, to a lesser degree, the case level variable of drug offending were predictors of severe outcomes for minorities compared to whites.

The Application of Sampson and Laub's Perspective to Account for DMC in Iowa

Leiber and colleagues' (1995, 1999) research extended Sampson and Laub's conflict perspective by identifying not only the structural factors associated with each jurisdiction but also decision makers' beliefs in a punitive response to crime and delinquency and in racial differences in involvement in crime, family structure, and cooperation with justice proceedings. In both studies, Leiber and Jamieson and Leiber and Stairs attempted to provide a more direct test of Sampson and Laub's perspective by quantitatively assessing the attitudes of decision makers and the relationship these attitudes have with structural factors and with the social control of youth. The research by Leiber and Stairs also assessed the extent the structural perspective could explain race and decision making in more homogeneous settings.

Prior research typically has examined either case outcomes nationwide (e.g., Sampson and Laub, 1993) or in numerous counties within a single state (e.g., Tittle and Curran, 1988) where variation in the independent variables was maximized. No research had been conducted employing more regional, homogeneous jurisdictions to understand juvenile justice decision making and social control using a structural framework. The limited variation in the independent variables used in the two studies allowed for a conservative test of Sampson and Laub's perspective but had the potential to add great validity to such an approach and/or to provide information concerning the issue of generalizability across populations and circumstances (Popper, 1968).

On the basis of Sampson and Laub (1993) and the distributions of the structural and attitudinal measures, there were a number of expectations concerning the presence of race bias and increased social control of youth. For example, it was anticipated that greater evidence of race bias and increased social control of youth would occur in jurisdictions classified as poorer and as having greater racial inequality and a higher incidence of racially stereotypical beliefs. Alternatively, race differences were not expected in communities that scored lower on these indices. The results from Leiber and his colleagues' previous studies (1994, 1995, 1999), however, reveal partial support for these hypotheses and raise questions regarding the extent a structural and/or an organizational perspective alone can account for the presence of race effects in case processing and outcomes.

Leiber (1994) discovered race effects in a community that could not be explained solely by legal and extralegal factors. Leiber and Jamieson (1995) found that racial stereotyping and other contextual factors structured the case outcomes of whites and African Americans. The direction of the effects, however, varied, and the influence of the contextual variables was not always statistically significant.[6] Leiber and Stairs (1999) examined the structural characteristics of three jurisdictions and found that youth were subjected to more social control in jurisdictions evidencing greater social and racial inequality and beliefs in racial differences. In addition, African American youth were more likely than white youth to receive more severe outcomes in these jurisdictions. In one jurisdiction, race had a direct and major effect on decision making, while in another, race interacted with family structure. These findings were consistent with expectations.

African Americans were also more likely than their counterparts to be recommended for further court processing in a jurisdiction identified as relatively low in terms of the structural and attitudinal measures. For youth who received diversion as part of an informal adjustment at intake, there were few racial differences in the amount of social control among jurisdictions. African Americans, however, were subject to less juvenile court intervention in the form of participation in diversionary options than whites in a jurisdiction with greater inequality and beliefs in racial differences. These results were contrary to expectations.

There have been a limited number of structural contextual analyses conducted relative to microlevel case research. The results from these studies parallel those of Leiber (1994, 1995, 1999) and reveal inconsistent support for macrolevel effects on race and decision making in criminal and juvenile justice proceedings (for a contrary opinion see Sampson and Lauritsen, 1997; Engen et al., 2002). The prior research on the structural contexts of race and decision making is reviewed in the following section.

PRIOR RESEARCH INVOLVING THE COMMUNITY CONTEXTS OF DECISION MAKING

Research on the effects of the social characteristics of the community on decision making generally has relied on Weber's (1969) notion of rationality and bureaucratic justice and/or more elaborated inquires based on versions of Blalock's (1967) minority group threat thesis. The following review of the literature covers quantitative assessments of the mediating effects of structural contingencies on the social psychological processes of decision making and is not meant to be comprehensive. More thorough reviews can be found elsewhere (e.g., Tittle and Curran, 1988; Chiricos and Crawford, 1995; Sampson and Lauritsen, 1997; Engen et al., 2002; Bishop, 2003).

The Urban/Rural Distinction

Earlier research that examined the effects of community characteristics on criminal justice decision making focused on the interrelationship between urbanization and bureaucratization and its effect on social control. This research has yielded contradictory evidence. Relying on Weber (1969), the degree of bureaucratic organization (formal vs. substantive rationality) varies with the setting, especially urban versus rural. Urban environments are characterized by rational formal justice and by greater adherence to legal criteria. Rural environments, on the other hand, are thought to depend on substantive rationality, whereby formal bureaucracy is lacking and informal criteria and legally irrelevant factors inform decision making. Thus, African Americans should experience lower rates of intervention in urban settings than rural settings once differences in levels of crime are considered.

Others, however, have argued just the opposite: urban courts will evidence greater racial discrimination than rural courts. According to this view, adherence to a formal rationalized system may imprison individuals in an "iron cage." Decision-makers will unquestioningly accept the procedure and substance of the law as binding and just and rely on legal factors that may be biased. In the act of following the rules, decision-makers will reinforce inequities in case processing (Zatz, 1987a). Some have also argued that because urban courts must contend with large volumes of cases, to increase efficiency decision-makers must classify offenders into "routine types." The routine types often are based on stereotypes reflecting assumptions about African Americans, the poor, individual moral character, motivation, and behavior (Sudnow, 1965; Cicourel, 1968; Emerson, 1969; Swigert and Farrell, 1977; Farrell and Holmes, 1991). Consequently, the influence of race and other extralegal attributes on outcomes will be greater in urban than in rural settings (Bridges et al., 1987; Chambliss and Seidman, 1971).

Some research has revealed that rural courts are less formal and more likely to discriminate against minorities in sentencing than urban courts (e.g., Pope, 1976; Hagan, 1977; Austin, 1981). Other research, however, has shown just the opposite: urban courts are more punitive and discriminatory than rural courts (e.g., Miethe and Moore, 1985; Myers and Talarico, 1986b). In Pennsylvania, urban courts were more biased against African Americans in the initial decision to incarcerate, while suburban courts were found to racially discriminate in terms of the length of imprisonment (Kempf and Austin, 1986). Myers and Talarico (1986b) analyzed felony convictions in Georgia and found that urbanization was a contextual determinant of differential treatment independent of bureaucratization. The effects of urbanization were conditioned by, or interacted with, race, sex, age, and offense type, and the result was not always in the expected direction. While urbanization increased the likelihood for imprisonment for African Americans, it decreased their length of imprisonment: whites received longer sentences in urban courts than African Americans.

Minority Group Threat/Racial Threat Thesis

Another theoretical strategy for understanding the contextual influence of place on race and decision making is Blalock's (1967) minority group power threat thesis and its elaborations (see also, Spitzer, 1975; Liska, 1992). Traditional interpretations of conflict theory have focused on the subordination and powerlessness of minorities. This is in contrast to the pluralistic conflict approach of minority group threat where the focus is on the perceived or actual threat such groups pose to the dominant group. A group threat orientation typically considers two interrelated factors: the size of the minority population and the economic situation of minorities compared to the advantaged group.

Blalock (1967) argues that the larger the proportion of the population made up by the minority group, the greater the competition over resources (i.e., money, property, prestige, and voting rights) and the perceived challenges to the dominant group's status. The second group-level factor linked to minority group threat is economic equality. The traditional interpretation of this concept is that increases in the income and wealth of minorities relative to whites should make the latter group feel more threatened.[7] Consequently, prejudicial attitudes will develop and discriminatory practices will be employed by the dominant group to diffuse the minority group threat. The likelihood of the dominant group perceiving and acting upon a minority group threat is dependent on the existing political and economic relations between the groups.

Little research has been conducted that utilizes the minority group threat theory to explain case processing and outcomes of minorities relative to whites, especially in juvenile court settings.[8] Results predicated upon the power threat thesis have also been inconsistent. Dannefer and Schutt (1982), for example, used the power threat thesis in their study of two counties and three police bureaus from each county in New Jersey. They discovered that in the community with the higher proportion of minorities, police responded in a biased manner toward minority youth. In this same county, the bias was corrected, to some extent, by the courts.

Frazier and his colleagues (1992) examined the case processing of Florida youth with the specific objective of testing Hawkins's (1987) version of the power threat thesis. Hawkins (1987) called for a revised conflict theory incorporating the historical contexts of race and punishment (Adamson, 1983; Peterson and Hagan, 1984) and the concept of Blalock's (1967) power-threat thesis to account for the anomalous findings in the criminal justice system. He argues that as minority populations gain greater visibility through increased numbers and gains in social, economic, and political domains, their threat to the advantage of majority groups becomes more intense as does competition for resources. Under these conditions, the criminal justice system will exert greater social control as a method of diffusing this perceived or actual threat. Discriminatory treatment will be more evident in settings with greater minority presence and economic equality.

Frazier and his colleagues argue that Hawkins's thesis stands in direct opposition to several traditional conflict theories that posit that a lower proportion of minorities in the population allows this relatively powerless group to be subjected to greater social control. Hawkins's argument is that racial differences in social control will be evident in communities with greater numbers of minorities and racial economic equality. Frazier and his colleagues (1992) tested this thesis by incorporating case-level variables and a number of social contextual variables (e.g., racial income inequality, percentage whites, white/black poverty, index crime rate, and juvenile arrest rate) to assess the case outcomes of blacks compared to whites at intake, court referral, and court dispositions.

Although not always consistent, the contextual variables were significant determinants of case outcomes. Racial disparity in each of the three case outcomes was evident and, to some degree, conditioned by the percent of whites living in a jurisdiction. However, the result was consistent with a traditional conflict interpretation rather than a power threat thesis, where Frazier and his colleagues (1992) argued that as white majority populations increase in a jurisdiction, so does their ability to exert social control over minorities (see also Bridges and Crutchfield, 1988). Frazier and his colleagues concluded that black powerlessness may be a better explanatory factor of black disadvantage in juvenile justice proceedings than the notion of power threat.

Bridges and his colleagues (1995) also found mixed support for the effects of macrolevel contexts in their examination of the rates of confinement in juvenile correctional facilities for whites and minorities for all counties in the state of Washington for the years 1990 through 1991. The racial composition of a community and urban concentration did not affect the level of confinement for minority youth. Both structural factors, however, had inverse statistically significant effects on the rate of confinement for white youth. Bridges and his colleageus *did* find that youth in communities that experienced higher levels of violent crime were more likely to be confined, and the effect was strongest for minorities living in violent crime communities. The pattern held even after controlling for differences in white and minority rates of referral to juvenile court.

Crawford and his colleagues (1998) relied on Blalock's (1967) concept of minority group threat and Sampson and Laub's (1993) emphasis on the perceptions of African Americans as racially threatening to "mainstream America" to examine African Americans' likelihood of being classified as habitual offenders, especially for crimes involving drugs and violence. They found race effects for drug offenses and property offenses. All significant race effects, however, were found in communities that were low in terms of racial threat (i.e., low in terms of percent of African Americans, racial income inequality, drug arrest rates, and violent crime rates). The racial threat was greatest where the actual threat of crime itself was low.

SUMMARY

Research employing contextual frameworks that quantitatively assesses the characteristics of the community on decision-making outcomes for minorities compared to whites has yielded mixed and inconsistent results that confirm those discovered by Leiber (1994, 1995; Leiber and Stairs, 1999) in his studies of DMC in Iowa. Although not discussed in great detail, the same can be said of studies that examined the effects of organizational contingencies on case processing and outcomes.[9] Dixon (1995), for example, found no evidence of race effects in her study of decision making in seventy-three counties in Minnesota. Legal variables were important determinants of sentencing irrespective of organizational context, while the degree of court bureaucratization influenced guilty pleas and sentence reductions. Cohen and Kluegel (1978) also failed to find support for their expectation of race effects in a Memphis juvenile court, where rehabilitation and informality were practiced, compared to a Denver juvenile court, which was more formal and oriented to due process. Prior record and the type of offense strongly influenced case dispositions for whites and nonwhites in both jurisdictions.[10]

Prior research in this area has failed to provide consistent evidence that minorities are treated differently than whites in settings that vary in terms of community characteristics and/or organizational factors and in the expected directions (e.g., Crawford et al., 1998). Perhaps because of the inclusive effects of these mediating variables on decision-making outcomes, researchers disagree on what kinds of contexts are most important and exactly how or why they are linked with race and social control (Bridges and Myers, 1994).

An analytic framework that includes structural and organizational contingencies, however, provides greater insight into the relationship between race and decision making beyond the traditional focus on microlevel case determinants (Sampson and Laub, 1993; Sampson and Lauritsen, 1997; Ulmer, 1997). The results from previous analyses lend some support for this claim (e.g., Albonetti and Hepburn, 1996; Steffensmeier et al., 1998). Still, prior research, including Leiber's (1995, 1999) work in Iowa, indicate that such a contextual approach alone may not provide a complete picture of the factors that influence decision-makers in the case processing and outcomes of whites and minorities, particularly in more homogeneous communities. In Iowa, race effects are evident in the four jurisdictions under study in the present research (Leiber, 1994; Leiber and Stairs, 1999). There are a number of explanations that might account for the incompleteness of the structural approach.

The presence of racial disparity across all four jurisdictions, for example, could suggest that the sites are more similar than different on the structural and organizational variables. However, variation in the contextual indexes, while limited, is evident. Differences by jurisdiction in the case processing of youth, as predicted by Sampson and Laub's theory (1993), were also present (table 2 in Leiber and Stairs, 1999; chapter 5 in this volume). The results could also suggest that a contextual analysis is not an appropriate framework for studying the influence of race on juvenile justice decision making. It could be that due to the tremendous amount of discretion decision-makers can exercise and the varied factors they can rely upon to arrive at decisions, it is too difficult to identify and control for all of these factors solely by quantitative assumptions and methods (e.g., Sanborn, 1996; Mears, 1998).

Although there is some validity to each of these contentions, a contextual analysis can offer insights into the situations in, and conditions under which, race influences juvenile justice decision making, but refinement is needed conceptually and in application. The results from Leiber and his colleagues (1994,

1995, 1999) and others (e.g., Bridges et al., 1995) suggest that the effects of race on justice outcomes are variable and point to the need to broaden the focus of the factors that impact juvenile justice case processing and outcomes. An analytic strategy is also needed that uses both quantitative and qualitative methods to examine and capture the intricacies involved in decision making. While not bound by any specific theory, the present research is driven by these needs.

Chapter 3

Correctional Orientations, Race, Crime, Family, and Respect for Authority

Despite differences in theory and/or the sources for the increased social control of youth, a common theme within contextual analyses pertinent to this study is how decision-makers perceive minorities. Prior contextual frameworks place an emphasis, explicitly or implicitly, on the social interactions between decision-makers and youth and the meanings derived from the contacts. Stereotyping plays a significant role in this process as does the extent these perceptions interact with the stated or perceived correctional goals of the court. While historical, structural, and organizational contingencies have also been treated as central factors, the primary concern of this book is the further development and scrutiny of the mid-to-microlevel aspects of the contexts of decision making.

EXPANDING THE FOCUS TO INCLUDE ADHERENCE TO MULTIPLE CORRECTIONAL ORIENTATIONS

Research has shown that organizational contingencies appear to yield inconclusive results in terms of understanding differences in the treatment of whites and minorities (see chapter 2). The courtroom work group has been found to impact organizational arrangements, case processing, and sentencing strategies (e.g., Sudnow, 1965; Eisenstein et al., 1977, 1988, Ulmer, 1997). Herbert Packer's (1968) description of the administration of criminal justice as proceeding from either a due process or a crime control model aids in understanding the views and values of the court as a group and responses toward youth within the juvenile justice system.

Courts that emphasize a due process model focus on formal procedures, respect for the individual liberty and autonomy of the accused, and providing the accused with his or her full array of legal rights. A crime control model approach is concerned with the repression of crime, the rights of the victims, and the protection of society from criminals. Informal administration procedures, discretionary decision making, and the disposition of cases quickly are all characteristics of a court practicing a crime control approach to justice.

Attempts to apply Packer's models of the criminal process to the juvenile court have typically contrasted "social welfare" or "treatment" models and a "just deserts" or "due process" model (Cohen and Kluegel, 1978; Stapleton et al., 1982; Hasenfeld and Cheung, 1985; Feld, 1999: 111). As discussed by Feld,

> In a welfare model, youths bear little responsibility for their misdeed and officials decide informally and without extensive public scrutiny whether a youth requires intervention and what form it should take. Professionals respond to a youth's "needs" rather than "deeds" and provide indeterminate, nonproportional rehabilitative dispositions to promote his future welfare. By contrast, the juvenile just deserts model reflects neoclassical assumptions of criminal law and characterizes youths as substantially responsible and accountable for their behavior. . . . Questions of guilt, innocence, blame and punishment occupy the central focus; the court uses formal criminal procedures to determine legal guilt. Determinate and proportional sanctions emphasize personal responsibility, foster equality among similarly situated youthful offenders, and sentence for past offenses rather for future welfare. (1999: 111–112, cite omitted)

The social welfare model is often referred to as the "traditional" model or the "rehabilitative" model while the just deserts model is implied within studies of juvenile justice decision making that focus on the court's emphasis on punishment, represented by youth receiving more severe outcomes and greater social control.

The overreliance on the role of the just deserts model or punitiveness within contextual analyses of social control can be traced to a number of factors, including increased support for the punishment of adult and juvenile offenders, rising crime rates, and the "war on drugs." Beginning with the late 1970s, public opinion (Gallup Report, 1985; Maguire and Pastore, 1997), research (Cullen et al., 1985; Grasmick et al., 1993; Mears, 1998), and legislative reforms (Irwin and Austin, 1994) reflected a societal intolerance of crime and support of punitive interventions for offenders.

The "get tough" movement not only impacted the treatment of adult criminals (e.g., Clear, 1994) but juvenile delinquents as well (Rubin, 1985; Feld, 1987; Bernard, 1992; Merlo, 2000; Moon et al., 2000; Triplett, 2000). Many states enacted provisions to transfer youth more easily from juvenile to adult jurisdiction (Feld, 1993; Snyder and Sickmund, 1999). For example, many of these waiver provisions lowered the age at which youth could be transferred to adult court and in some instances permit a change in jurisdiction based on the severity of the offense rather than age (Griffin et al., 1998). States also expanded the number of offenses that justify transfer, raised the maximum age of the juvenile court's jurisdiction over juvenile offenders, and created blended sentences that allow the imposition of both juvenile and adult correctional sanctions on certain young offenders (Snyder and Sickmund, 1999). Feld, for example, points out that California's presumptive waiver legislation was amended seven times between 1977 and 1993 to include a greater number of crimes that excluded youth from juvenile court jurisdiction and permitted transfer to adult court (1999: 219). The juvenile justice system also underwent other changes that emphasized the rights of victims, the use of fingerprinting, shifts from closed to open proceedings, and the use of multiple sanctions (Torbet and Szymanski, 1998; Moon et al., 2000).

In the 1980s, celebrity criminal cases, sometimes involving youth, and increases in crime, especially among juveniles in general and younger youth in particular, paved the way for the growing dissatisfaction with the traditional *parens patriae* approach of the juvenile justice system (Rubin, 1985; Bernard, 1992; Snyder and Sickmund, 1999). Coupled with findings from the career criminal research and from its focus on age at onset, a greater emphasis was placed on early intervention into youth misconduct and holding youth more accountable for their actions (e.g., Wolfgang et al., 1972; Hamparian et al., 1978; Petersilia, 1980; Blumstein et al., 1986; Farrington, 1986; Champion, 1994; Fagan and Zimring, 2000).

The increase in the levels of accountability, together with the "war on drugs," had dramatic consequences for the detection and involvement of minorities especially, African Americans, in both the criminal and juvenile justice systems (Chambliss, 1995; Tonry, 1995; Miller, 1996; Humphries, 1999; Stahl, 1999). McGarrell (1993:33), for example, found that from 1985 to 1989, the number of nonwhite youth detained for drug offenses increased by 235% while the number of white youth detained for similar violations declined by 17.2%. Similar disproportionate minority overrepresentation also existed in state training schools and in other secure facilities (e.g., Hamparian and Leiber, 1997; Snyder and Sickmund, 1999; chapter 1 in this volume).

It is easy to see why theory development and contextual analyses focused on concerns for punishment (e.g., Sampson and Laub, 1993; Albonetti and Hepburn, 1996). But research also reveals that the public and decision-makers adhere to and support models of decision making in addition to punishment. In a series of studies conducted during the last fifteen years, Cullen and his colleagues (1985, 1997, 1999), Moon et al. (2000), and Applegate et al. (2000), for example, report that the general public support retributive as well as rehabilitative strategies for dealing with criminals. The author and his colleagues (1995; 1997; 2000; 2002) found similar responses among juvenile justice personnel in Iowa and King County, Washington. Adherence to fundamentalist Christian beliefs was a significant determinant in explaining attitudes toward both correctional orientations, especially among female juvenile justice personnel in Iowa (Leiber, 2000). Leiber and Woodrick (1995) also discovered the presence of a conservative subgroup that believed in a literal interpretation of the Bible, racial and gender stereotyping, and punitive responses to crime.

None of the aforementioned studies examined the extent religion and conservative attitudes influenced the actual treatment of minorities relative to whites or youth in general. Gibson (1978) found that southern judges who were affiliated with a fundamentalist church were likely to sentence adults more punitively. Myers (1988), however, found that fundamentalist judges were not more likely than other judges to discriminate against African Americans or against other disadvantaged offenders. In fact, fundamentalist judges displayed greater leniency in their sentencing of African Americans in criminal justice proceedings.

Although not focusing on race or religion, Davis and his colleagues (1993) discovered that liberal juvenile justice personnel supported a rehabilitative ideology; believed in an external causality of crime (i.e., situational attributions); adhered to a nontraditional view of women; and held a positive prognosis for the offender. Two conservative groups were also identified among the respondents. One conservative group was younger; focused on the severity of the crime; supported a punitive response to crime; adhered to an internal causality of crime (i.e., dispositional attributions); and sentenced the most harshly of the three groups. The other conservative group advocated an internal crime attribution, held a traditional view of women, and were between the other two groups on sentencing goals. This group sentenced youth the least harshly.

Results from follow-up interviews with decision-makers in Washington by Bridges and his colleagues (1987, 1995) also reveal that adherence to correctional strategies other than punitiveness has consequences for responses toward minorities. Bridges and his colleagues (1987) discovered a reliance on the stereotyping of minorities as dangerous by justice officials that were used to determine that minorities posed significant threats to the public and to the moral order of a community. They argue that this may result in the adoption of formal and informal policies to control the perceived threat and consequently, exacerbate racial disparities in confinement. Bridges and his colleagues also point out that while the respondents discussed minority youth and crime in terms of threats, they placed more of an emphasis on the cause of crime as a consequence of unmet welfare needs of the poor and of the other disadvantaged in their community. This "child-saving" orientation often resulted in the differential rate of detention and confinement for minority youth (Bridges et al., 1995: 151). The finding of adherence to a "child-saving" orientation is not surprising, given that the juvenile justice system was founded on the premise of *parens patriae* (Platt, 1969) that continues to be, in conjunction with retribution, the guiding principle for interacting with system- involved youth (Feld, 1993, 1999).

In summary, an overview of the literature reveals that the general public and juvenile justice personnel support both punitive and rehabilitative correctional strategies. A variety of factors including religion and casual attributions appear to be predictors, or at the minimum correlates, of adherence to one, both, or slightly different "takes" of these correctional strategies. The extent varying correctional ideologies interact with beliefs concerning minority youth or have implications for the treatment of racial groups in juvenile justice proceedings have not been fully assessed. The limited research that has been conducted, however, has shown this area to be a promising avenue for further development and inquiry (Bridges et al., 1995).

An objective of the present research is to identify the correctional strategies or orientations adhered to by juvenile court personnel, assess the extent to which these orientations influence decision making and the handling of minority youth relative to white youth, and vary by each of the four juvenile courts. Next, the discussion centers on the need to expand the notion of racial stereotyping beyond the relationship between being African American and involved in drug offending.

EXPANDING THE FOCUS TO INCLUDE RACE, CRIME, FAMILY, AND RESPECT FOR AUTHORITY

In this section, data are first presented to establish the factual basis of the associations between race, crime, family, and respect for authority. The discussion then covers literature that indicates that these associations have been racially stereotyped to apply to most, if not all, African Americans and are often used to promote fear, self-interest, differentiation, and control.

The Statistical Picture

Minority groups have been cast as a "problem population" (Spitzer, 1975) affiliated with "gangs" (Jackson, 1992); dangerous (Bridges et al., 1987); and differentially involved in delinquency (Frazier et al., 1992) and drugs (Myers, 1989; Snyder, 1990; Blumstein, 1993; McGarrell, 1993) and there is evidence that African Americans in particular are disproportionately involved with gangs, serious delinquency, and drugs (e.g., Hindelang et al., 1981; O' Brien,

1985; Chiricosi, 1996; Farrington et al., 1996; Esbensen and Winfree, 1998; Hawkins et al., 1998).

Table 3.1 provides arrest information differentiated by whites, African Americans, Hispanics, Native Americans, and Asians for the years 1980, 1985, 1990, and 1995. Recall, minority youth make up 30% of the general juvenile population age 10 to 17. African Americans represent 15%, Hispanics 12%, Native Americans 1.2%, and Asians 3.3%.

The greatest overrepresentation in arrests is for African Americans, followed by Hispanics. Native Americans and Asians, for the most part, are arrested in proportion to their representation in society. In 1995, African American youth, for example, were involved in 28 percent of all juvenile arrests. These youth represented 49 percent of the violent crime index, 27 percent of the property crime index, and 26 percent of the nonindex crimes. With some exceptions, arrests for each racial group have remained relatively stable since 1980.

African American youth are most overrepresented in arrests for murder (58%) and forcible rape (60%). The gap between white youth and African American youth for these crimes and others has remained constant throughout the last twenty years. As previously discussed, the most notable exception is for murder. Arrests for murder increased for both whites and African Americans in the 1980s, but between 1984 and 1991, the rate at which white juveniles committed murder increased by 64 percent, while the African American juvenile murder rate increased by 211 percent (Snyder and Sickmund, 1995: 56).

Another exception is arrests for drug violations (Snyder and Sickmund, 1995). The increase in arrests for drug violations is directly linked to the disproportionate increase in the numbers of minority youth referred to the juvenile court, detained and/or committed to juvenile secure corrections, and transferred to adult court (Snyder, 1990; Miller, 1996:86). McGarrell found that the largest increase in referrals, detentions, petitions, and placements for drug offenses was for African Americans (1993:47 note 2). While juvenile cases waived to adult court between 1985 and 1994 involving whites involved mostly person offenses, drug violations surpassed these offenses among African American youth transferred to adult court during 1989 through 1992 (Sickmund et al., 1997:31). Overall, confinement rates for minority youth in the juvenile justice system have increased over the last twenty years, and the overrepresentation is greatest for African Americans (Synder and Sickmund, 1995; see also, chapter 1 in this volume).

For the most part, the results from victimization surveys concerning race parallel those from the Uniform Crime Reports. For example, in 1984, African American juveniles were 4 times more likely than white juveniles to be homicide victims: among juveniles age 14 to 17, the homicide victimization rate for African American males was 3 times that of their female counterparts, 5 times that of white males, and 9 times that of white females. By 1991, the homicide

TABLE 3.1
Arrest Rates by Race

Category	Year	Percent White	Percent Black	Percent Nat. Am.	Percent Asian	Percent Hispanic
U.S.						
Population	1980	78.6	14.7	0.7	1.8	8.8
(17 & under)	1990	74.9	15.1	1.2	3.3	12.2
Total Arrests	1980	76.7	21.7	0.9	0.7	10.7
	1985	74.9	23.2	0.9	1.0	11.7
	1990	71.3	26.2	1.1	1.5	—[a]
	1995	69.2	27.9	1.2	1.8	—
Index Crimes						
Violent	1980	47.6	51.2	0.6	0.6	15.8
	1985	46.3	52.4	0.6	0.7	14.5
	1990	47.8	50.5	0.6	1.1	—
	1995	48.5	49.3	0.8	1.5	—
Property	1980	71.5	26.6	0.9	1.0	9.9
	1985	72.1	25.7	1.1	1.2	11.0
	1990	71.7	25.4	1.2	1.7	—
	1995	69.3	27.3	1.3	2.1	—
Nonindex						
Crimes	1980	81.7	16.9	0.9	0.5	10.7
	1985	78.3	20.0	0.8	1.0	11.8
	1990	73.0	25.0	1.0	1.4	—
	1995	70.8	26.3	1.2	2.0	—

Source: FBI Uniform Crime Reports for the United States, 1980, 1985, 1990, 1995: Washington, DC: U.S. Government Printing Office.
[a]Information not available.

victimization rate for African American males was 7 times that of African American females, 8 times that of white males, and 29 times that of white females (Synder and Sickmund, 1995: 25). Furthermore, African American youth had the highest chance of becoming a victim of a violent crime in 1991 with a rate of 84 per 1,000 people, compared to a rate of 69 for both white non-Hispanic and white Hispanic (Synder and Sickmund, 1995:22). In short, African Americans are disproportionately involved in official statistics both as offenders and as victims.[1]

A variety of factors are believed to account for African American participation in crime, including economic deprivation, joblessness, family disruption, segregation, residing in isolated and disorganized communities, and cultural adaptations (e.g., Sampson, 1987; Jencks, 1992; Massey and Denton, 1993; Peeples and Loeber, 1994; Heimer, 1995; Sampson and Wilson, 1995; Tonry,

1995). These potential causes of delinquency are interrelated, but the two that have the most significant implications for influencing juvenile decision-makers are youth coming from female-headed households and being perceived as lacking respect for authority and the law (e.g., Cicourel, 1968; Frazier, 1979; Pope and Feyerherm, 1990). Both are often seen as part of a subculture tolerant of sexually promiscuous lifestyles and disregard for other middle-class values, including conformity to the law and respect for authority (e.g., Clark, 1965; Liebow, 1967; Wolfgang and Ferracuti, 1967; Wilson, 1987; Anderson, 1990, 1999; Duneier, 1992; Hacker, 1995).

Ever since Moynihan's (1965) report on the social pathologies of ghetto life, the African American family has been a topic of concern and debate (compare Wilson, 1987, with Bailey, 1996).[2] Bennett and his colleagues, for example, argue that African American delinquency and criminality is the result of "moral poverty" (1996:13) or the "lack of loving, capable, responsible adults who teach the young right from wrong" (46). While the traditional two-parent household is less evident today than in the past for all racial groups (Lugaila, 1998), the situation is most acute for African Americans. It has been estimated that 75% of African American children, compared to 40% of white children, will experience parental separation or divorce by age 16 (Bray and Hetherington, 1993). Single-parent households have been increasing over the last thirty years, but almost 60% of African American homes are headed by a female compared to 19% for whites (Hacker, 1995).

The rise of female-headed families, in particular among African Americans, parallels the increase in out-of-wedlock births (Wilson, 1987). Every year more than 900,000 young women age 15 through 19 become pregnant (U.S. Department of Health and Human Services, 1999). Out-of-wedlock births are especially evident among African American females under age 18 (Jaynes and Williams, 1989). The significance of the single-parent family and "kids having kids" is the increased likelihood of living in poverty, being on welfare, and being involved in crime (Murray, 1984; McLanahan, 1985; Jencks, 1992; Moffitt, 1995; Maynard and Garry, 1997; Thornberry et al., 1999).

Results from both surveys and studies reveal that racial groups also differ in their beliefs about the legitimacy of the law and the police and respect for authority in general (e.g., Kluegel and Smith, 1986; Anderson, 1999). African Americans are also far more likely to perceive criminal injustice and express distrust (Jaynes and Williams, 1989; Hacker, 1995; Bureau of Justice Statistics, 1998). In fact, Weitzer and Tuch (1999) report that being African American is the strongest determinant of perceptions of racial bias on the part of the police and the criminal justice system. A 1994 *USA Today* poll, for example, showed that 74% of African Americans agreed and 65% of whites disagreed with the statement that blacks are treated more harshly than whites by the criminal justice system.

Several observers have noted that the differences in values and attitudes may be contingent not only upon cultural norms but also upon social structures and social events that differ across racial as well as class lines (Hagan and Albonetti, 1982; Frank et al., 1996; Sampson and Bartusch, 1999; Taylor, 2000). For example, Leiber and his colleagues (1998a) found that race and community characteristics were useful in explaining juveniles' unfavorable view of police fairness and police discrimination. The findings also implied that, quite aside from the nature of police encounters with juveniles, the imposition of legal authority and social control in certain neighborhoods engendered a pervasive resentment and resistance and that youthful residents of those neighborhoods harbored a general disrespect for the law itself. Sampson and Bartusch discovered that African Americans are more dissatisfied with the police because they are more likely to reside in concentrated disadvantaged neighborhoods. They argue that neighborhood context is a stronger explanatory factor of attitudes toward the police than race. For the present research, however, it is not important whether race has a direct or mediated effect on attitudes unfavorable toward legal authority. What is important is that race is associated with more negative attitudes of the law and of those who enforce the law.

The brief review of the evidence suggests that as society has endorsed a punitive correctional orientation, African Americans have received the brunt of the "get tough" response toward crime. African Americans also appear to be more likely to be involved in crime and to be victims of crime and are more likely to live in households headed by single females and experience out-of-wedlock births and at a younger age. Furthermore, African Americans, for a variety of reasons, may be more likely to lack respect for the law and legal authorities than whites. These particular factors characterize the theoretical foundations of both Sampson and Laub (1993) and Tittle and Curran (1988), who both emphasize the symbolic significance of these behaviors that run counter to middle-class norms and to the reaction of juvenile justice personnel to "aggressiveness, sexuality, and the lack of personal discipline." How decision-makers perceive minorities, the factors that shape the perceptions, and the extent they vary by court guide the analytic strategy used in the present study.

Decision-makers' attitudes about crime, the family, and respect for authority and the law are factors believed to influence juvenile justice decision making and are important for understanding the treatment of African Americans compared to whites. Each factor is associated more with African Americans than whites and are, to a varying degree, legitimate criteria that can be relied upon by juvenile justice decision-makers to assess the need for intervention. For example, the juvenile court was established on the premise that the poor and minority youth came from families that lacked moral character and that were incapable of providing proper parental guidance and "that everything the government could do to instill these children with proper values was for the better"

(Schlossman, 1977:17; Odem, 1995). Furthermore, the principle of individualized justice still underlies the juvenile court to varying degrees and allows for the determination of a disposition based on the "full understanding of the client's personal and social character" and "individual needs" that includes assessments about the family, respect for authority, and the offense (Matza, 1964, 114–115; Feld, 1999).

The actual or perceived racial differences in crime, family, and respect are viewed by some as having been racially stereotyped and result in the differential handling of African Americans compared to whites. Next, literature representing this line of thought is discussed.

Racial Stereotyping

Politicians, law enforcement officials, and the media have been primarily responsible for the creation and maintenance of criminal imageries that often result in moral panics (Fishman, 1978; Leiber et al., 1993, 1998b; Mears, 1998; Humphries, 1999; Muzzatti, 2003) and racial stereotyping and racial oppression (Swigert and Farrell, 1977; Zatz, 1987b; Chambliss, 1995; Chiricos, 1996; Miller, 1996; Rome, 1998). Omi and Winant indicate that the media "have been notorious in disseminating images of racial minorities which establish for audiences what people from these groups look like, how they behave, and 'who they are.' The power of the media lies not in their ability to reflect the dominant racial ideology, but in their capacity to shape that ideology in the first place"(1986: 63). This point is highlighted by the Building Blocks for Youth coalition that conducted a survey of almost one hundred research studies that examined the coverage of crime by news media—local and network television, newspapers, and broadcast and print news magazines.

The report indicates that the proportion of crime committed by African Americans was overreported and that crimes involving minority victims were underrepresented. Concomitantly, media coverage of crime overrepresent African American involvement by underreporting crimes committed by whites (Dorfman and Schiraldi, 2001). Media coverage of crimes committed by minorities raises the level of fear among viewers including juvenile justice decision-makers and politicians, and reinforces support for retributive crime policies (Gans, 1995).

The criminal imagery has led "to the perpetuation of racial caricatures, as racial stereotypes serve as shorthand for scriptwriters, directors, and actors" (Omi and Winant, 1986: 63; see also Quinney, 1970; Barak, 1994; Mann and Zatz, 1998). Within the criminal and juvenile justice arenas, racial stereotyping has resulted in the ability of decision-makers to differentiate and control. For example, through interviews, Steffensmeier and his colleagues (1998) found that decision-makers were strongly influenced by fear and by the social attributes of the defendants, especially African Americans. African Americans were seen as poor, unemployed, on welfare, less educated, dangerous, and poor risks for rehabilitation. Young male African American defendants in particular were typecast as even more "dangerous, committed to street life, and less reformable" (see also, Spohn and Holleran, 2000). Swigert and Farrell (1977) found similar racial stereotypes in homicide convictions where African Americans were typecast as "normal primitives."

Utilizing both quantitative and qualitative methods, Bridges and Steen (1998) discovered that probation officers attributed African Americans' delinquency to internal explanations (i.e., "feeling no remorse," "uncooperative") while for whites external or environmental attributions were stressed (see also, Cicourel, 1968). African American youth were perceived as dangerous and more often guilty than whites because decision-makers believed that the causes of crimes by African American youth were linked to these personality traits. Consequently, internal attributions were found to be stronger predictors of officers' assessments of re-offending than offense severity and criminal history. The only factors to influence sentencing recommendations were internal attributions and the assessment of re-offending (see also, Carroll, 1978).

Although Bridges and Steen (1998) discovered that the three courts examined differed in structure and ideology, there was no evidence that the courts varied in attributions about juvenile offenders or recommended dispositions. In short, they reveal that differences in probation officers' assessments of the causes of crime mediated the effects of race on punishment. By also exploring the subjective qualities of legal decision making, they were able to determine how the values and beliefs of decision-makers created a recognizable but racially stereotypical image of an offender that influenced the decision-making process.

Race stereotyping goes beyond crime and includes sexuality and the family. Over a half century ago, Myrdal (1944) spoke of the relationships between sex, race, and racist beliefs, and the castration and lynching of blacks, including the insistence on the part of white men that they needed to protect women from the sexual advances of black men. Hacker argues that whites still have racist beliefs concerning the sexuality of African Americans and may even be envious of the alleged sexual prowess of African Americans. "Compounding the ordinary insecurities most men have in this sphere, white men face the mythic fear that black men may out-rival them in virility and competence. At issue, of course, is not whether this is actually true but the fact that the stereotype persists" (1995:67). Furthermore, Hacker states:

To be white is to be "civilized," which brings acceptance and imposition of sexual constraints. True, the freedoms that arose with the sexual revolution permit more experimentation than in the past. Still, fantasies persist that black men and women are less burdened by inhibitions and can delight in primal pleasures beyond the capacities of whites (68).

These views coincide with the underlying premises of Tittle and Curran's (1988) symbolic threat thesis.

Historical and legal precedent allow probation officers within the juvenile court to make assessments of the family's ability to provide a "good" home environment, socialize, and supervise youth in arriving at decisions as to how to proceed (Feld, 1999). Research has shown that family considerations have important implications for the handling of youth (e.g., Molgaard et al., 2000). It has been the prevailing view that youth from two-parent households may be treated more leniently by the court than youth from single-parent homes (e.g., Dannefer and Schutt, 1982) because such homes are assumed to exert greater supervision over their children than single-parent homes (e.g., Arnold, 1971). Or it may be that preferential treatment results because the court is unwilling to break up families by placing youth in secure facilities (e.g., DeJong and Jackson, 1998). A third possibility, is that decision-makers respond differently to youth from single-parent homes because of perceived notions that such households are threatening to middle-class standards because they do not conform to idealized notions of sexual relations and the traditional nuclear family (e.g., Leiber and Mack, 2003).

Pope and Feyerherm argue that the "family situation" may in fact be a typescript for "race" within juvenile justice proceedings. They question whether this racially tainted factor should be relied upon by juvenile justice decision-makers and whether assessments about the family ought to produce the degree of difference between majority and minority youth that it appears to produce (1993: 3). Pope and Feyerherm discovered that youth from single-parent female-headed homes often faced more severe dispositions than those from two-parent homes. Since African American youth are more likely to reside in such homes, they were more likely to receive severe sanctions (1993: 11).

Results from interviews with juvenile justice personnel in Florida support the findings and sentiments of Pope and Feyerherm (1993). Frazier and Bishop state that the views of decision-makers "about minority families indicate racial bias, attitudes that feed on and support racial bias, and they ultimately operate to justify the system's bent toward treating youths from minority families more formally and more harshly" (1995: 35). Furthermore, decision-makers viewed nonwhite single-parent families as more problematic than their similarly situated white counterparts. DeJong and Jackson (1998), however, discovered that while living with only one parent influenced the likelihood of white youth being placed in secure detention, family status had no effect on decision making involving African American youth. Fagan and his colleagues (1987), on the other hand, failed to find any significant differences in the treatment of white and minority youth by family status.

Cicourel (1968) also discovered in his study of police, juvenile court personnel, and teacher interactions with troubled youth that parents of minorities and minority youth were more likely to be viewed as lacking respect for authority and as inappropriate candidates for gaining the trust of probation officers. Minority youth were also more likely to be judged on general style of life, appearance, and demeanor than white youth (see also, Piliavin and Briar, 1964).

Frazier (1979) observed that juvenile offenders who were unconventional in appearance and less respectful in demeanor had a greater chance of receiving a more harsh outcome. Although race was not explicitly examined in the Frazier study, Mann argues that the implications of these findings for minorities are clear:

> In the first place, there is no escaping the fact that minorities in custody look "different," not only because of skin color and physiognomy, but also, since most are poor, their speech and manner of dress do not coincide with those of the middle-class and, in many cases, highly educated judges they face. Frazier . . . defined "nonconventionals" as "those who wore their clothes sloppily, had uncombed or dirty hair, and appeared unkempt." [Puerto] Rican "naturals" or "Afro" hairstyles would be suspect, and the Jamaican dreadlocks and "Frankenstein" haircuts worn by young African Americans today would certainly be looked at with judicial disfavor. (1993: 211)

Miller suggests that the involvement of the criminal and juvenile justice system into the lives of African Americans has contributed to a "culture of opposition." According to Miller, African Americans are "now routinely socialized to the routines of arrest, booking, jailing, detention, and imprisonment that it should come as no surprise that they bring back into the streets the violent ethics of survival which characterize these procedures" (1996: 97). The "culture of opposition" referred to by Miller is taken from Anderson (1990, 1995, 1999), whose ethnographic studies provide insights into racism and adaptations of the ghetto poor, especially African Americans, to subcultural values where being treated "right" and expressions of "manhood" are of great importance and where violence is accepted (see also, Clark, 1965; Liebow, 1967).

Both Miller and Anderson believe that a vicious cycle has been created where the oppositional culture confirms the stereotypical and negative images that whites and middle-class African Americans have of ghetto African Americans. These racist beliefs, in turn, legitimize the oppositional culture among African Americans. Until the cycle is broken, the middle class will continue to view poor African Americans in a negative light.

Some contend that a social distance exists between whites and African Americans and that this social distance comes from whites' perceptions of African Americans' "criminality, lack of intrinsic worth, and threat to the social order" (Taylor, 2000:203; Georges-Abeyie, 1990). Furthermore, Taylor argues that a "cultural mistrust becomes an operating mechanism for assessing and dealing with what has become for some, everyday perceptions or cultural markers" (2000: 203). According to this line of thought, African Americans will continue to lack respect for the law and for the personification of the law represented by middle-class juvenile court personnel. Their perceived or actual failure to abide by middle-class values can be relied upon by officials to "legally" justify the differential treatment of African American youth compared to the more cooperative and deferent white youth.

The extent to which African Americans truly are more criminal, reside in dysfunctional families, are sexually promiscuous, are disrespectful, and act as a result of their place in an oppositional culture or a "culture of mistrust" is not at issue for the present research. What is important for the present research and for a contextual analysis is the extent to which decision-makers rely on these factors, *perceive* African Americans to differ on these factors and, in turn, note how the perceived differences influence decision making and the treatment of African Americans relative to whites. This book also assesses whether these perceptions are fostered by structural and court contexts including adherence to correctional philosophies with the case processing and outcomes of minorities in each of the four juvenile courts.

THE NEED FOR A DIRECT EXAMINATION
OF THE ATTITUDES OF DECISION-MAKERS

Too often, the microlevel interpretations of interactions with youth that reflect structural, cultural, and organizational contexts are overlooked or at best inferred. For example, Tittle and Curran (1988) did not directly test their notion that young, sexually active minorities represent symbolic threats to decision-makers. Similarly, Sampson and Laub (1993) infer support for their macrolevel structural theory of social control from findings of a race interaction with drugs and for those receiving a severe outcome in certain communities. Albonetti and Hepburn's (1996) finding that decision-makers rely on racial stereotypes to reduce or minimize uncertainty in the decision to divert felony drug offenders is also inferred from results of a statistically significant interaction between minority status, prior record, and age. Little research has been conducted that inquires into the actual beliefs of decision-makers regarding minorities and how they, along with aspects of community and organizational structures, affect decision making (Bridges et al., 1995: 151–152).

Underlying the relationship between stereotyping and structural or organizational contingencies is the belief that involvement in a specific crime results in discriminatory outcomes. The outcome differential between African Americans and whites is thought to be indicative of racist beliefs and of attitudes supportive of punitiveness on the part of decision-makers. For example, minorities accused of drug offenses are perceived as serious offenders in need of stronger social control, while the same is not true for similarly situated whites (e.g., Sampson and Laub, 1993). This represents an implied connection between stereotypes and decision-making outcomes rather than an explicit test of the relationship between individual attitudes and the treatment of minorities relative to whites.

This point is addressed in a critical analysis of macroperspectives on crime control by Liska:

Rather than measuring ruling class interests and threats to these interests directly, by measuring people's perceptions and beliefs, researchers measure them indirectly, by the structural conditions (economic inequality, crime rates, and percentage nonwhite) assumed to threaten these interests. Such indirect measures of the central theoretical concept yield only weak tests of the central theoretical propositions. (1987:85–86)

Bridges and Steen echo a similar point: "Despite the importance of perceived threat to sociological explanations of legal decision making, few studies have examined how officials' assessments of offenders or their crimes influence their perceptions of threat. Indeed, most studies focus on legal outcomes . . . without regard to the perceptual processes involved" (1998: 556–557; cf. Bortner, 1982; Drass and Spencer, 1987; Steffensmeier et al., 1998). In the present research, this limitation is addressed by querying decision-makers on their attitudes concerning correctional ideologies, race, crime, family, and respect for authority. Each of these factors is interrelated, possibly influenced by structural and organizational factors, and directly or indirectly associated with race and decision making.

Research on race and juvenile justice decision making has generally employed either quantitative (e.g., Sampson and Laub, 1993) or qualitative (e.g., Mann, 1984) techniques. More recent contextual analyses have relied exclusively on official statistical data (e.g., Frazier et al., 1992). However, a "variable orientation" alone may not fully capture the subtleties of the factors associated with race and decision making (Crew, 1991; Conley, 1994; Bridges and Steen, 1998). Underlying a variable orientation are the assumptions that the contents of cases are factual and represent an objective reality.

Accordingly, researchers assume that they can classify cases as alike or similar on the basis of legal criteria, such as severity of the offense and prior record, and make comparisons between offenders to determine if they are treated alike or receive similar types of outcomes. This positivistic model has been criticized on a number of grounds. First, the unexplained variance in decision making (i.e., the dependent variable) is large (Hagan et al., 1979). Second, factors that influence decision making are often omitted from the analysis (Sanborn, 1996), and/or not all of the decision-making stages are examined (Pope and Feyerherm, 1993) or are measured incorrectly (Leiber and Stairs, 1999). Third, a quantitative approach often fails to detect informal procedures and practices that are not conducive to variable inquiry (Georges-Abeyie, 1990). The most damaging criticism of the quantitative method, however, is the failure to recognize that decision-makers are active participants in the construction of official records and the case in general (e.g., Maynard, 1982; Crew, 1991). Research has shown that decision-makers negotiate, process, and respond to cases as part of a larger set of shared expectations or characterizations that may be based on familiarity, mental images, and stereotypes (e.g., Sudnow, 1965; Emerson, 1969; Drass and Spencer, 1987; Albonetti and Hepburn, 1996; Bridges and Steen, 1998; Leiber and Mack, 2002).

Qualitative techniques involving observations and interviews have been suggested as an alternative method for overcoming the limitations of quantitative methods (e.g., Mann, 1989). Qualitative methods are believed to be better suited for the discovery of insights into how decision-makers think, interpret, and respond to interactions with offenders and whether race and stereotyping play roles in the process (Maynard, 1982). Qualitative techniques, however, have their weaknesses. The most notable shortcomings of a reliance solely on qualitative inquiries are a lack of reliability and the inability to generalize the results. Consequently, many have argued for the utilization of both quantitative and qualitative methods (e.g., Pope and Feyerherm, 1993; Leiber, 1994; Mears, 1998).

Research relying upon both quantitative and observational, ethnographic, or other qualitative methods have provided greater insights into how decision-makers perceive and respond to minorities (e.g., Bridges et al., 1995; Bridges and Steen, 1998; Steffensmeier et al., 1998). The present research uses both quantitative and qualitative methodologies to assess when and under what conditions race and stereotyping influence case processing and decision-making outcomes.

SUMMARY

Research has long recognized that adherence to a variety of correctional philosophies, such as "due process" versus "therapeutic," may account for court variation in the case processing and in outcomes of criminals (e.g., Packer, 1968) and delinquents (e.g., Stapleton et al., 1982). Similarly, research has found that decision-makers often employ typifications to achieve shared definitions of cases as "normal crimes" (Sudnow, 1965; Emerson, 1969) that may be based on the offender's demeanor and appearance (Cicourel, 1968; Frazier, 1979) and race (Swigert and Farrell, 1977; Bridges and Steen, 1998). It has not been until recently that structural, organizational, and social-psychological contextual analyses of race and decision making have focused on the relationship between decision-makers' adherence to correctional orientations and perceptions of minorities with the imposition of sanctions (e.g., Sampson and Laub, 1993). These contextual perspectives generally have emphasized structural and organizational contingencies, punishment-oriented ideologies, and the casting of minorities as threats to community safety or as symbolic threats to middle-class standards.

The objective of the present study is to build upon previous contextual analyses to account for the presence of race effects in four homogeneous juvenile courts in Iowa. The contextual framework is refined by expanding the focus of inquiry beyond punitive ideologies and race and drugs to include multiple correctional orientations and the views of decision-makers concerning race, crime, family, and respect for authority. Both quantitative and qualitative methodologies are employed to discover the perceptions of minorities by decision-makers and to how these perceptions may explain race differences in case processing and outcomes.

Chapter 4

Methods

The present research examines the extent adherence to a dominant correctional orientation(s) and perceptions of minorities as criminal, coming from dysfunctional families, and lacking respect for authority by decision-makers influence decision making and vary by juvenile court. The examination of these social-psychological processes should broaden our understanding of the contexts of decision making including when and under what conditions race matters. In this chapter, the data and samples, the structural and organizational characteristics of the jurisdictions, the decision-making stages, the case-level variables, and analysis procedures used to accomplish this objective are discussed.

DATA AND SAMPLES

Multiple strategies are needed to fully search for the existence of racial bias and to provide explanations as to why and under what conditions it exists in each of the four jurisdictions. Therefore, the present research uses information from the Census and juvenile court case files and from semistructured interviews with juvenile court personnel.

A random sample of court referrals identified as white (n = 5,883) was selected and disproportionate random sampling was used to select African American (n = 1,049) and Native American referrals (n = 276). Since sampling procedures varied across the four jurisdictions, different weight factors were used for whites, African Americans, and Native Americans to obtain sample proportions that reflect the racial distribution of all delinquency referrals in each court.[1] The weighted sample size used in the present research is 7,208. The weighted sample for Bond is 2,020, Jackson 1,967, King 1,798, and Parks 1,423.[2]

African Americans were selected since it is this population that is most overrepresented in the system in Iowa (chapter 1 in this volume) and nationwide (Hamparian and Leiber, 1997). African Americans also comprise the largest group of minority youth in three of the four jurisdictions (70 percent or more). Native Americans were included in the study because they make up a sizable percentage of minority youth in Jackson (22 percent) and there is a lack of research on the case processing of this racial group (Pope and Feyerherm, 1990; Pope et al, 2001). Although each of the four jurisdictions have the greatest number of minorities compared to all other jurisdictions in Iowa (Bureau of the Census, 1990), the overall small number of minority youth in each required the selection of delinquency referral cases for a twelve-year period from 1980 to 1991.

Juvenile court personnel in each of the four jurisdictions were interviewed through semi-open-ended questions that focused on their beliefs concerning crime, family, the role of the juvenile court, disproportionate minority confinement (DMC), and findings specific to the quantitative component of the study (Leiber, 1993). The interviews were taped and transcribed and ranged in length from one to two hours. The personnel were interviewed in late 1991 and early 1992. Juvenile court probation officers (n = 72), public defenders (n = 4), prosecutors (n = 4), and judges (n = 4) comprise the nonrandom sample for a total of 84.[3]

Most of the juvenile court personnel participated in the study (90 percent) and a large majority are white (94 percent). The respondents are on average forty-one years old, male (64 percent), work in the social sciences (74 percent), and have ten years of job tenure. Cross-tabulations and analysis of variance (ANOVA) failed to show statistically significant differences on these background characteristics by jurisdiction (not shown).

THE STRUCTURAL CHARACTERISTICS
OF THE JURISDICTIONS

Because of the importance that structural contexts have in increasing our understanding of race, decision making, and social control, information is provided that distinguishes each community on these indexes. The structural characteristics discussed were selected on the basis of theory and previous research (e.g., Tittle and Curran, 1988; Albonetti, 1991; Sampson and Laub, 1993).

Table 4.1 provides the distributions on the population for each jurisdiction and race concentration. King has the largest population (n = 315,158), followed by Parks (n = 155,500), Bond (n = 130,224), and Jackson (n = 98,276). Eighty percent of the county's population, however, lives in the largest city within Bond and Jackson, while the percentage is over 60% in the remaining two jurisdictions.

The largest minority presence within the largest city is in Bond, followed closely by King and Parks. African American youth comprise 19 percent of all

TABLE 4.1
Community Characteristics—Population and Minority Concentration,
Distributions by Jurisdiction

| | *Jurisdiction* | | | |
	Bond	*Jackson*	*King*	*Parks*
I. Population	130,224	98,276	315,158	155,500
% Persons age 17 and younger	24.1	28.1	26.0	27.1
II. % of All Youth				
African American	11.0	2.8	6.1	8.3
Hispanic	1.7	4.0	2.8	2.0
Native American	0.2	3.0	0.3	0.3
Asian	0.5	1.8	2.8	0.9
Other	0.4	0.9	0.5	0.4

| | *Largest City within Jurisdiction* | | | |
	Bond	*Jackson*	*King*	*Parks*
III. Population	106,536	81,254	192,095	99,298
% Persons age 17 and younger	30.1	28.7	25.8	28.9
IV. % of All Youth				
African American	19.0	3.4	10.0	12.8
Hispanic	0.8	4.7	3.7	3.2
Native American	0.2	3.5	0.4	0.3
Asian	0.7	2.0	3.6	1.0
Other	0.4	1.2	0.9	1.5

youth in the largest city within Bond and about 13 percent in Parks. Jackson and its largest city are the most racially diversified, with Hispanics and Native Americans making up the largest minority groups, followed by African Americans.

Table 4.2 presents the distributions for the structural indexes represented by underclass poverty, racial inequality, moral/sexual promiscuity, and wealth. Underclass concentration is represented by the percentage of persons below the poverty level, the rate of unemployment, and the percentage of employed persons age 16 and older. Racial inequality is captured by the ratio of African American to white families below the poverty level and the percentage of minorities in poverty. The variable morality/sexual promiscuity is included to represent Tittle and Curran's claim that "nonwhites and youth symbolize to white adults resentment-provoking or fear-provoking qualities like aggressiveness, sexuality, and absence of personal discipline" (1988:52). Morality/sexual promiscuity is measured by the percentage of babies born out-of-wedlock to

TABLE 4.2
Community Characteristics—Inequality and Juvenile Crime, Distributions by Jurisdiction

| | Jurisdiction | | | |
Definitions	Bond	Jackson	King	Parks
I. Underclass				
% persons in poverty	11.65	12.10	8.67	9.83
Unemployment (rate)	9.44	6.56	5.64	7.61
% of 16 and older employed	61.90	63.40	70.70	66.90
Racial Inequality				
Ratio of African American persons to white persons in poverty	4.08	3.85	3.43	4.37
% minority in poverty	23.80	14.75	20.05	21.45
Morality/Sexual Promiscuity				
% babies born out-of-wedlock to teenage mothers	39.64	37.90	37.14	40.33
II. Wealth				
Per capita personal income ($)	12,932	13,038	16,026	14,352
Average family income ($)	28,619	26,239	31,784	31,130
III. Juvenile Crime				
% juvenile arrests	34.70	33.30	24.10	33.70
CJ $ resources (police expenditures, $ per person)	10.81	9.89	9.47	14.83

teenage mothers. The wealth of a community is measured by per capita income and by the average family income.

Two variables represent the extent of juvenile crime in a community and the financial commitment to crime control. The percentage of juvenile arrests for each county is included in the analysis since the severity of case outcome may be influenced by the proportion of serious crime in a specific locality (Frazier et al., 1992). A community's commitment to crime control is measured by the variable criminal justice resources and reflects police expenditures per person in each county. Spending on criminal justice resources may shape court processing and social control in general (Hasenfeld and Cheung, 1985; Sampson and Laub, 1993).[4]

The economic measures and the crime measures are based on Census information that represent population parameters. Because these are population parameters as opposed to samples of the populations, any differences in the contextual variables are true differences and negate problems associated with chance and with the use of tests for significance. Bond can be characterized overall as poorer and as having greater racial inequality. The jurisdiction ranks second in terms of unwed teenage pregnancy and in the amount spent on criminal justice resources slightly behind Parks. In Bond, juveniles make up the highest percentage of arrests.

Jackson closely resembles Bond in terms of impoverishment. King stands out from the other three jurisdictions ranking lower on poverty, racial inequality, sexual promiscuity, and the crime measures while ranking higher on wealth. For example, in 1987 the per capita personal income (PCPI) for King was ranked 1st in the state while Bond ranked 60th, Jackson ranked 34th, and Parks ranked 9th (Bureau of the Census, 1990). Parks evidences greater racial inequality, unmarried teen pregnancy, and spends on average the most on criminal justice resources.

THE ORGANIZATIONAL CHARACTERISTICS OF THE JURISDICTIONS

Previous research suggests that organizational contingencies that include correctional orientations may be also fruitful in the study of decision making, especially in more homogeneous communities, such as the four jurisdictions under study in the present research (Matza, 1964; Cicourel, 1968; Emerson, 1969; Albonetti, 1991). For example, Ulmer (1995), Ulmer and Kramer (1996), and Steffensmeier et al. (1998) found that county court differences in personal relationships among the courtroom work groups and sponsoring agencies interacted with ideologies about case processing and sentencing that resulted in racial differences in case outcomes. Sampson and Laub (1993) also, to a limited degree, controlled for possible organizational contingencies. Five variables represent the organizational characteristics of each juvenile court: types of referrals, average number of all referrals per year, rate of delinquent referrals per year, average caseload, and court ideology. The distributions for these variables by jurisdiction are presented in table 4.3.

Both Jackson and King handle referrals (e.g., children in need of supervision) in addition to delinquent cases. Possibly reflecting the population size of the jurisdiction, King and Parks on average handle more overall referrals per year. Few differences are evident between the jurisdictions in terms of the rate of delinquent referrals per year. Still, King and Parks have on average higher caseloads.

One focus of the present study is the importance of court ideology on case processing and outcomes. Court ideology will be measured in two ways. The first measurement reflects the correctional goals as stated by the chief juvenile court officer in each jurisdiction (Leiber, 1992a,b). The second measurement of correctional orientations represents the responses from the

TABLE 4.3
Juvenile Court Characteristics at the Organizational Level by Jurisdiction

Definitions	Jurisdiction			
	Bond	Jackson	King	Parks
Types of Referrals				
Delinquent	yes	yes	yes	yes
Children in need of supervision		yes	yes	
Mental health at issue			yes	
Parental termination rights			yes	
Average Number of All				
Referrals Per Year	900	894	3,742	1,100
Rate Delinquent Referrals				
Per Year (youth referred to	2.87	2.90	3.29	2.63
youth < age 17 per 100)				
Average Caseload	50	35	90	70
(based on x number of				
personnel and all referrals)				
Court Ideologies[1]	Account-ability	Rehabili-tation	Maintain order	Account-ability
	Inter-vention	Protection of society	Protection of society	Inter-vention

[1]As stated by chief juvenile court officer.

individual court officers. The results from the individual decision-makers will be presented later in the book.

Before the start of the initial DMC study, the chief juvenile court officer in each jurisdiction was asked to comment on the overall ideology of his or her juvenile court and all four of the respondents spoke of rehabilitation. Each of the officers, however, also emphasized other correctional objectives. As can be seen in table 4.3, differences exist in the espoused ideology. Holding youth accountable and intervention are the main objectives in Bond. In Jackson, rehabilitation and the protection of society from further delinquency are emphasized. The latter objective and the maintenance of order are stressed in King. Both jurisdictions de-emphasized the use of diversion as a form of intervention at the stage of intake. Accountability and intervention are seen as important in Parks.[5]

DECISION-MAKING STAGES

Following the suggestions of Bortner and Reed (1985) and others (e.g., Bishop and Frazier, 1988), decision making in the juvenile justice system is viewed as a process consisting of many successive stages rather than simply one or two discrete decisions. The five decision-making stages in the juvenile justice system in Iowa are presented in a flow chart (figure 4.1). Each stage constitutes a dependent variable, with the most severe decision outcome representing the reference category for analysis purposes.[6]

Intake

Despite prior inquiry on race and intake decision making, the relationship between the two is unresolved. This occurrence, in part, is the result of previous research that has conceptualized decision making at intake as a dichotomy, typically differentiated in terms of unofficial versus official (Cohen and Kluegel, 1979; Thornberry, 1979; Frazier and Bishop, 1995; DeJong and Jackson, 1998) and has failed to consider differences that may exist between the decision to release and the use of diversion (cf. Bell and Lang, 1985; Leiber and Stairs, 1999).

In grouping release with diversion, researchers, for example, treat the decision to release and the use of the diversion options as one and the same. Yet, at intake youth typically may be released, agree to some form of diversion in exchange for a promise that further proceedings be dismissed (if youth successfully abides by the conditions of the agreement), or be recommended for further court processing. Clearly, different factors, such as the severity of the offense, may be related to the use of a simple release or the decision to have the referral move further into the proceedings (Bell and Lang, 1985).

In Iowa, juvenile court officers make the decision to release, to offer an informal adjustment in the form of diversion, or to recommend further court processing. Diversion was used in the majority of the cases (53 percent). State statute requires an admission of guilt as a prerequisite for diversion or as an informal adjustment (Iowa Juvenile Code Statute 232.29). To overcome the shortcoming of past conceptualizations of decision making at intake, this stage in the process is measured in two ways: (1) release/diversion versus further court processing and (2) release versus diversion/further court processing.[7]

Petition

The decision to seek further formal court processing is made by the prosecutor. An official petition is a charging instrument that specifies the offenses

FIG. 4.1.
Decision-Making Stages and Distributions Representing Four Juvenile Court Jurisdictions in Iowa

INTAKE

Release 1,741 (24%)

Diversion 3,842 (53)

⬆ Further processing 1,625 (23)

PETITION

Dismissed 114 (7)

⬆ Further processing 1,511 (93)

INITIAL APPEARANCE

Diversion 396 (33)

⬆ Further processing 807 (67)

ADJUDICATION

Dismissed 85 (10)

⬆ Delinquent 722 (90)

JUDICIAL DISPOSITION

Community treatment 438 (45)

⬆ Change of placement/541 transfer (55) adult court

aThe discrepancy between youth petitioned and those at the initial appearance hearing is due to the omission of youth transferred to adult court (n = 257) and missing cases (n = 51).

52

against the juvenile and that initiates formal court proceedings. A significant majority of the juveniles (93 percent) in the jurisdictions under study were petitioned.

Initial Appearance

At this stage of the proceedings, decision-makers again have the option of diversion or they may process the juvenile to the adjudication stage.[8] Analogous to the use of diversion at intake, over one third of the cases in the present sample were diverted at initial appearance. As with the intake stage, these youth must admit guilt, and those who fail to adhere to the stipulated conditions may be subject to further juvenile court proceedings.

Adjudication

This decision-making stage is operationalized as dismissed and as the adjudication of delinquency. Ninety percent of the cases reaching this stage were adjudicated delinquent.

Judicial Disposition

Next to the death penalty, transfer to adult jurisdiction can be the most severe sanction given to a youth and disproportionately involves African Americans relative to whites (Stahl, 1999). In the present research, youth transferred to adult court are included within the definition of judicial disposition (see also, Bishop and Frazier, 1988). Judicial disposition is defined as an outcome that resulted in a change of placement (e.g., training school, residential facility, or group home) or transfer to adult court versus probation and/or treatment within the community.[9] Fifty-five percent of youth at this stage received a disposition involving a change of placement/transfer to adult court.

CASE CHARACTERISTICS

The independent variables include extralegal and legal factors regarding current offense, previous history, and social characteristics. Previous research on the influence of race on juvenile justice decisions includes similar variables (e.g., Kempf-Leonard and Sontheimer, 1995). Table 4.4 presents the variables, the coding scheme, and the distributions differentiated by jurisdiction.

TABLE 4.4
Case-Level Characteristics, Codes, and Distributions by Jurisdiction

		Jurisdiction							
		Bond		Jackson		King		Parks	
Independent Variable	Code	N	%	N	%	N	%	N	%
Social Traits									
Race[a]	0 = White	1,818	90	1,593	81	1,476	82	996	70
	1 = African American	202	10	98	5	322	18	427	30
	2 = Native American			275	14				
Gender	0 = Male	1,644	81	1,455	74	1,405	78	1,148	81
	1 = Female	376	19	511	26	393	22	275	19
Age	Years Mean =	15.5		14.3		15.3		14.3	
Family status	0 = Two parents present	1,193	59	1,211	62	871	49	774	54
	1 = One parent present	827	41	756	38	927	51	649	46
School status[b]	0 = Attend—no problems	1,436	71	1,439	74	1,489	83	1,083	76
	1 = Attend—problems	394	20	362	18	117	6	261	18
	2 = Not attending	190	9	166	8	192	11	78	6
Legal									
Prior referrals	Number Mean =	1.6		1.3		0.9		0.8	
Court authority	0 = No	1,543	76	1,832	93	1,633	91	1,259	89
	1 = Yes	477	24	134	7	166	9	164	11
Charges	Number Mean =	1.3		1.1		1.1		1.3	
Crime severity	0 = Misdemeanor	1,559	77	1,690	86	1,390	77	1,006	71
	1 = Felony	461	23	277	14	408	23	417	29
Crime type[c]	0 = Other	442	22	454	23	355	20	279	20
	1 = Property	1,027	51	1,100	56	966	54	813	57
	2 = Person	260	13	153	8	325	18	245	17
	3 = Drugs	290	14	258	13	152	8	85	6

[a]When necessary, race will be treated as two dummy variables with white as the reference category.
[b]School status will be treated as a dummy variable with attending—no problems as the reference category.

The social traits are represented by race, gender, age, the family living status of the youth, and school status. Race is operationalized as white versus African American. In Jackson, race is represented by the dummy variables African American and Native American with white the reference category. Family living status is defined by two-parent household versus one-parent household. School status is measured by two dummy variables: attending school but having problems and not attending. The reference category is attending school.

Two measures of the juvenile's previous history include the number of prior contacts with the juvenile justice system (interval) and whether she was under court authority at the time of the current referral (no = 0, yes = 1). Characteristics of the current offense are the number of charges against the youth (interval), the seriousness of the offense (misdemeanor = 0, felony = 1), and the type of delinquency. Because of the theoretical importance of drug offending in a contextual analysis of race and decision making (Sampson and Laub, 1993), dummy variables were created to distinguish between property, person, and drug offenses. Referrals consisting of disorderly conduct, resisting arrest, and so forth. comprise the reference category. Most cases are classified as misdemeanors (78 percent) and involve property crimes (54 percent).

A comparison of the legal and extralegal variables reveals few statistically significant differences by jurisdiction, but there are a few exceptions. The juvenile court in Bond handles more youth that are under court authority at the time of the most recent referral compared to the other three jurisdictions. Youth also evidence a greater mean number of prior referrals than those in the jurisdiction referred to as Parks. In comparison to the other jurisdictions and especially Parks, the court in Jackson deals with less serious delinquency as measured by activity charged as a misdemeanor.

ANALYSIS PROCEDURES

Following Bishop and Frazier (1988), Sampson and Laub (1993), and Leiber and Stairs (1999), the first step in the analysis assesses the movement of youth through each stage of the system. The movement of youth through the system is examined so as to compare decision making across jurisdictions and to determine if jurisdictional differences exist in exerting social control over youth, in particular, African Americans and, when appropriate, Native Americans (Jackson) and at what stage(s) in the proceedings. Cross-tabulations and proportions are used to accomplish these tasks. The results are presented in chapter 5.

Next, multivariate analyses are performed using logistic regression procedures to determine if the effects obtained from the bivariate comparisons hold once legal and extralegal factors are controlled. In addition to estimating additive models for each stage of the proceedings, models that include two-way interactions for race and each independent case-level variable will be estimated (Farnworth and Horan, 1980; Spohn et al., 1980–1981). These interactions are reported only when their inclusion in the model yields a statistically significant race interaction effect that improves the overall fit of the model. If a race inter-action with an independent variable is found to meet this criteria, separate mod-els will be estimated for each racial group so as to observe the relationship more clearly (Zatz, 1987a; Jaccard et al., 1990). I also calculated a probability estimate using the regression coefficient for race (when a statistically significant effect was present) and the mean of the dependent variable for each equation (Peter-son, 1985). The results from the logistic regression are presented in chapter 6.

The results from zero-order correlations and from the collinearity diag-nostic statistics revealed acceptable levels of shared correlation among the vari-ables (Belsley et al., 1980). The zero-ordered relationships among the variables are provided for each jurisdiction and are presented in the appendixes.

The process of excluding youth in a systematic manner at various stages may create a more homogeneous population as youth move from one stage in the proceedings to the next. This may result in sample selection bias (Berk, 1983). Although there are unsettled issues and disagreement about solutions to correct for sample selection bias (e.g., Stolzenberg and Relles, 1990; Kempf-Leonard and Sontheimer, 1995), Heckman's (1974) two-stage procedure is em-ployed whereby a probit model is estimated to assess the probability of inclusion in the sample. Estimates from this equation are then utilized to cre-ate a hazard rate. Next, the hazard rate or lambda is added to the second equa-tion to adjust for selection bias.

A hazard rate is included in the logistic regression equations for the four decision stages following intake to correct for the possibility of sample selection bias (Kempf-Leonard and Sontheimer, 1995). Selection bias is controlled be-tween (1) intake decisions and the filing of petitions, (2) petitions and initial appearance decisions, (3) initial appearance and adjudication, and (4) adjudica-tion and judicial disposition.[10]

Underlying a contextual analysis is the belief that subtle forms of racial bias are hidden or masked in the makeup of the community, organizational practices, situational factors, and the stereotypical attitudes and fears of deci-sion-makers. Thus, step 2 of the analysis involves the use of the information obtained from the semistructured interviews to tease out the more indirect forms of racial bias. The analytic framework is organized around the logistic re-gression results and the responses of decision-makers concerning race, crime, family, and respect for authority and the interrelationships with the perceived role of the juvenile court (i.e., retribution and rehabilitation). Decision-makers' explanations for minority overrepresentation in the system, their reactions to the specific findings from the quantitative analysis of the case files, and their suggestions for reducing the presence of minorities in the juvenile justice system are included within the framework. Each of these topics are believed to be interrelated and individually or in total should allow for further insights into the subtleties of the associations between race, crime, family, and respect for authority that may not be as evident in the results obtained from the quantitative analysis. The qualitative analysis is based on the assumption that inquiries into the perceptions of decision-makers regarding correctional ideologies, crime, family, and respect for authority will enhance our understanding of the case processing and outcomes of minorities relative to whites and the variability of the possible relationships within each jurisdiction. The results have implications for expanding the view of context, especially where structurally and organizationally communities and courts are more alike than different and where race effects exist. The information from the interviews is presented in chapters 7 through 10 with each of the four jurisdictions represented by one chapter. Chapter 11 presents a summary and discussion of the results that include directions for a contextual framework, research, and policy.

SUMMARY

Although the state and the jurisdictions examined in the present study consist mostly of whites, Iowa and the four communities are representative of areas elsewhere in the country. For example, the four jurisdictions experienced dramatic increases in unemployment and single-female households in the 1980s, similar to the rest of the country. Thus, minority economic experiences in the jurisdictions under study reflect similar trends at the national level (Iowa Department of Economic Development, 1990). In addition, offenses of this sample of juveniles parallel national aggregate arrest statistics (Snyder and Sickmund, 1995) and are somewhat limited in severity (see also, Sampson, 1986).[11] Also, recall that the rate incarceration for African American adults and youth in Iowa ranks well above the national average (Hamparian and Leiber, 1997; Des Moines Register, 2000). Therefore, an examination of the contexts of juvenile justice decision making should not be dismissed on the basis of a smaller proportion of nonwhites and/or the lack of major urban areas in Iowa.

On the basis of Sampson and Laub (1993) and other structural contextual approaches (e.g., Crawford et al., 1998) and organizational analyses (e.g., Steffensmeier et al., 1998) and the distributions, one could expect differences in decision making and social control. For example, race effects and greater social control should be evident in Bond and possibly in Parks compared to King and Jackson. The lower scoring on the underclass measures and the degree of urbanization and relative high-average caseload suggest that King approximates a highly bureaucratic urban setting, where a justice orientation exists.

Similarly, Jackson does not have a strong minority presence and ranks low on racial inequality relative to the other three communities. We would not anticipate race differences to be present once relevant legal and extralegal considerations are controlled. Recall that results from Leiber and his colleagues' previous research (1994, 1995, 1999), however, failed to provide strong support for these hypotheses and pave the way for further inquiry into the contexts of decision making that include historical, structural, organizational, and social-psychological contingencies.

Chapter 5

Movement through the Juvenile Justice System

This chapter examines decision making in each jurisdiction to assess the movement of youth from referral at intake to a dispositional outcome involving a change of placement or transfer to adult court. There are two objectives in tracing this movement through the proceedings. The first is to treat juvenile justice decision making as a process that spans multiple stages. Researchers generally focus on only one or two decision-making points (e.g., DeJong and Jackson, 1998); most commonly disposition (or severity of disposition); and detention (e.g., Aday, 1986). The failure to examine all relevant decision-making points may obscure selection bias that occurs either earlier or later in the proceedings. Furthermore, the initial effect of selection bias may be small, and possibly statistically insignificant, but cumulative effects may be significant in their impact on outcomes for minority youth (e.g., Bortner and Reed, 1985; McCarthy and Smith, 1986; Fagan et al., 1987; Hamparian and Leiber, 1997).

A second objective in tracing the movement of youth through the proceedings is to determine the extent the jurisdictions differ in exerting social control, particularly in responses to African Americans relative to whites. Theory and prior research (e.g., Sampson and Laub, 1993) would lead us to anticipate that youth in general and African Americans specifically would be subject to greater social control in Bond and perhaps Parks than would their counterparts in the other two jurisdictions, especially King. Recall that Bond and Parks ranked high on minority concentration, racial inequality, and criminal justice resources and expressed organizational ideologies predicated on accountability and intervention. King could be characterized as more of an urban setting, where cases are handled quickly and relatively informally. Jackson is more similar to King than different, despite being smaller and poorer. The organizational philosophies of these jurisdictions emphasized the protection of society. Jackson also emphasized rehabilitation, while King expressed concerns for the

maintenance of order. In short, we expect less social control in these two jurisdictions compared to Bond and Parks.

Cross-tabulations are used to determine if jurisdictional differences exist
in decision-making outcomes and in the exertion of social control over youth,
particularly minorities, at each of the five stages in the proceedings. Part A of
each table presents the distributions of decision-making outcomes for each
stage in the proceedings for all youth by jurisdiction. Part B provides decision-
making outcomes by jurisdiction and race. By utilizing this method I will be
able to compare the racial makeup of the cohort moving through the juvenile
justice system in each jurisdiction and calculate probabilities of youth receiving
a change of placement/transfer to adult court (see Bishop and Frazier, 1988).

DECISION-MAKING STAGES

Intake

Recall that at intake, decision-makers have three outcomes to choose from: release, participation in diversion, and recommendation for further court processing. As can be seen in part A of table 5.1, referrals for further court processing at
intake are more prevalent in Bond (34 percent) and Parks (29 percent) than in
Jackson (12 percent) and King (15 percent). Diversion is the most common outcome at the intake stage in three of the four jurisdictions. King is the exception.
Jackson ranks by far the highest on the use of diversion (69 percent), followed by
Parks (58 percent), Bond (54 percent), and King (32 percent). While King ranks
fourth in the use of diversion, the jurisdiction uses the option of release more frequently than any other jurisdiction. For example, 53 percent of the youth in King
are released at intake compared to 12 percent of the youth in Bond.

In part B of table 5.1, it is evident that African American youth are more
likely to receive a recommendation for further court processing at intake than
are white youth in Bond. Of the African Americans, 42 percent are likely to
be referred to the stage of petition compared to 33 percent of the whites. No
statistically significant association is present between race and the likelihood of
being referred for further proceedings in the remaining three jurisdictions.
African Americans are less likely than whites to participate in diversion in all
four jurisdictions, although the effect is statistically insignificant in Parks. In
Jackson, both white youth (70 percent) and Native American youth (71 percent) are more likely than African American youth (58 percent) to be diverted
at intake. No substantive differences in the jurisdictions are evident between
the racial groups and the decision to release.

In short, these data suggest that Bond and Parks exert greater social control over youth than the other two jurisdictions. Bond scores highest on refer-

TABLE 5.1
Intake Decision Making by Jurisdiction

Part A: All Youth

| | Jurisdiction | | | |
Intake	Bond	Jackson	King	Parks
Release	241[1]	364	949	186
	(12)	(19)	(53)	(13)
Diversion	1,088	1,360	571	823
	(54)	(69)	(32)	(58)
Further Court Processing	691	242	278	414
	(34)	(12)	(15)	(29)

[1]Represents N, followed by percent within a jurisdiction (Chi-square Pearson value = 1369.680, $p = .00$). Percent does not add up to 100 due to rounding.

Part B: Differentiated by Race

| | Jurisdiction | | | | | | | | |
| | Bond | | Jackson | | | King | | Parks | |
Intake	W.[1]	A.	W.	A.	I.	W.	A.	W.	A.
Release	212[2]	29	283	26	56	765	184	130	56
	(12)	(14)	(18)	(26)	(20)	(52)	(57)	(13)	(13)
Diversion	1,000	88	1,109	57	194	494	77	585	238
	(55)	(44)	(70)	(58)	(71)	(33)	(24)	(59)	(56)
Further Court Processing	605	85	201	16	25	217	61	281	133
	(33)	(42)	(13)	(16)	(9)	(15)	(19)	(28)	(31)

[1]W. represents white youth; A. represents African American youth; I. represents Native Americans.
[2]Represents N, followed by percent within a racial group. Comparisons between whites, African Americans and, when appropriate, Native Americans within jurisdictions reveals statistically significant associations (for Bond Chi-square Pearson value = 9.465, $p = .001$; for Jackson Chi-square Pearson value = 9.468, $p = .050$; for King Chi-square Pearson value = 12.633, $p = .001$; for Parks Chi-square Pearson value = 1.349, n.s.).

rals for further proceedings, followed by Parks. Jackson ranks highest on the use of diversion, and release is the most common option used in King. At intake, decision making appears to be more similar in Bond and Parks, while Jackson and King are more alike.

As far as race is concerned, African Americans are subject to greater social control in Bond. No statistically significant race differences are evident in the other three jurisdictions in recommendations at intake for further court proceedings. Whites receive diversion more often than African Americans in three of the four jurisdictions, except Parks. In Jackson, Native Americans receive diversion on par with whites and more so than do African Americans.

Petition

Table 5.2 provides the distributions for youth referred to the petition stage. At this stage, proceedings may be dismissed or continued in the form of a petition of delinquency. In all four jurisdictions, youth are likely to be petitioned if they are not diverted or released at intake (table 5.2, part A). Still, slight jurisdictional differences are evident. Youth in Jackson are not petitioned as frequently (14 percent) as youth in the other three jurisdictions, but over 94 percent or more of youth receive the more severe outcome.

Only one statistically significant association occurs when decision making at the petition stage is differentiated by race and jurisdiction (table 5.2, part B). In Parks, African American youth are less likely to be petitioned than are white youth.

Initial Appearance

An examination of decision making at initial appearance by jurisdiction reveals that differences exist in the extent to which youth are referred further into the system instead of being diverted (table 5.3, part A). Bond (78 percent) and Jackson (83 percent) use the more severe outcome of referral to adjudication proportionately more often than King (38 percent) and Parks (63 percent). Furthermore, King is the only jurisdiction to practice diversion at this stage more often than referrals to adjudication.

African American youth are disproportionately more likely to be referred for further court processing than are white youth in Parks (table 5.3, part B). Eighty-one percent of the African Americans at this stage are referred to adjudication, compared to only 56 percent of the whites. No other statistically significant associations exist between race, jurisdiction, and decision making at initial appearance.

Adjudication

Table 5.4, part A details decision making involving the adjudication of delinquents and dismissals. Similar to decision making at the stage of petition (table

TABLE 5.2
Petition Decision Making by Jurisdiction

Part A: All Youth

	Jurisdiction			
Petition	Bond	Jackson	King	Parks
No Petition	42[1]	35	12	24
	(6)	(14)	(4)	(6)
Further Court Processing	649	207	266	389
	(94)	(86)	(96)	(94)

[1]Represents N, followed by percent within a jurisdiction (Chi-square Pearson value = 25.556, p = .00). Percent does not add up to 100 due to rounding.

Part B: Differentiated by Race

	Jurisdiction								
	Bond		Jackson			King		Parks	
Petition	W.[1]	A.	W.	A.	I.	W.	A.	W.	A.
No Petition	35[2]	7	25	4	6	10	2	10	14
	(6)	(9)	(12)	(28)	(22)	(5)	(3)	(3)	(11)
Further Court Processing	571	78	176	11	20	206	59	271	118
	(94)	(91)	(88)	(72)	(78)	(95)	(97)	(97)	(89)

[1]W. represents white youth; A. represents African American youth; I. represents Native Americans.
[2]Represents N, followed by percent within a racial group. Comparisons between whites and African Americans and, when appropriate, Native Americans within jurisdictions reveals a statistically significant association (for Bond Chi-square Pearson value = .981, n.s.; for Jackson Chi-square Pearson value = .132, n.s.; for King Chi-square Pearson value = .221, n.s.; for Parks Chi-square Pearson value = 8.909, p = .001).

5.2, part A), a clear majority of youth who reach this stage receive the more severe outcome. However, youth are more likely to be adjudicated delinquent in Jackson and King compared to the other two jurisdictions. In Jackson, 98 percent of youth receive the more severe outcome.

An examination of the breakdown of adjudication decision making by race and jurisdiction indicates no statistically significant race differences (table 5.4, part B). Although the numbers are small, every African American (n = 6) and Native American (n = 14) youth who reached the adjudication stage in Jackson were adjudicated.

TABLE 5.3
Initial Appearance Decision Making by Jurisdiction

Part A: All Youth

| | Jurisdiction | | | |
	Bond	Jackson	King	Parks
Initial Appearance				
Diversion	107[1]	30	157	102
	(22)	(17)	(52)	(37)
Further Court Processing	383	149	98	175
	(78)	(83)	(38)	(63)

[1]Represents N, followed by percent within a jurisdiction (Chi-square Pearson value = 145.099, p = .00). Percent does not add up to 100 due to rounding.

Part B: Differentiated by Race

| | Jurisdiction | | | | | | | | |
| | Bond | | Jackson | | | King | | Parks | |
Initial Appearance	*W.[1]*	*A.*	*W.*	*A.*	*I.*	*W.*	*A.*	*W.*	*A.*
Diversion	96[2]	11	25	2	2	124	33	87	15
	(22)	(17)	(16)	(28)	(13)	(62)	(60)	(44)	(19)
Further Court Processing	331	52	129	6	15	76	22	110	65
	(78)	(83)	(84)	(72)	(87)	(38)	(40)	(56)	(81)

[1]W. represents white youth; A. represents African American youth; I. represents Native Americans.

[2]Represents N, followed by percent within a racial group. Comparisons between whites and African Americans and, when appropriate, Native Americans within jurisdictions reveals a statistically significant association (for Bond Chi-square Pearson value = .823, n.s.; for Jackson Chi-square Pearson value = .924, n.s.; for King Chi-square Pearson value = .099, n.s.; for Parks Chi-square Pearson value = 15.516, p = .000).

Judicial Disposition

The dispositional outcome of change of placement/transfer to adult court is used more frequently than a disposition involving community-based treatment (table 5.5, part A). Bond and Parks sanction youth the most severely: 60 percent of youth reaching the disposition stage in Bond and 57 percent in Parks receive a change of placement or transfer to adult court. Conversely, Jackson sanctions less harshly relative to the other jurisdictions. Of youth that reach the judicial dispo-

TABLE 5.4
Adjudication Decision Making by Jurisdiction

Part A: All Youth

		Jurisdiction		
Adjudication	Bond	Jackson	King	Parks
Dismissed	49[1]	4	6	26
	(13)	(2)	(6)	(15)
Delinquent	334	146	94	149
	(87)	(98)	(94)	(85)

[1]Represents N, followed by percent within a jurisdiction (Chi-square Pearson value = 18.134, p = .00). Percent does not add up to 100 due to rounding.

Part B: Differentiated by Race

				Jurisdiction					
	Bond		Jackson			King		Parks	
Adjudication	W.[1]	A.	W.	A.	I.	W.	A.	W.	A.
Dismissed	42[2]	7	3	0	0	4	2	14	12
	(13)	(13)	(2)	(4)	(2)	(6)	(7)	(13)	(19)
Delinquent	289	45	126	6	14	73	21	96	53
	(87)	(87)	(98)	(96)	(98)	(94)	(93)	(87)	(82)

[1]W. represents white youth; A. represents African American youth; I. represents Native Americans.
[2]Represents N, followed by percent within a racial group. Comparisons between whites and African Americans and, when appropriate, Native Americans within jurisdictions reveals no statistically significant association (for Bond Chi-square Pearson value = .002, n.s.; for Jackson Chi-square Pearson value = .048, n.s.; for King Chi-square Pearson value = .069, n.s.; for Parks Chi-square Pearson value = 1.11, n.s.).

sition stage in Jackson, 59 percent receive community treatment. Slightly over half of youth receive a change of placement/transfer to adult court in King.

Differentiating decision making at judicial disposition by race and jurisdiction reveals few differences (table 5.5, part B). African American youth, however, are more likely than their white counterparts in Parks to receive the more severe dispositions. The association is weak but statistically significant. Recall that African Americans in Parks were more likely than whites to receive the more severe outcome at their initial appearance (table 5.3, part B).

TABLE 5.5
Judicial Disposition Decision Making by Jurisdiction

Part A: All Youth

	Jurisdiction			
Judicial Disposition	Bond	Jackson	King	Parks
Community Treatment	193[1]	101	49	95
	(40)	(59)	(49)	(43)
Change of Placement/	294	71	50	125
Transfer Adult Court	(60)	(41)	(51)	(57)

[1]Represents N, followed by percent within a jurisdiction (Chi-square Pearson value = 19.381, p = .00). Percent does not add up to 100 due to rounding.

Part B: Differentiated by Race

	Jurisdiction								
	Bond		Jackson			King		Parks	
Judicial Disposition	W.[1]	A.	W.	A.	I.	W.	A.	W.	A.
Community	166[2]	28	91	2	7	39	9	70	25
Treatment	(39)	(46)	(62)	(27)	(46)	(53)	(37)	(48)	(34)
Change of	262	32	57	6	8	35	15	75	50
Placement/	(61)	(54)	(38)	(73)	(54)	(47)	(63)	(52)	(66)
Transfer Adult									
Court									

[1]W. represents white youth; A. represents African American youth; I. represents Native Americans.
[2]Represents N, followed by percent within a racial group. Comparisons between whites and African Americans and, when appropriate, Native Americans within jurisdictions reveals statistically significant associations (for Bond Chi-square Pearson value = 1.295, n.s.; for Jackson Chi-square Pearson value = 5.073, n.s.; for King Chi-square Pearson value = 1.789, n.s.; for Parks Chi-square Pearson value = 4.236, p = .039).

Summary

It is clear that decision making varies by jurisdiction; the variation does not appear to be the result of jurisdictional differences in case-level variables (e.g., crime severity) (see chapter 4). The findings appear to lend initial support for the influence of community characteristics on decision making. As predicted by Sampson and Laub's (1993) macrolevel structural perspective, Bond and Jackson exert greater social control over youth than the other two jurisdictions that score lower on structural inequality and that evidence a smaller minority presence in the community. In addition, race differences are found in both jurisdictions. However, race associations with decision-making outcomes are also evident in Jackson and King. These results are contrary to the claims of Sampson and Laub.

The following section takes a closer look at the issue by examining changes in the racial composition of the cohort moving through the system. Probabilities are also presented to provide a clearer picture of the likelihood youth referred at intake receive a change of placement at judicial disposition or a transfer to adult court.

RACIAL COMPOSITION OF COHORT MOVING THROUGH THE SYSTEM

Figure 5.1 presents information on the initial racial composition of the cohort referred to juvenile court and changes in the racial makeup of youth moving through the system. The discussion centers on decision making at each stage within a jurisdiction.

In Bond, African Americans comprised 10 percent of the initial cohort, while whites made up the difference. The proportion of African Americans referred for further processing at intake is 12 percent, representing a 2 percent increase in the African American composition of the cohort. In Jackson, white youth constituted 81 percent of the referrals, African Americans 5 percent, and Native Americans 14 percent. The composition of the cohort referred for further proceedings increased by almost 2 percent for both whites and African Americans, while Native American representation decreased by 4 percent. White youth made up 82 percent of the initial referrals in King, and African Americans constituted 18 percent. The African American representation in the cohort moving further into the system increased by 4 percent. In Parks, African American youth initially comprised 30 percent of the cohort. The proportion of African Americans among all youth referred for further processing at intake is 32 percent, representing a 2 percent increase in the makeup of the cohort. Overall, there are slight increases in the representation of African American youth in the cohort moving further into the system from intake in all four jurisdictions and a decrease for Native Americans in Jackson.

Tracing the movement of youth from petition reveals little change in the composition of the cohort in each jurisdiction. In Bond, African Americans, for example, still represent 2 percent more of the cohort than they did at the initial referral. The composition of the cohort referred further into the system at petition has decreased by 2 percent for African Americans and remained the same for Native Americans as at intake (10 percent).

FIGURE 5.1.

Racial Composition of Cohort Moving through System by Most Severe Outcome and Jurisdiction

Initial Cohort Size

	Bond		Jackson			King		Parks	
	African Americans	*Whites*	*African Americans*	*Native Americans*	*Whites*	*African Americans*	*Whites*	*African Americans*	*Whites*
	10%	90%	5%	14%	81%	18%	82%	30%	70%

INTAKE	PETITION	INITIAL APPEARANCE	ADJUDICATION	JUDICIAL DISPOSITION
Further processing ⬆	Further processing ⬆	Further processing ⬆	Delinquent ⬆	Change of placement/ Transfer Adult Court

% Change in racial composition of initial cohort[a]

		PETITION	INITIAL APPEARANCE	ADJUDICATION	JUDICIAL DISPOSITION
Bond	African Americans	+2	+2	+3	+1
	Whites	−2	−2	−3	−1
Jackson	African Americans	+2	0	−1	+3
	Native Americans	−4	−4	−4	−1
	Whites	+2	+4	+5	−2
King	African Americans	+4	+4	+4	+12
	Whites	−4	−4	−4	−12
Parks	African Americans	+2	0	+7	+10
	Whites	−2	0	−7	−10

[a]Derived from comparing percent within an outcome to percent of racial makeup of initial cohort.

The cohort of youth referred from initial appearance to the next stage in the proceedings (adjudication) increased to 13 percent for African Americans in Bond, representing a gain of 3 percent from the initial cohort of referrals. Slight changes in the racial composition of the cohort are evident in both Jackson and King. The most significant change in the makeup of the cohort is evident in Parks, where the African American proportion of the cohort grew by 7 percent.

Also, few changes are evident in the composition of the cohort in each jurisdiction receiving the more severe outcome and moving further into the system at adjudication. African American youth remain overrepresented in Bond (+3%), King (+5%), and Parks (+6%). Both African Americans (−1%) and Native Americans (−4%) are underrepresented in Jackson.

At the disposition stage, the composition of the cohort in Bond receiving the more severe outcome is slightly overrepresented by African Americans (+1%). An increase in the African American component of the cohort (+3%) is also evident in Jackson while the Native American component decreased (−1%). The most dramatic growth in the composition of the cohort receiving a change of placement/transfer to adult court exists in King and Parks. In King, African Americans comprise 30 percent of the cohort at this point—a 12 percent increase in comparison to their initial referral composition. African Americans make up 40 percent of the cohort receiving the more severe outcome, representing a 10 percent growth in their component of the cohort in Parks.

Overall, African American youth in each jurisdiction have a greater likelihood of moving through the system than white youth. These associations vary by stage and jurisdiction. Native Americans in Jackson have a lower likelihood of social control compared to African Americans and whites.

PROBABILITIES OF RECEIVING OUTCOME OF CHANGE OF PLACEMENT/TRANSFER TO ADULT COURT

The probabilities of youth moving through the system and receiving an outcome of involving a change of placement or transfer to adult court are provided in table 5.6. Part A of the table presents the probabilities for all youth by jurisdiction, while part B differentiates the results by racial group and jurisdiction.

The probability of a youth referred to intake receiving an order of change of placement/transfer to adult court is .15 in Bond (part A). Once a youth is referred from intake to petition, the chances of receiving a change of placement/transfer to adult court are quite high (.42). Similarly, youth in Parks have the second highest probability of receiving a change of placement/transfer (.09, .30, respectively). Conversely, youth in Jackson and King have relatively lower probabilities. These findings support expectations and the claims by Sampson and Laub (1993): jurisdictions with greater economic and racial inequality, minority concentration, and a focus on crime control exercise greater social

TABLE 5.6.
Probability of Youth Receiving Change of Placement/
Transfer to Adult Court by Jurisdiction

Part A: All Youth

	Jurisdiction			
Change of Placement/ Transfer Adult Court	*Bond*	*Jackson*	*King*	*Parks*
Initial Sample[1] (referred to intake)	.15	.04	.03	.09
Referred to Petition Stage from Intake[2]	.42	.29	.18	.30

[1]Initial sample for Bond = 2,020, Jackson = 1,967, King = 1,798, and West = 1,423. Figure based on youth who received change of placement/transfer at judicial disposition (table 5.5., part A) divided by initial sample.

[2]Youth referred at intake to petition (table 5.1., part A). Bond = 691, Jackson = 242, King = 278, and Parks = 414. Figure based on youth that received change of placement/transfer at judicial disposition (table 5.5., part A) divided by referred to petition from intake.

Part B: Differentiated by Race

	Jurisdiction								
	Bond		*Jackson*			*King*		*Parks*	
Change of Placement/Transfer Adult Court	*W.*[1]	*A.*	*W.*	*A.*	*I.*	*W.*	*A.*	*W.*	*A.*
Initial Sample[1] (referred to Intake)	.14	.16	.04	.06	.03	.02	.05	.08	.12
Referred to Petition Stage from Intake[2]	.43	.38	.28	.37	.32	.16	.25	.27	.38

[1]Figure based on race-specific youth who received change of placement/transfer at judicial disposition (table 5.5., part B) divided by their initial sample (table 5.1., part B). Race-specific initial sample at intake Bond = W (1,817), A (202); Jackson = W (1,593), A (99), I (275); King = W (1,476), A (322); Parks = W (996), A (427).

[2]Figure based on race-specific youth who received change of placement/transfer at judicial disposition (table 5.5., part B) divided by referred to petition at intake (table 5.1., part B). Race-specific youth referred to petition from intake Bond = W (605), A (85); Jackson = W (201), A (16), I (25); King = W (217), A (61); Parks = W (281), A (133).

control. However, closer inspection of the probabilities of receiving the more severe outcomes for different racial groups reveals some findings contrary to Sampson and Laub.

As predicted by Sampson and Laub, greater social control of African Americans is evident in Bond and Parks (part B). For Bond, the probability of African Americans referred to juvenile court receiving a change of placement/transfer to adult court is .15, compared to .14 for whites. In Parks, almost 7.5 out of every 100 white youth referred to juvenile court receive an outcome involving a change of placement/transfer to adult court; for African Americans, the figure is almost 11.75.

In Jackson, African Americans have a probability (.06) of receiving the more severe outcome at judicial disposition that is one and a half that of whites (.04) and two times that of Native Americans (.03). The probability of a white youth from referral at intake receiving an outcome of a change of placement/transfer to adult court in King is .02, while the probability for African Americans is .05.

Thus, as expected, Bond and Parks exercised the greatest amount of social control in general and specifically in terms of African Americans relative to the other two jurisdictions. This race/social control association, however, appears to be the result of residing in communities where social control is greater. Although social control is not as evident in Jackson and King, African Americans still experience an increased probability of receiving the more severe outcome than whites. In fact, the racial gap is quite significant in these two jurisdictions. Sampson and Laub's (1993) perspective, for example, is not able to account for this occurrence.

SUMMARY

The findings concerning decision making and the movement of minorities through the system confirm the claims stated in chapter 2. Contextual analyses based on structural and organizational factors alone may not be able to explain race differences and social control in general in more homogeneous communities and court settings. The results suggest that juvenile justice decision making is much more complex than anticipated and justify the need for further inquiry into the causes of disproportionate minority confinement in Iowa.

The findings discussed in the preceding pages support the view that juvenile justice decision making and social control are variable and cannot be totally explained by jurisdictional differences in legal and extralegal factors. Recall that the jurisdictions, for the most part, did not vary on these case-level characteristics (chapter 4). Jurisdictional differences do exist in outcomes for youth in general and minority youth in particular. Even within a juvenile court, no clear patterns emerge between decision making at one stage compared to another stage. Still, some general summary statements can be made concerning the handling of youth in each jurisdiction.

Bond, for example, appears to exercise the greatest amount of social control over youth relative to the other three jurisdictions. Bond ranked highest on referrals to petition at intake, referrals for further proceedings at the initial appearance hearing, and an order of change of placement/transfer to adult court at judicial disposition.

Decision making in Parks is more difficult to classify. On the one hand, the jurisdiction ranked second in referring youth for further court proceedings at intake, and youth referred to intake have the second highest probability of receiving a change of placement or transfer to adult court. On the other hand, Parks was second in the use of diversion at both the initial appearance hearing and the judicial disposition hearing.

Conversely, options involving less severe sanctions (i.e., release, diversion, and community-based treatment) are used disproportionately in King and to a lesser extent in Jackson. These two jurisdictions exert the least amount of social control.

At some decision-making stages, African Americans receive the more severe outcome, while at others they are the recipients of more lenient outcomes. Race effects are most evident at intake. In Bond, African American youth are more likely than white youth to be referred for further court proceedings. With the exception of Parks, African Americans are also less likely than whites at this decision-making point to participate in diversion. In Jackson, Native Americans are diverted at intake at the same rate as are whites. African American youth in this jurisdiction, however, are less likely than whites and Native Americans to be petitioned. In Parks, African Americans are more likely than whites to receive the more severe outcome at initial appearance and judicial disposition.

The findings about the relationship between race and social control presented in the foregoing pages were not entirely anticipated. Race effects should have been present only in Bond and perhaps Parks. In addition, the cumulative effects of the race differences in outcomes resulted in a growth of the minority composition of all youth moving through the system in all four jurisdictions. Similarly, despite variation by jurisdiction in exerting social control, African Americans have a greater probability of receiving a change of placement or transfer to adult court than do whites. In the following chapters, multivariate analysis is performed to determine if these relationships remain once the effects of legal and extralegal variables on decision making are considered. A qualitative inquiry is also employed to delve further into the roles that correctional orientations and decision-makers' perceptions of minorities have on decision making and the relationships between race and social control.

Chapter 6

The Influence of Legal and Extralegal Factors on Decision Making

In this chapter, a summary of the results from the examination of the race associations with each decision-making stage for each jurisdiction is presented. Next, the discussion centers on the findings from the multivariate analysis in the form of logistic regression to determine if the bivariate relationships remain once legal and extralegal factors are considered.

BOND

In this jurisdiction, African American juveniles are more likely than white youth to be referred to petition at intake and less likely to be diverted from further juvenile court involvement via an informal adjustment (table 6.1). Bond has a strong emphasis on intervention, and while this has consequences for African American youth, the relative effect is not as dramatic as in the other jurisdictions.

After controlling for legally relevant case characteristics and extralegal considerations, the effect of race on intake decision making remains for referrals to petition (table 6.1). African American youth have a 12 percent higher likelihood than white youth to receive a recommendation for further court processing. Of the remaining social characteristics and indicators of school involvement, age and not attending school impact intake decision making. Five of the seven legal variables are also predictors of the dependent variable, and the effects are in the expected direction.

Most of the significant predictors of decisions to recommend further court proceedings also explain the use of diversion, with four exceptions (column 2). Race is not a statistically significant determinant of the use of informal adjustments in Bond. Thus, the finding that African Americans are

TABLE 6.1
Logistic Regression Results for Intake for Bond

Variable	Release/ Adjustment vs. Further Court Processing (1)	Release vs. Adjustment/Further Court Processing (2)
Social Characteristics		
Race	.50**	−.21
	(.19)	(.23)
Gender	.06	−.06
	(.15)	(.18)
Age	.11**	−.04
	(.04)	(.04)
Family status	.06	−.08
	(.12)	(.15)
School		
Attending, but problems	.08	.03
	(.15)	(.18)
Not attending	.62**	.28
	(.20)	(.28)
Legal		
Number of prior referrals	.26**	−.06*
	(.03)	(.03)
Court authority	1.37**	.43*
	(.14)	(.20)
Number of current charges	.26**	.40**
	(.08)	(.15)
Crime severity	1.74**	.53*
	(.15)	(.22)
Property	.20	.50**
	(.16)	(.18)
Person	.58**	−.37**
	(.20)	(.21)
Drugs	.19	.14
	(.20)	(.22)
−2 log likelihood	1,876.85	1416.78
N	2020	2020

NOTE: Regression coefficients, standard error ( ).
*$p < .05$. **$p < .01$.

less likely to participate in diversion than whites appears to be the result of legal factors—such as offense type—rather than racial bias.

The number of prior referrals and type of crime also have different effects on the use of release or diversion compared to referrals for further court processing. Youth with fewer past referrals to juvenile court are more likely to be released. While being charged with a personal offense is a predictor of recommendations for further court processing, offenses involving property and drugs influence participation in diversionary outcomes.

Recall that in the early analysis, race was not found to be associated with decision making at any stage following intake in Bond. Similarly, race is not a statistically significant determinant of decision making at petition, initial appearance, adjudication, and judicial disposition once legal and extralegal factors are controlled (table 6.2).

Age is predictive of decisions at petition (column 1), initial appearance (column 2), and judicial disposition (column 4). Older youth are more likely to be petitioned and receive a change of placement/transfer to adult court.[1] Younger youth have a greater chance of being diverted at the initial appearance hearing than older youth. Family structure is not a statistically significant determinant of decision making at any stage in Bond.

Of the legal factors, the number of prior referrals, being under court authority, the number of current charges, and being charged with property and drug crimes predict decision making at various stages in the proceedings, and the effects are in the anticipated directions. For example, youth charged with either a property offense or a drug offense are more likely to receive community treatment instead of a change of placement at judicial disposition or transfer to adult court (column 4).

In summary, legal factors, and to a lesser degree, the extralegal characteristic of age, are determinants of decision making at every stage in the proceedings in Bond. While legal and extralegal factors appear to explain the race differences in the use of diversion at intake, African American youth are still more likely to receive a referral for further court proceedings at this stage than are similar white youth. Legal factors alone do not account for African Americans receiving the more severe outcome at the intake stage. Thus, the race effect at intake appears to be a contributing factor to the overrepresentation of African American youth moving through the system and receiving a change of placement/transfer to adult court (chapter 5).

JACKSON

Race associations are evident in Jackson at the stages of intake, petition, and initial appearance (table 6.3.). African Americans are also more likely than

TABLE 6.2
Logistic Regression Results Predicting Multiple Case Processing Outcomes for Bond

Variable	Petition (1)	Initial Appearance (2)	Adjudication (3)	Judicial Disposition (4)
Social Characteristics				
Race	−.00	.45	−.06	−.25
	(.63)	(.40)	(.49)	(.33)
Gender	−.77	.30	.99	.56
	(.41)	(.39)	(.59)	(.53)
Age	.31*	−.27**	.20	.31**
	(.14)	(.10)	(.15)	(.09)
Family status	−.01	.06	−.20	−.43
	(.36)	(.24)	(.33)	(.24)
School				
Attending, but problems	−.34	−.06	.19	.39
	(.41)	(.30)	(.43)	(.25)
Not attending	−.20	.18	−.53	.75
	(.70)	(.39)	(.45)	(.46)
Legal				
Number of prior referrals	.30	.31**	−.12	.29**
	(.21)	(.08)	(.12)	(.05)
Court authority	1.00	.42	.77**	.39
	(1.25)	(.29)	(.45)	(.64)
Number of current charges	1.05*	−.07	.09	.09
	(.44)	(.14)	(.21)	(.12)
Crime severity	1.31	.13	.58	.53
	(1.47)	(.27)	(.36)	(.37)
Property	1.58**	−.33	−.35	−1.03**
	(.51)	(.52)	(.60)	(.37)
Person	.64	.18	−.48	−.63
	(.67)	(.47)	(.67)	(.47)
Drugs	.10	.07	−1.05	−1.42*
	(.54)	(.48)	(.67)	(.68)
Hazard rate	−4.51	6.75	4.60	−3.45
	(4.39)	3.73	3.38	5.25
−2 log likelihood	275.75	459.22	268.99	537.527
N	691	491	383	523

NOTE: Regression coefficients, standard error ( ).

$p < .05.$ $**p < .01.$

whites to move throughout the system. Native Americans appear to be shunted out of the system at both intake and petition, but from that point on, the size of their composition at the judicial disposition stage is comparable to African Americans. Consistent with these results, race effects remain once legal and extralegal factors are taken into account. Being a white youth and having more prior contacts with the juvenile court, for example, increases the likelihood of moving further into the proceedings by 16 percent (table 6.3, column 2).[2]

Table 6.4 more closely examines this relationship. When comparing the effect of prior referral on the dependent variable for each racial group, it can be seen that there is a significant relationship only for whites (column 1, $p <$ .01), and the effect is positive.

Early results indicate that Native Americans were as likely as whites to receive an informal adjustment in Bond, and both racial groups did so proportionately more often than African Americans (table 5.1). An examination of the logistic regression results reveals that the effects of being Native American and white are statistically insignificant (table 6.3, column 3). Race interaction effects are present when estimating models to predict decisions involving release and the use of diversion (column 4). Native American youth who are either younger or charged with a serious crime are more likely to be released than participate in diversion. The probability of receiving diversion decreases by .03 for younger Native Americans and by .23 for those charged with a serious crime.

Conversely, among Native American youth under court authority at the time of the referral, diversion is increased by 15 percent. Whites not attending school are more likely to be released (probability $= -.34$), while the likelihood of receiving an informal adjustment is increased for white youth accused of committing a property offense (probability $= -.13$). Separate models for each racial group were estimated to provide a clearer picture of these relationships. The logistic regression results are presented in columns 4 through 6 of table 6.4.

An examination of the impact of age, court authority, and crime seriousness on the intake measure for each of the three racial groups shows the effects to be statistically significant only for Native American youth. Similarly, the relationships between not attending school and property offending with the decision to release or use diversion are statistically significant only for white youth. As in the interaction model, the effects with the dependent variable are negative with the exceptions of the positive association between being Native American and under court authority and being white and charged with a property offense.

Thus, under some conditions, Native American youth are more likely to receive either an informal adjustment or be released compared to African Americans and, to a less extent, whites. For white youth, not attending school increases the chance of release, while involvement with property crimes increases the likelihood of participation in diversion. Additionally, whites with a

TABLE 6.3
Logistic Regression Results for Intake for Jackson

Variable	Release/Adjustment vs. Further Court Processing		Release vs. Adjustment/ Further Court Processing	
	(1)	*(2)*	*(3)*	*(4)*
Social Characteristics				
Race				
Native American	−.44	−.29	.43	2.55**
	(.41)	(.40)	(.28)	(.93)
White	−.02	−.32	.47	−.18
	(.34)	(.35)	(.25)	(.31)
Gender	−.71**	−.67**	−.04	−.07
	(.23)	(.23)	(.14)	(.14)
Age	.20**	.19**	.01	.05
	(.04)	(.04)	(.03)	(.03)
Family status	−.08	−.15	−.12	−.09
	(.17)	(.17)	(.13)	(.13)
School				
Attending, but problems	.81**	.83**	.15	.15
	(.19)	(.19)	(.17)	(.17)
Not attending	.43	.39	−.31	.87
	(.25)	(.25)	(.21)	(.52)
Legal				
Number of prior referrals	.04	−.02	−.01	−.02
	(.02)	(.04)	(.02)	(.02)
Court authority	−.35	−.46	.00	−.44
	(.28)	(.29)	(.25)	(.27)
Number of current charges	.29	.29	−.05	−.02
	(.17)	(.17)	(.14)	(.15)
Crime severity	2.05**	2.05**	−.13	.11
	(.17)	(.17)	(.18)	(.21)
Property	.03	.01	.41**	−.61*
	(.21)	(.21)	(.15)	(.29)
Person	.29	.21	−.80**	−.87**
	(.29)	(.29)	(.21)	(.22)
Drugs	−.67*	−.74*	−.49**	−.59**
	(.34)	(.34)	(.19)	(.20)

(continued)

greater number of prior contacts with the system are likely to be referred for further court proceedings. The finding that a slight increase in the number of African American youth moving further into the system at the intake stage appears to be the result of the legal variable crime severity. Interestingly, the model for African American youth produced statistically insignificant effects for every independent variable with decisions to release versus diversion/further

TABLE 6.3 (*cont.*)
Logistic Regression Results for Intake for Jackson

Variable	Release/Adjustment Further Court Processing		Release vs. Adjustment Further Court Processing	
	(1)	(2)	(3)	(4)
White × Prior Referral		.16**		
		(.05)		
Native American × Age				−.17**
				(.07)
Native American × Serious				1.70**
				(.65)
Native American × Serious				−1.11**
				(.45)
White × Not Attending				−1.59**
				(.56)
White × Property				1.30**
				(.30)
−2 Log Likelihood	1,147.01	1,136.56	1,820.67	1,773.52
N	1966	1966	1966	1966

NOTE: Regression coefficients, standard error ( ).
$^*p < .05$. $^{**}p < .01$

court proceedings suggesting that factors other than those controlled for in the analysis are influencing the decision-making process.

Of the remaining social characteristics, gender and age have statistically significant main effects on intake decision making. Females are less likely than their male counterparts to be referred for further court proceedings (table 6.3, column 1). The effect of gender is of particular importance for whites (table 6.4, column 1), but the association is not statistically different in its effect compared to the other two racial groups. Older youth are more likely than younger youth to receive the more severe outcome at intake (table 6.3, column 1). Having problems in school is predictive of referrals for further court proceedings, as is crime seriousness. Surprisingly, being charged with a drug offense results in receiving a more lenient rather than a more severe outcome at intake.

Contrary to expectations, involvement in either a personal offense or a drug offense decreases the likelihood of receiving diversion in Jackson (column 3). Instead, youth charged with these offenses have a greater chance of being released.

The results up to this point reveal that intake decision making is multi-faceted and complex. Social and legal factors operate quite differently when

TABLE 6.4
Regression Results from the Estimation of Separate Models for Whites, African Americans,
and Native Americans for Jackson

	Intake 1		
Variable	White (1)	Black (2)	Native Americans (3)
Social Characteristics			
Gender	−.86**	.04	−.09
	(.27)	(.94)	(.55)
Age	.19**	.25	.16
	(.05)	(.16)	(.10)
Family status	−.12	−.06	−.09
	(.19)	(.65)	(.50)
School			
Attending, but problems	.81**	.73	1.08*
	(.21)	(.78)	(.54)
Not attending	.32	.83	.63
	(.28)	(1.14)	(.75)
Legal			
Number of prior referrals	.15**	−.08	−.02
	(.04)	(.14)	(.04)
Court authority	−.95**	.11	.47
	(.38)	(.86)	(.59)
Number of current charges	.49**	.27	−.17
	(.19)	(.57)	(.47)
Crime severity	2.12**	1.91**	1.81**
	(.19)	(.75)	(.50)
Property	−.00	.05	.27
	(.23)	(.90)	(.68)
Person	.07	.34	.79
	(.33)	(1.06)	(.85)
Drugs	−.70*	−.52	−1.77
	(.37)	(1.86)	(1.49)
−2 log likelihood	927.25	66.75	129.88
N	1594	98	276

(continued)

TABLE 6.4 *(cont.)*
Regression Results from the Estimation of Separate Models for Whites, African Americans, and Native Americans for Jackson

	Intake 2		
Variable	*White* *(4)*	*Black* *(5)*	*Native Americans* *(6)*
Social Characteristics			
Gender	−.15	.19	.09
	(.16)	(.63)	(.35)
Age	.05	.09	−.13*
	(.03)	(.08)	(.06)
Family status	−.06	−.14	−.22
	(.15)	(.48)	(.35)
School			
Attending, but problems	.09	.36	.16
	(.20)	(.63)	(.38)
Not attending	−.68**	.10	.94
	(.24)	(1.14)	(.61)
Legal			
Number of prior referrals	−.06	−.05	.01
	(.03)	(.11)	(.03)
Court authority	−.37	−.24	1.21*
	(.31)	(.74)	(.62)
Number of current charges	−.05	.37	−.05
	(.18)	(.71)	(.28)
Crime severity	.11	−.10	−.91*
	(.22)	(.70)	(.42)
Property	.62**	.23	−.59
	(.17)	(.59)	(.46)
Person	−.90**	−.09	−.87
	(.24)	(.75)	(.66)
Drugs	−.71**	1.04	−.16
	(.22)	(1.74)	(.59)
−2 log likelihood	1,398.62	109.58	256.39
N	1594	98	276

NOTE: Regression coefficients, standard error ( ).

$*p < .05.$ $**p < .01.$

examining the various options available to juvenile justice officials at this stage. Next, the discussion focuses on decision making at the stages of petition, initial appearance, and judicial disposition. These findings are presented in table 6.5.

Both Native Americans and African Americans are more likely than whites to be denied petitions for further processing. The probability of being released at petition is .34 for African Americans and .27 for Native Americans. These findings support those observed from the bivariate analysis (table 5.2).

A significant relationship also exists between African Americans and decisions at the initial appearance hearing in Jackson (column 2). The chances of African American youth participating in diversion at this stage increases by a staggering 79 percent. There is no evidence of a race difference at judicial disposition (column 3).

Of the remaining social characteristics, age has associations with decision making at the stages of initial appearance and judicial disposition. Older youth are more likely to participate in diversion at initial appearance than are younger youth. Conversely, being older increases the probability of receiving the more severe outcome at judicial disposition. Having problems in school or not attending school increases the likelihood of being petitioned and referred for further proceedings at initial appearance.

The impact of the legal factors on decision making at each of the three stages is modest at best. Youth with greater prior contact with the system have a greater chance of receiving a change of placement/transfer to adult court.[3] Youth charged with more serious crimes and those involved with drug offenses are less likely to be referred for further court proceedings at initial appearance.

Results for decision making at initial appearance are somewhat contrary to those found at intake. For example, youth charged with drug offenses are less likely to participate in diversion at intake but more likely at the initial appearance. This discrepancy could exist because of plea bargaining or because the diversion option was withheld until this stage. Concomitantly, the involvement of the prosecutor at this point in the proceedings, in addition to juvenile court personnel, might explain the differences in the factors associated with the likelihood of diversion at initial appearance compared to intake.

In short, while legal factors explain some of the decision making at each of the four stages examined, race is a strong determinant of case outcomes and processing at intake, petition, and initial appearance. The effects of both race and the legal factors are not consistent and appear to reflect the widespread discretion that juvenile justice personnel have in arriving at decisions. All three racial groups receive the more severe outcome and/or the more lenient outcome, depending on the conditions and the stage studied. The effects of the legal variables were found to act in a similar fashion.

TABLE 6.5
Logistic Regression Results Predicting Multiple Case Processing Outcomes for Jackson[a]

Variable	Petition (1)	Initial Appearance (2)	Judicial Disposition (3)
Social Characteristics			
Race			
Native American	−1.44*	−3.26	.43
	(.72)	(1.81)	(.73)
African American	−1.75**	−4.89*	1.53
	(.74)	(2.29)	(.99)
Gender	−.27	−.03	−.58
	(.83)	(.76)	(.89)
Age	−.16	−.67**	.49**
	(.19)	(.28)	(.14)
Family status	.04	−.60	.78
	(.49)	(.63)	(.42)
School			
Attending, but problems	1.93**	4.35*	.36
	(.82)	(1.97)	(.47)
Not attending	3.03**	7.91**	−.64
	(1.10)	(2.98)	(.53)
Legal			
Number of prior referrals	−.09	.07	.21*
	(.09)	(.23)	(.09)
Court authority	1.02	2.79	.82
	(.93)	(1.92)	(.65)
Number of current charges	.86	.70	.02
	(.66)	(.91)	(.48)
Crime severity	−.23	−2.15**	.65
	(1.52)	(.89)	(.39)
Property	.67	−.97	−.51
	(.54)	(1.70)	(.50)
Person	.37	−.07	−1.43*
	(.75)	(1.82)	(.68)
Drugs	.56	−5.48**	−6.46
	(1.38)	(1.78)	(.68)
Hazard rate	−1.00	−11.93	−1.96
	(4.27)	(7.94)	(5.11)
−2 log likelihood	169.76	105.88	182.885
N	242	179	144

NOTE: Regression coefficients, standard error ( ).

[a]Too few cases at adjudication precluded estimation of models.

*$p < .05$.   **$p < .01$.

KING

In King, African American youth were less likely than white youth to participate in diversion at the intake stage. In addition, the size of the African American composition of the cohort moving from referral to each subsequent stage
increased initially at intake and continued to grow as youth moved through the
system. Relative to the other three jurisdictions, the racial gap was quite significant in terms of the probability of being referred to intake and receiving a
severe outcome at disposition.

Table 6.6 provides logistic regression results for decision making at intake,
initial appearance, and judicial disposition. The lack of variation in decision
making at petition and adjudication precluded estimation of models for these
stages.

Contrary to the findings from the bivariate analysis (table 5.1), African
Americans are more likely than whites to be referred for further court proceedings at intake once legal and extralegal factors are taken into account (table 6.6,
column 1). African Americans are .07 times more likely than whites to be recommended to the petition stage in the proceedings in King.

No race differences are evident in decisions involving release and participation in diversion (column 2). Gender, however, is associated with participation in diversion: males are more likely to be diverted instead of released.
School factors and legal variables, such as the number of prior referrals, court
authority, and the severity of the crime, are also statistically significant predictors of intake decision making.

Consistent with the bivariate results, race is not a determinant of decision
making at initial appearance and judicial disposition. Most of the decision
making at initial appearance appears to be influenced once again by school factors, prior contact with the system, and type of offense (property and person).
Possibly because of the relatively small number of cases at judicial disposition
(n = 110), only one statistically significant effect is evident: prior referral has a
positive association with the dependent variable.[4]

Legal factors and school problems appear to explain most of the decision
making at intake, initial appearance and, to less extent, judicial disposition.
African American youth are more likely to be referred for further court proceedings at the intake stage than white youth. Thus, the initial increase in the
size of the African American composition of the cohort moving further into
the system is not explained entirely by differential involvement in crime and
other legal considerations. Legal and relevant extralegal factors appear to explain decision making at subsequent stages. In fact, prior contact with the system has a positive statistically significant effect on decision making at every
stage examined. The consistent relationship between prior record and decision
making is not evident in the other three jurisdictions. The significance of this

TABLE 6.6
Logistic Regression Results Predicting Multiple Case Processing Outcomes for King[a]

	Intake			
Variable	Release/ Adjustment vs. Further Court Processing (1)	Release vs. Adjustment/ Further Court Processing (2)	Initial Appearance (3)	Judicial Disposition (4)
Social Characteristics				
Race	.44*	−.22	−.23	.79
	(.20)	(.14)	(.37)	(.62)
Gender	−.24	−.26*	.30	−1.24
	(.21)	(.13)	(.45)	(.93)
Age	.12**	.04	.02	−.24
	(.05)	(.03)	(.11)	(.19)
Family status	.04	.03	.14	−1.02
	(.15)	(.10)	(.29)	(.54)
School				
Attending, but problems	1.66**	1.30**	.89*	−.03
	(.24)	(.23)	(.46)	(.71)
Not attending	1.28**	.46**	.81*	.22
	(.20)	(.17)	(.36)	(.03)
Legal				
Number of prior referrals	.11**	.09**	.20*	.33**
	(.03)	(.03)	(.09)	(.11)
Court authority	.84**	.64**	.39	.05
	(.23)	(.20)	(.40)	(.57)
Number of current charges	.21	.16	−.09	−.45
	(.13)	(.10)	(.27)	(.65)
Crime severity	1.92**	1.13**	.50	.55
	(.16)	(.13)	(.35)	(.58)
Property	.24	.11	1.53*	1.45
	(.25)	(.14)	(.74)	(1.44)
Person	.62*	−.03	1.78*	.56
	(.28)	(.17)	(.81)	(1.48)
Drugs	.20	.14	.87	1.19
	(.36)	(.20)	(1.03)	(1.91)
Hazard rate			−1.66	−.78
			(4.67)	(4.00)
−2 log likelihood	1,183.06	2,272.10	300.09	111.271
N	1798	1798	255	110

NOTE: Regression coefficients, standard error ( ).

[a]Too few cases in categories of petition and adjudication precluded estimation of models.

*$p < .05$.　**$p < .01$.

relationship and its implications for the treatment of minority youth will be discussed in chapter 9.

PARKS

African Americans are more likely than whites in Parks to receive the more severe outcome at initial appearance (referral to adjudication) and judicial disposition (change of placement/transfer to adult court). Conversely, African American youth are less likely than their white counterparts to be petitioned. Thus in Parks, as in Jackson, African Americans appear to receive both more severe and less severe outcomes than whites depending on the stage in proceedings.

While race does directly affect intake decision making in Parks (table 6.7, column 1), there is a positive statistically significant interaction between race and family status with decisions to recommend further court proceedings once legal and extralegal factors are controlled (column 2). African American youth who live in a single-parent household have a 16 percent increased likelihood of being subject to greater social control at intake than other youth. The interaction effect between race and family status is clearer when examining the results from separate models for each racial group (table 6.8). As can be seen in columns 1 and 2 of table 6.8, family status has effects for both racial groups, but the association is only statistically significant for African Americans ($p < .01$).

Of the remaining social characteristics, age has a positive statistically significant effect on the likelihood of being referred for further court proceedings (table 6.7, column 2). Not attending school also increases the chances of greater social control at intake. Of the seven legal indicators, only property offending is insignificant. The other six have positive effects on the dependent variable.

Being female and from a single-parent household increases the probability of receiving an informal adjustment at intake (column 3). Attending school with evidence of problems and property offending also are determinants of decisions involving release or diversion.

The regression results for the remaining stages are provided in table 6.9. The lambda or hazard rate in each model is statistically insignificant, indicating that decision making at a previous stage did not influence decisions at the next stage in the proceedings. However, there is one exception: decision making at adjudication (columns 3 and 4) appears to be influenced by earlier decisions at the initial appearance hearing (lambda $p < .01$).

Similar to the results from the bivariate analysis, African American youth are less likely than white youth to be petitioned once legal and extralegal factors are controlled (column 1). The probability of not being petitioned decreases by .11 for African Americans. A relationship is evident between the number of current charges and a likelihood of being petitioned.

TABLE 6.7
Logistic Regression Results for Intake for Parks

Variable	Release/Adjustment vs. Further Court Processing		Release vs. Adjustment/Further Court Processing
	(1)	(2)	(3)
Social Characteristics			
Race	.01	−.44	−.07
	(.17)	(.30)	(.19)
Gender	−.23	−.23	.63**
	(.20)	(.20)	(.25)
Age	.26**	.27**	.07
	(.04)	(.04)	(.04)
Family status	.45**	.29	.39*
	(.15)	(.17)	(.17)
School			
Attending, but problems	.05	.04	.55*
	(.18)	(.18)	(.25)
Not attending	.62*	.61*	−.01
	(.29)	(.29)	(.38)
Legal			
Number of prior referrals	.41**	.41**	−.10
	(.06)	(.06)	(.06)
Court authority	.76**	.76**	.45
	(.22)	(.22)	(.31)
Number of current charges	.43**	.42**	.19
	(.08)	(.08)	(.14)
Crime severity	1.56**	1.57**	.17
	(.16)	(.16)	(.20)
Property	.16	.15	.63**
	(.21)	(.21)	(.20)
Person	.80**	.80**	.45
	(.24)	(.24)	(.25)
Drugs	1.34**	1.31*	.50
	(.31)	(.31)	(.38)
Race × family status		.68*	
		(.36)	
−2 log likelihood	1,253.73	1,250.00	1,056.29
N	1423	1423	1423

NOTE: Regression coefficients, standard error ( ).
*$p < .05$.   **$p < .01$.

TABLE 6.8
Regression Results from the Estimation of Separate Models for White
and African American Youth for Parks

Variable	White (1)	African American (2)
Social Characteristics		
Gender	−.47	.16
	(.26)	(.33)
Age	.28**	.26**
	(.05)	(.07)
Family status	.30	.95**
	(.18)	(.31)
School		
Attending, but problems	.15	−.28
	(.21)	(.35)
Not attending	.57	.78
	(.35)	(.52)
Legal		
Number of prior referrals	.48**	.29**
	(.08)	(.09)
Court authority	.67**	.91**
	(.27)	(.38)
Number of current charges	.36**	.85**
	(.09)	(.23)
Crime severity	1.67**	1.38**
	(.19)	(.29)
Property	.10	.32
	(.25)	(.43)
Person	.18**	.88*
	(.30)	(.45)
Drugs	1.33**	.99
	(.33)	(.91)
−2 log likelihood	878.35	359.30
N	995	427

NOTE: Regression coefficients, standard error ( ).
$*p < .05.$ $**p < .01.$

The association found earlier between race and decisions at the initial appearance hearing is not evident once multivariate techniques are employed (column 2). The growth in the size of the composition of the cohort moving on from this stage (+7%) appears, in part, to be the result of greater prior contact with the system, being under court authority at the time of the referral, and drug involvement.

Regressing adjudication on extralegal variables and legal factors yields a statistically significant race effect (column 3). African Americans are .31 times

TABLE 6.9
Logistic Regression Results Predicting Multiple Case Processing Outcomes for Parks

Variable	Petition (1)	Initial Appearance (2)	Adjudication (3)	Judicial Disposition (4)
Social Characteristics				
Race	−1.14*	.83	−1.56*	.32
	(.52)	(.58)	(.74)	(.37)
Gender	−.00	−.08	1.28	.57
	(.65)	(.46)	(.90)	(.54)
Age	.33	.05	.25	.52**
	(.23)	(.10)	(.17)	(.14)
Family status	−.19	.05	−.85	.34
	(.60)	(.32)	(.62)	(.36)
School				
Attending,	.09	.34	.01	1.03*
but problems	(.59)	(.36)	(.67)	(.43)
Not attending	−.10	.47	−.77	.23
	(.79)	(.61)	(1.00)	(.52)
Legal				
Number of prior	−.16	.55**	−.10	.46**
referrals	(.26)	(.17)	(.20)	(.12)
Court authority	1.17	1.32**	−.95	.14
	(.87)	(.56)	(.94)	(.43)
Number of current	1.48*	.09	.76*	−.17
charges	(.63)	(.20)	(.40)	(.22)
Crime severity	.78	−.02	1.73*	.52
	(1.13)	(.35)	(.62)	(.47)
Property	.86	−.73	1.35	−.52
	(.66)	(.63)	(.86)	(.60)
Person	1.45	.47	.51	−.17
	(.88)	(.72)	(.85)	(.64)
Drugs	1.41	−1.47*	10.29	.65
	(1.31)	(.76)	(18.83)	(.90)
Hazard rate	−3.46	1.01	9.66**	−3.72
	(3.78)	(5.52)	(3.06)	(2.68)
−2 log likelihood	161.52	279.55	104.51	248.15
N	413	277	175	229

NOTE: Regression coefficients, standard error ( ).
*$p < .05$. **$p < .01$.

more likely than whites to have their cases dismissed. The legal variables number of current charges and crime severity are also predictors of adjudication decision making.

At judicial disposition and contrary to the results from the bivariate analysis, race is a statistically insignificant determinant (column 4). Age, attending school but having problems, and prior referral increase the probability of receiving a disposition involving a change of placement/transfer to adult proceedings.

In Parks, race impacts decision making at several stages in the proceedings and African Americans appear to receive both the more severe and the more lenient outcomes relative to whites. At intake, African American youth who come from single-parent households are more likely than other youth to be referred for further court proceedings. Conversely, African Americans are less likely than whites to be petitioned and adjudicated delinquent. No race effects are evident at either initial appearance or judicial disposition once legal and extralegal considerations are taken into account.[5] Thus, the initial bump in the size of the composition of the cohort consisting of African Americans appears to be the result of possible race bias at intake. The disproportionate overrepresentation of African Americans moving beyond that stage, however, is accounted for by factors other than race (i.e., problems at school, prior record, and number of charges).

SUMMARY

The results from the multivariate analyses confirm those from the bivariate comparisons and prior research that decision making and juvenile justice outcomes vary by jurisdiction. Although legal factors were found to explain much of the decision making in each jurisdiction and at each stage of the proceedings, race also impacted the treatment of youth in all four jurisdictions even after crime severity, age, and so forth are controlled for the analyses. The extent race influences decision making differs by the racial group, the stage in the proceedings, and the jurisdiction. Prior record was also a significant determinant of decision making, especially in King. Next, information is used from the interviews to provide insights and a context for these findings.

Chapter 7

Accountability and Intervention

Decision making in Bond is more closely examined through the use of data gathered from interviews with nineteen decision-makers. Fifteen juvenile court officers, a judge, two public defenders, and a prosecutor were interviewed. Twelve of the respondents are male and, with the exception of two African Americans, all are white. The mean age is thirty-eight. The mean length of time on the job is twelve years. Recall that of the four jurisdictions, Bond has

- the largest African American population;
- the greatest amount of inequality;
- the most arrests;
- relatively high racial inequality, unwed teenage pregnancy, and criminal justice expenditures;
- an organizational philosophy of accountability and intervention; and
- the greatest emphasis on the social control of youth.

Furthermore, African American youth are more likely than white youth to be referred for further court processing at intake once controls for relevant legal and extralegal factors are considered.

The theme of this chapter is the heavy emphasis placed by Bond on holding youth accountable for their actions through a legalistic orientation that includes a desire to rehabilitate troubled youth. The effects of social structure on decision making are subtle and tied to history and beliefs that youth are more troubled and commit crime at younger ages than in the past. African Americans are seen as requiring greater intervention because they commit more crime due to a variety of factors that range from impoverishment to living in dysfunctional families. Suggestions for addressing their overrepresentation of African American youth in the juvenile justice system focus on the prevention of delinquency.

91

PERCEIVED ROLE OF THE JUVENILE COURT
AND VIEWS OF THE SYSTEM

Almost all of the respondents believe in a "law and order" approach for handling youth within a rehabilitative context. Underlying this view is the belief that youth should be held accountable for their behavior, and intervention is one method to accomplish this objective.

1. I think today's kids require more active involvement. I used to think that you could just sit down and talk to them and they would end up being good and I learned over the years, well actually I learned that really quickly, that talking didn't get you anywhere and the thing that kids need most in their life is someone putting some limits on them and saying that this is how you have to run your life. . . .

2. We used to do preventive education kinds of things, we do very little of that now. It used to be here in the office that we had discussions about who we were, were we social workers, were we counselors, or were we probation officers, meaning that we were more law and order like policemen. We used to have these debates back and forth, and people aligned with those certain groups and certain people including me, thought that we were probation officers and probation officers to them were like part of the arm of the police department and we would go in different directions. But, we no longer have debates like that . . . I think that more people aligned with the law and order part. . . .

The legalistic/rehabilitation orientation reflects the perception that delinquent behavior is caused by an inability to control impulses, free choice, and a lack of parental supervision and parental discipline. Youth referred to juvenile court, however, are seen as multiproblematic. Many personnel also believe that youth are committing more serious crime and entering the system at a younger age. As stated by one respondent,

I think that our job has become more difficult. I think we really are working with more disturbed kids coming into the system, kids that are just more difficult in a lot of ways to deal with. . . . We always had them before, but I think there are more numbers and I think they are coming at a younger age that requires more significant intervention.

The assumptions that youth have multiple problems and are getting into trouble at a younger age are perceptions shared by juvenile justice personnel nationwide and by the public in general (e.g., Jones and Newman, 1997; chapter 3 in this volume). Relying on data from the Uniform Crime Reports and the

National Juvenile Court Data Archive, Butts and Snyder (1997) show that an increased proportion of offenders under age fifteen were arrested for violent crime between 1980 and 1995. Youth in this age category comprised 30% of all juvenile arrests, compared to 25% in 1980. The proportion of person offense cases that involved youth age 12 or younger, however, was the same in 1994 as in 1985 (12%). For property offense cases, the proportion was slightly less in 1994 (13%) than in 1985 (14%). Thus, perceptions that youth referred to juvenile court are younger than in the past is conditional at best.

One reason for the perception of a greater presence of youth who are younger and who evidence multiple problems is the belief that families do not get involved, and/or that the caretakers lack parenting skills in order to provide adequate supervision. Changes in the family structure and family dynamics are seen as factors influencing the quality of supervision and discipline provided to youth. Underlying this phenomenon is that children referred to juvenile court have children themselves.

> Since I have been in the field there has been a dramatic increase in single-parent homes. When I first got involved there were some kids in their early teens having children, but families were helping them raise those children. Each year it has multiplied, the number of kids having children younger. . . .

Some believe that both female and male teenagers have children in order to achieve self-worth and status among their peers and that this may be generational and part of a subculture.

The belief that today's delinquents are younger, more problematic, lack family supervision and guidance, and are more likely to be parents themselves justifies a correctional philosophy that centers on intervention and holding youth accountable for their behavior. Demands placed on the juvenile court by the schools are also seen as contributing factors to this orientation.

> Our referrals are up, some of our referrals never would have been referred to us 10 years ago. Some of the kids we are working with have gotten into fights at school. That used to be handled by the school authorities, and now that becomes a disorderly conduct [issue]. Schools are depending on the police and the juvenile court for control.

The perceived or actual pressure from schools may explain the presence of the statistically significant effect between dropping out of school and the likelihood of referral at intake to petition (table 6.1, column 1).

Added pressure to intervene and treat troubled youth was also noted by decision-makers as coming from the community, prosecuting attorneys and judges in their court, and legislators at the state level. A recent study of criminal justice sentencing in the state of Iowa echoes these sentiments where the community of Bond was found to send minor felons to prison more than most areas and for drug offenses nearly twice the state average. Interviews with criminal justice personnel from Bond indicate that the county "has a history of aggressive county attorney offices dating back to the '60s, mirroring the desire of the public to treat crime seriously" (Eby, 2001: A1, A7).

Race, Crime, Family, and Distrust of the System

Three quarters of the respondents did not believe that African American youth are involved in more serious crime than white youth. However, almost half of the decision- makers indicated that African Americans commit more crime and "more of them are getting caught." For the majority of the respondents, the main reason cited for the differential involvement in crime and the system is the breakdown of the family. Some officers felt that African American youth arc more likely than white youth to come from a dysfunctional family unit. In particular, decision-makers believe that African Americans are more likely to come from single-parent households that are dysfunctional.

1. The numbers of minorities on probation, placements, and in secure institutions is too high of a percentage of the minority population in this community. . . . One of the things that seems to be very common to black youth that we see on probation is broken families and most of them are being raised in matriarchal families where it is either a mom or an aunt or a grandmother or some combination, so I certainly think that plays a part in it.
2. Well, I think that it goes back to the fact that there is a lot of disintegration in the family unit and I don't know the statistics, but I guess I think that there are a higher percentage of babies being born out of wedlock in minority populations. And when you see a family like this, you are looking at economics and deprivation financially. . . .

For some personnel out of wedlock births among African Americans is seen to be acute, especially among teenagers. The following highlights this concern and highlights why teenage pregnancy is more prevalent among this population:

1. For the young black man, it is a badge of their manhood to have children. We had a boy who was 15. He had two kids and three more on the way from five separate girls and he is quite proud of this . . . So, you have got a fifteen-year-old that instead of this being some-

thing to avoid, it is a mark of their adulthood, and they don't really have any intent or knowledge that they can be a parent to this kid, the child that is coming along. And, again, you get that with white kids, . . . but it seems too disproportionate among black kids.

2. Young black females, who have been raised in their mother's home without the solid family connection would see it as more natural to raise children in a home without a father and therefore, may see it as being more acceptable to begin their family without a male counterpart in the picture.

3. I suspect that white females see a brighter future for themselves as opposed to a minority female and if that is true . . . some of your minority females are more vulnerable and get tied into the relationships, and for some there is also a money angle and freedom.

The viewpoints of the juvenile justice personnel concerning race, sex, and pregnancy parallel the findings by Anderson (1990) in his study of race, class, and urban life and in particular, the description of sex codes and family life. Specifically, Anderson contends that due to the poor socioeconomic conditions of the community and the lack of jobs and promising opportunities for conventional life, sex and pregnancy become important symbols for both boys and girls. For boys, sexual conquests represent proof of manhood (Anderson, 1990: 112; see also Liebow, 1967). For girls, sex allows for the attention of a young man, passage into adulthood, and status (125–126). As stated by Anderson, "The baby may bring her a certain amount of praise, a steady welfare check, and a measure of independence" (1990: 137).

The strength of the African American family and its importance to family members also differs. While some suggested that African American families are weaker than white families and that members lack a sense of the family as a cohesive unit, not all agreed with these views. In fact, some argued that the African American family is stronger than white families. "I would say that their [African American's] family is more important to them. . . .Their kin, their aunts, uncles, grandparents . . . I think the extended family is still there, the importance of the family is still there."

This view is consistent with the contentions of Willie (1991), who argues that people focus too much on the negative aspects and consequences of African American life and overlook the significant and positive features, including the significant role played by relatives and other reference groups. Anderson in his ethnographic study (1990) and follow-up inquiry of inner-city life, for example, echoes this point when he states that both the mother and the grandmother are significant sources of support for the black family. The black grandmother, in particular, "holds a special place among her people, both in folklore and in real life," and through "the generations, many have characterized her as the anchor holding in place the family and indeed the whole kinship structure" as well as the community, in general (Anderson, 1999: 206 footnote omitted). The inner-city African American grandmother provides among other things a sense of commitment to family, an orderly life, and faith in religion (Anderson, 1999; chapter 6 in this volume).

Most of the respondents felt that African American youth are more distrustful of the system than white youth. Much of this mistrust is believed to stem from the family and from past discriminatory practices.

1. Well, I think that for some of our minority youth, there are parents that aren't real trusting of the system, either they have been involved in the system or for various reasons they are just not trustful, and I think they provide an attitude for the kids that they don't have to do or isn't important that they do what we say down here.

2. . . . if I'm just dealing with the kid, it doesn't seem to be an issue . . . you get a lot of distrust of me being white from the parents or from the grandparents. They'll project a lot of that several different times in the situation. They think I'm sending the kid up the river because I'm white and part of the system. . . . That's where you get a lot of the distrust, from the older generation. There's more history there.

Although most of the decision-makers believed African American youth may be more distrustful of the system, 65 percent did not see these youth as more likely to deny guilt or unwilling to cooperate with the proceedings than white juveniles. Though, as one probation officer stated,

A kid is more likely to be given the benefit of the doubt when they are arrested if they say "yes, sir" and "no, sir" and "whatever you want, sir" than the kid who spits in your face and stomps on your foot.

Q. And, you think that minority youth are more likely to spit in your face and stomp on your foot?

A. Yeah.

In addition to crime, family, and distrust of the system, the respondents offered a wide range of opinions regarding the factors that may account for the overrepresentation of minorities in secure facilities. For some, it simply is not an issue, and in some cases the respondents answered the question by voicing their concerns regarding "reverse discrimination."

I think there is probably race bias in the juvenile justice system and if anything, I think that the race bias at this point and time is probably pro-black than it is against black. I think that people are probably more sensitive to being called prejudiced and being called racist and that if we are doing anything we are probably being more lenient and giving more chances to blacks than we are to whites, and I think that goes along with the whole minority hiring as well, management has to fill quotas and even if you are just as well as qualified, you probably won't get it instead of the black. So, I think that there is reverse prejudice kinds of issues going on, sometimes . . . I believe that there are probably instances where blacks have encountered prejudice as well. I can only assume that is probably true. I don't think it is done intentionally here.

This respondent is thinking of racial bias in overt terms and anything less, such as unintentional, indirect bias, does not fall within the realm of bias.

A small percentage of the respondents cited deficiencies in the juvenile justice system as contributing to the overrepresentation of minority youth. The deficiencies named ranged from a lack of cultural sensitivity among treatment staff to having primarily an all-white staff to a lack of innovative programs. Recall that of the nineteen juvenile justice personnel in Bond, there are only two African Americans.

1. . . . I think that you have to adapt some of your services to the population that you are serving, and I do not believe that some of the traditional things we do probation-wise, I don't think that some of our black youth can identify with that. They don't see it as important.

2. . . . [I]t is probably more of an economic difference than it is race, to get out of secure detention you need to have either the economics to have a phone or one or two parents who will stand up in court and say that they are going to control and supervise this kid 24 hours a day, and I will report any violations and that is where the black kids come up short. They either come in and they can't get out because they have a single parent and they don't have a phone, or they have a single parent and the mom can't say that she is going to be able to watch him for 24 hours and that she will report if he violates [his probation] because she is going to have to be at work. So, what you have, is a lot of black kids in detention because they can't get out using the same exit devices that the middle-class white kids can or even the poor white kids because they at least usually have a phone and poor black kids usually don't.

Frazier and Bishop (1995) in their study of disproportionate minority confinement (DMC) in Florida also attributed relative access of nonwhites and the poor to telephones to call parents or to single-parent households and mothers who could not leave the other children at home when they came to pick up their delinquent-detained child.

Overall, a large majority of the decision-makers did not feel that the race of a delinquent influenced the likelihood of referral once youth are in the system, but more than half of the respondents argued that the police respond differently to African American youth than to white youth. Some of the interviewees cited differential involvement in criminal activity on the part of African Americans and the attitude of minority youth toward the police as explanations for this occurrence.

Other decision-makers believe that the police act in a discriminatory fashion toward African Americans.

> I saw police picking up blacks, and it seemed that they were getting more serious charges than whites. It seemed like for a brief period that there was kind of a slowdown on things like that, but just like the race relations kind of things, for a while it seemed to cool down and now it is coming back, so it is like a rolling ball. I actually think that these racial things make a difference. Because usually after something happens racial, then there is a whole surge of police picking up blacks, it seems sometimes just for nothing.

Interestingly, but not surprising, some decision-makers see the police acting in a discriminatory fashion but they do not believe that they themselves might act in a discriminatory manner.

In summary, juvenile justice personnel in Bond do not necessarily believe the African American youth are involved in different crimes than white youth, although they do believe the former commit more crime. The race differential in delinquent behavior is seen as the result of families being dysfunctional—characterized as lacking in supervision and headed by an unwed teen single parent. African American youth and their parents are also seen as distrustful of juvenile justice proceedings but not less likely to cooperate or to show remorse than whites. Most of the respondents contend that the police respond differently toward African American youth and, for the most part, this is the result of youths' participation in crime and lack of respect for the police.

EXPLANATIONS FOR THE QUANTITATIVE FINDINGS

As discussed in chapter 6, quantitative analysis of decision making in Bond revealed that a large number of youth are referred to court at intake, and African Americans are more likely than whites to receive the more severe outcome at intake. The respondents were asked for their interpretation of these results.

Most of the responses focused on the overall philosophy of the court that emphasizes early intervention, holding youth accountable for their behavior, and treatment.

1. We are a pretty aggressive county in terms of reacting. I think there is a feeling that you attempt to provide initial services informally, and then if they come back into the system that is considered that they have ongoing problems, and part of the way to deal with an ongoing problem is to initiate the court involvement. We are just more aggressive in our programming and more aggressive as far as services and intervention.

2. I think that traditionally [Bond] has had a service-intensive mindset in dealing with juvenile offenders, and I think that it goes to history for explanation that the presiding juvenile judge for many years here . . . was a past president of the National Council of Juvenile and Family Court Judges, . . . and the judge raised the juvenile court system over a 15-year period . . . where the emphasis was on intervene early and provide as much and as good . . . treatment as possible.

Relative to the other three jurisdictions, Bond had developed and implemented a wide range of specialized services and programs for treating youth that reflected the service mind-set of the court. These services and programs included a joint effort between the Juvenile Court and Area VII Job Training for youth to improve self-esteem, life skills, and employment opportunities (Leiber and Mawhorr, 1995). In addition, there was a volunteer juvenile court officer program, mandatory tours of the Men's Reformatory and the State's Training School for boys, a restitution program, a shoplifting program, a tutoring program, community service work, and victim services.

The respondents were less consistent in their responses concerning the findings involving racial differences in referrals at intake. The explanations for the finding that African American youth are more likely to receive the more severe outcome at intake included African Americans' unwillingness to admit guilt and the family's unwillingness to ensure that the youth will abide with the conditions of diversion. The following highlights these perceptions:

1. . . . if you have a kid come in with two offenses we might give an informal adjustment agreement at intake, however, you need to have some level of trust for the system in order to just admit to the charges. Black families don't trust the system, and then they are further into the system than the white kid who just agreed with things.

2. I have a number of black kids on my caseload that come in on offenses that shouldn't be a big deal, but they end up being a really big

deal because the kids don't come in for appointments, they don't do their community service, they don't go to school, they don't do that when you don't have the family or their support . . . and because of the probation violations, not really the crime, because they don't do what is expected of them, they end up going away. A number of blacks tend to not be really time oriented, whites tend to be more so. Blacks may come in for their appointment a day late or a week late, and it is no big deal.

This respondent is basically saying that African American youth are getting in trouble because they won't do as they're asked—instead of looking at the content or structure of what it is they are told to do.

The discussion of cultural differences between African Americans and juvenile justice decision-makers in terms of abidance to norms, demeanor, dress, and speech is a prominent theme that emerges in the jurisdiction of Jackson and will be discussed in greater detail in chapter 8. However, the question that should be considered is whether decision-makers interpret failures on the part of whites to adhere to middle-class standards in the same way as for African Americans. Prior research suggests that a dual standard applies for racial groups, with African American youth responded to more severely than whites (e.g., Bortner, 1982).

Despite evidence of race differences at intake, some of the interviewees denied that such differences actually exist. Underlying this view was once again a reliance on understanding bias only in terms of overt acts instead of its more indirect and subtle forms. As one juvenile court officer stated, "I can't see that the intake officer would look at the kid and say that if you are black you are going to be more trouble for us." Unfortunately, the failure to recognize the possible existence of indirect racial bias is a common occurrence among decision-makers (e.g., Zatz, 1987a; Hamparian and Leiber, 1997) and the general public.

A number of the juvenile court personnel discussed the role of the family in arriving at a decision as to what to do with a particular youth, and many view the African American family in a negative light in this regard. African American families are perceived as less cooperative and more mistrustful of the system. These factors increase the likelihood of youth receiving more severe outcomes and going further into the system.

1.   They might receive less family pressure to get this thing cleared up. A white family probably wants to keep their kid out of the court system. I think that is a big value to them, and they will do [anything] to keep the kid out whereas I don't think that a black family gives it that much weight. . . . If my [child] comes in here after committing a crime and denies it and I know that he did it, we are going to go

and have a little chat, and then he is going to come back in here and
then he is going to admit it. I don't know if I would feel that way if
I was a black male and didn't trust the system anyway and I thought
my kid was getting tagged by the police and I tended to believe him
over the rest of the world. . . .

2. Family therapy will likely be distrusted and discarded by black
   clients to whom it is offered, and therefore those kids eventually find
   their way to hard treatment sooner.

A small number of the respondents indicated that juvenile probation officers
may be less accepting of inappropriate comments and behavior on the part of
African American youth than white youth. The inappropriate behavior includes
the failure to attend appointments and other conditions of diversion. It was even
stated that white juvenile justice personnel may be more afraid of African Americans than whites, and this fear may affect decision making.

Well, if you look in this office, we only have two black officers, so we
are still dealing with the black/white issue when it comes to making
decisions. . . . In most cases whites will tolerate more from another
white than they will black and that is the truth. I have seen it happen.
They are more afraid of the blacks than they are the whites. And I
have seen some of the same kinds of threats made to the whites, and
a black would come along and make the same kind of threat and it
gets blown out of proportion.

The possible element of fear on the part of decision-makers toward African
Americans reflects the main tenet of the racial threat thesis (e.g., Tittle and
Curran, 1988; Steffensmeier et al., 1998) and, in particular, the emphasis on
how the interrelationships between imagery and stereotyping result in decision-makers interpreting and responding to similar kinds of behaviors differently for African Americans relative to whites (e.g., Bridges and Steen, 1998;
Mann and Zatz, 1998).

SUGGESTIONS FOR REDUCING MINORITY OVERREPRESENTATION IN THE JUVENILE COURT

The last component of the interview involved asking decision-makers what
they believed was needed in order to change the overrepresentation of minority youth in the juvenile justice system and, in particular, in secure facilities. The
responses primarily focused on suggestions for preventing African American
involvement in crime, with specific attention on ways to strengthen the African

American family. A greater use of parenting classes and other programs that instill family values emerge as central themes from those espousing this view. Some of the respondents also felt that reducing overrepresentation was not their responsibility.

The following statements illustrate some of these diverse opinions:

1. . . . we need more programs that provide for skill development . . . I also think there needs to be more pride for our minority population, more programs where they felt a sense of accomplishment . . . I think that is going to carry over into the values that parents instill in youth. So, some of the programs are not just for families of the kids in trouble, I think some of the programs really need to branch out as a preventive kind of thing . . . so that their skills as parents are improved. . . .

2. We need to provide more positive role models.

3. . . . I am not sure that it is the court's business to cure all of the social handicaps of the country or the community.

4. Probably the thing that concerns me and the thing that alarms me the most . . . is when you read in the paper that there are more blacks in jail and we have to get the black population down and this and that. I get real concerned . . . if we are going to say that we aren't going to hold you accountable because we have met our quota of blacks today . . . If someone has done wrong and if the system is to correct their behavior and protect the public then you better damn well do it . . . I think it is the family's responsibility to go back to family values. . . .

The sentiments expressed by this last respondent are common when dealing with DMC. There appears to be confusion and misunderstanding that efforts to address minority overrepresentation will translate into "quotas" or the release of delinquents who will jeopardize community safety.

A few of the respondents offered suggestions that attempt to address racial bias or at least to recognize that a problem may exist that goes beyond simply blaming the issue on differential involvement in crime. These suggestions ranged from an increase in cultural awareness to the creation of more community-based programs to the hiring of more African American personnel.

SUMMARY

In Bond, the stated organizational ideology and the views of the individual juvenile court personnel appear to be an emphasis on rehabilitation through intervention and accountability couched within a legalistic approach for dealing with youth. A perceived breakdown in family supervision and discipline and the growing number of single-parent homes are believed to justify a philosophy of social control for youth. Younger youth and more multiproblematic youth involved in crime are seen as causes for intervention. There is also belief among juvenile court personnel that historical precedent and the community as a whole requires them to provide help that carries with it the expectation of accountability on their part. No clear explanations were provided for why African American youth were more likely than their white counterparts to be referred for further court proceedings.

An understanding of this occurrence can be derived, however, from the subtle associations between decision making and beliefs that African Americans differentially participate in crime, reside in dysfunctional families, and to a lesser degree, fail to appear for meetings and agree to intake/court stipulations. These perceptions are heightened by the heavy reliance on a social control orientation. Accordingly, it is not surprising that solutions to addressing DMC are informed by strategies that focus on the prevention of crime and the enhancement of family responsibility.

Chapter 8

Rehabilitation, Protection of Society, and Adherence to Middle-Class Values

In Jackson, 23 adult juvenile court decision-makers were interviewed and consisted of juvenile court officers (n = 16), judges (n = 2), public defenders (n = 2), and prosecutors (n = 3). None of the decision-makers are minority; seven are female. The mean age of the personnel is 40. On average, they had worked for this juvenile court for eight years. Furthermore, a large percentage of them are Catholic and graduated from the same schools. A number of them are also related to one another (e.g., brothers and cousins).

Compared to the other three jurisdictions, Jackson also has the following characteristics:

- relatively high poverty and high average family income;
- smallest population and African American presence but the most racially diverse;
- emphasis on rehabilitation and the protection of society;
- ranked third in terms of the probability of youth at intake moving through the system and receiving the more severe outcome (only King had a lower probability); and
- heavy emphasis on the use of diversion at intake (69 percent) and at judicial disposition (59 percent).

Furthermore, race associations were evident at the stages of intake, petition, and initial appearance in Jackson, and African Americans were more likely than whites to move throughout the system. Native Americans are filtered out at both intake and petition, but from that point on, their representation at the judicial disposition stage is comparable to African Americans. Legal factors and race are strong determinants of case outcomes and processing at intake, petition, and initial appearance, but they are inconsistent: all three racial groups receive the more severe outcome and/or the more lenient outcome, depending on the conditions and the stage studied.

In this chapter, information is presented that shows decision making in Jackson to be complex, multifaceted, and couched within concerns for the rehabilitation of youth and the protection of the rules and norms of society. Historical factors and organizational policy shape beliefs that minimal intervention is best for implementing these goals. However, the court's reliance on a *parens patriae* approach for dealing with youth has direct and indirect implications for the social control of minorities. Minorities are perceived as gang members, criminal, and residing in dysfunctional families. Recent minority immigration into the community and beliefs in the decay of religious and moral values interact with these perceptions and ethnocentric views regarding appropriate language, dress, attitudes, and behavior to influence decision making and the case processing and outcomes of minorities. The decision-makers argue strongly for minority groups to acculturate into white, middle-class American society rather than for the recruitment of more diversified personnel and other methods to alleviate the disproportionate number of minorities in the juvenile justice system. A breakdown in the working relationships between juvenile probation officers at intake and prosecutors also contributes to petition decision making.

PERCEIVED ROLE OF THE JUVENILE COURT AND VIEWS OF THE SYSTEM

In Jackson, two themes emerge from the interviews of juvenile justice decision-makers regarding correctional orientations and their views of the juvenile justice system. The first theme is concern with rehabilitation and the protection of society, and the use of diversion and release to attain these objectives. The second interrelated theme is the emphasis placed on the failure of youth and families to adhere to white middle-class standards and values.

The chief juvenile court officer stated at the outset of the study that his court has adopted a philosophy of nonintervention, and the historical roots for this orientation come from a juvenile court judge. This judge advocated that only youth with serious problems should be involved in formal court proceedings. The chief juvenile court officer believed that a case outcome of release should be seen as the first option, followed by an informal adjustment, with referral for formal court intervention a last resort.

The following statements illustrates the emphases placed by the court on rehabilitation and the role of advocate:

1. I believe that the juvenile court officer's primary responsibility is in advocating for their client in making sure that there are programs

available for their families to be in that will help them . . . I think we
are good at placing the needs of the child first. What is in the best
interest of the child and how can we use what resources we have to
accomplish that.

2. The changes in the code . . . were initially put into effect to protect
    the rights of the children. . . . Many of the safeguards that were put
    into effect to protect the children in the end, end up harming the
    children in the long run. As more restrictions are put upon the work-
    ers, we can't help children who are having an increase in need. It has
    become more difficult and time-consuming.

The sentiment of the respondents in Jackson reflects the traditional philosophical emphasis on rehabilitation and informality (Champion, 1998: 339).
Contrary to Bond, where a legal orientation is the driving correctional orientation, the concept of *parens patriae* or the best interest of youth is the dominant ideology for interacting with juveniles.

Decision-makers in Jackson believe that the best interests of youth can be
best served by intervention(s) that includes family members as active participants in the treatment plan. Concomitantly, they view a dysfunctional family as
a major cause of delinquent behavior and justification for intervention services.

1. We look pretty seriously at the degree of control parents exercise
    over the child . . . what efforts have the parents made to alleviate the
    problems. Have they sought counseling, what has been the degree of
    involvement of the parents to control their kids and obtain services
    and follow through or have they sat back and basically make excuses
    for the kid? . . . If it's not a very serious offense for which society
    needs to be protected, and it looks like the parents are capable of
    controlling the child, we would look to a less restrictive form of in-
    tervention. Maybe an informal adjustment with community service,
    but with an effort to try to keep the kid in the home with the family.

2. Families are willing to let the peer groups take over. Today's
    teenagers are more mobile, have greater access to everything from
    very violent TV shows to alcohol or other types of drugs. . . . The
    parents don't spend a lot of time with the kids. . . . For the most
    part, some of it is cultural in terms of, let's say the . . . [Native
    Americans] [where] the grandparents tend to do a lot of the child
    rearing. With the situation as it exists here, that seems to be a very
    difficult situation for the elderly individuals to contend with these
    kids. They are out on the street, and they are kind of like street
    urchins. The delinquent kids that we see are pretty much disen-
    franchised from their own family.

In many ways the respondents' description of the ineffectiveness of extended family members in providing guidance and supervision, most notably the grandmother, reflects Elijah Anderson's portrayal and changing role of the grandmother in his study of African Americans in inner-city communities (1990, 1999). In particular, Anderson argues that the grandmother and her status as a "head" and guiding force has been weakened by the presence of crack cocaine, unemployment, persistent impoverishment, and role models or "new heads" that are the antithesis to everything she stands for and represents.

The movement of people from different cultures into the area (i.e., African Americans, Hispanics, Laotians, and Asians) and increased gang activity appear to augment and further justify the need for a rehabilitative philosophy. Some of the juvenile court probation officers and in particular, the intake unit, are very interested in gang activity, as is evident by the asking of youth for information on gangs, graffiti found at schools, on jackets, and so forth. Some officers, for example, collect and listen to rap music to pick out gang themes. Films are also watched for similar reasons (e.g., *New Jack City*). There seemed to be a split among the respondents whether gangs, however, are race specific. The following statement highlights these points:

> We have seen major influences of inner-city people moving here for a couple of different reasons. Specifically, a large number of Hispanics have been coming in because of one of our meat-packing plants have published in the *Los Angeles Times* for very cheap labor. They recruit. So suddenly we have a large number of people here. Housing is not adequate for them, social services are not adequate, and we are inadequate in terms of providing interpreting services. So we have a large number of people who are committing more crimes and usually against their own population, which suddenly sends them into a disproportionate crime rate. . . . They move their kids here to get them out of their gang involvement. Unfortunately, most of these kids only know the poor economic conditions in projects that they are used to and suddenly they are in a wide-open territory, and one of the first things they do is to begin forming gangs.

> Q. Who makeup the gangs, that is, racially?

> A. All races, white, black, Hispanic, . . . [Native American] and even Asian.

Overall, a number of the respondents believe that on a broader level there is a deterioration of values as indicated by a lack of respect for the court and a lack of religious values and morals in general.

1. The people don't adhere to standards. . . . You know [that] people that are involved with the court have the highest regard for the court and what it means and what the law means. . . . you see it so much when people come into court just in shorts, . . . I guess it's the air about it that, the court is a place of dignity and you're supposed to act appropriately in court. I think a lot of that's diminished and along with it the respect for the court and what the court means . . . I went to parochial schools and [there's] a lot of structure and, you know, respect for people involved in that setting, and I think it just carries along when you respect the court and what it stands for. . . .
2. Well, this is from my own observations, but the child that I see come in from the system, . . . and the ones that are repeat offenders and the ones that are really a problem are the ones that have no religion . . . I think that is reflecting upon their behavior and of the problems that they are getting into. Their spiritual growth. I see a black youth who just excels in sports, excels in music, but socially he's a misfit. Or, he goes out and steals. That tells you something, something is not right . . . we need more spiritual or religious guidance.
3. There's got to be more moral development.

The references on the part of decision-makers to youths' lack of spiritual or religious guidance, moral decay, and breakdown in structure and discipline as causes of delinquency reflect the respondents' concerns about the number of minority groups moving into the community and the decision-makers' parochial background and values in general. These occurrences and perceptions augment a historical precedent in Jackson whereby the intervention strategy is fostered by the best interests of youth and the family.

RACE, CRIME, FAMILY, AND DISTRUST
OF THE SYSTEM

Respondents in Jackson expressed a variety of opinions concerning what factors might account for the racial differences in referrals and the disproportionate confinement of minority youth. Although a very large percentage of the respondents did not believe minorities that commit different crimes, decision-makers indicate that minority youth commit more crime, a state of affairs precipitated by socioeconomic factors and by the large number of single-parent families among minorities.

Having a single parent in itself doesn't mean anything, but it does translate into a lesser ability to supervise the child due to simply the time and energy that's available to a single parent. . . . In some of the minority families we see a lack of male modeling . . . at the same time, I think they seem to de-emphasize education as a value.

Unlike in Bond, the police in Jackson are seen as only responding to where the crime exists. As stated by one interviewee, "Most things for the police are pretty clear cut." Overall, the juvenile justice personnel provided little information to suggest that the police are biased toward nonwhites.

Other decision-makers stated that they did not believe in the statistics that claim that minorities are overrepresented in secure facilities or believe that racial bias could be a cause. Some argued that African Americans adhere to racist attitudes and, because of the kind of music to which they listen, are likely to espouse values indicative of violence. Gang affiliation is also seen as a reason for differential involvement with the system. In the following, the theme of the failure of minority youth and their families to abide in general to the white middle-class norms of society again emerges as does the decision-makers' narrow view of racial bias and unwillingness to acknowledge and accept the possibility that racial bias exits. As will be evident, the decision- makers readily "blame the victim" for the disproportionate overrepresentation of minority youth in the system.

1. The Mexican community, a lot of it has to do with their cultural sensitivity. This was explained to me by one of the mothers. The Mexican male is supposed to be very macho. They have to prove themselves. They are taught that way by their parents, hence the gangs. Gangs encourage these kids to commit crimes, they get into drugs, and we start seeing a lot of them. . . . A lot of these people come into this country and come right up here. They don't have a chance to get used to the United States or understand how we work here.
2. I have never seen a racial incident with a police officer and a citizen. Throughout my twelve years at the police station and my time here have one of my co-workers come in and go, well, I've got this black kid. I've never heard a description of their color come into a conversation. Not once.
3. There's always racist people and they don't want to admit it, but I also think that blacks and Hispanics are racist against whites. It's a no-win situation. People use their race to get what they want. Poor me because I'm this color, poor me. . . . But if you look at it, the government tries to help those minorities much more now than whites. And the white male is the minority most of the time. I just hate that excuse . . . because they're Black or they're Hispanic.

Q. As an excuse for why they committed a crime and why they're in the system?

A. Right . . . I think that the attitude of the black community, as with rappers, has really slid. . . . A lot of the music plays a big part. . . . In fact, a center two years ago conducted a program where they gave kids any kind of music that they wanted for six months and then the next six months they took the music totally away. They found on that unit that their assaultive behavior were reduced by 300 percent by taking this music away. . . . Violence in television has also played a role.

Although a minority view, some of the decision-makers acknowledged that while minority youth commit more crime than white youth this occurrence might be stereotyped as applying to all minorities and by beliefs of affiliation with gang activity.

I think there seems to be more of them [minorities] committing crimes and there seems to be more group activity crimes linked to more minorities than for white kids. . . . Right now we have a phenomenon of gang activity. . . . A lot of times if a minority kid comes in with a particular dress style, they are pegged as a potential gangster. Whereas a supervisor's daughter comes in the same way and nobody thinks twice about it.

Recall that all of the decision-makers in Jackson are white.

A few of the personnel also linked minority youth overrepresentation in the system to the youth's and family's mistrust of the system. According to this view, African Americans are less likely to cooperate with the proceedings and/or to participate in diversionary programs. As a result, African American youth receive the more severe sanctions and move further into the system. The family more so than the youth is seen as the primary force influencing the behavior of the child and the decision-makers' perceptions of the situation. For example,

1. There might be a mistrust of authority. One of the more recent cases that I got, they skipped intake so that means that automatically a petition gets filed. I scheduled a meeting with them prior to the hearing, no-show on that. That means that they aren't going to get a formal adjustment at the initial appearance hearing. The young man is 13 years old. They missed some opportunities and that puts them right into the adjudication ball game.

2. . . . kids that come in with the parent, the message is that when you offer an informal to a child on a simple charge, a simple misde-

meanor, and the kids says they won't choose it because they're inno-
cent. The message that you generally hear is racism. The family be-
lieves that the child has been selected by the police solely on the
basis of race, that he is not in fact guilty. The child then, many times
even if he wants to, can't admit because the parent has basically already told the youth that they are not guilty and that everybody is
out to screw them over and that they will stand behind them. They
refuse the informal because they won't admit the offense . . . then the
court makes the decision. The problem is, in the majority of those
cases the kids are found guilty. . . . So they're found guilty and now
they are pulled into the court system . . . and this places them in a
situation that even on a simple misdemeanor they would be placed
outside the home.

Despite this view, very few of the interviewees acknowledged racial differences
in a willingness to admit guilt.

The following statements are presented to illustrate the complexities of the
interactions between minority youth, their families, and juvenile court officers.
Note the theme of youth failing to adhere to certain expected standards.

1. Sometimes I think they may react that way because of distrust of the
   police and the system and authority . . . one of the things you notice
   in the assimilation of the culture is that black parents use the same
   jargon that the kids do. They're very up on what the latest slang
   terms are. They seem to be much more involved in their kids' lives.
   They may not necessarily be doing activities, but taking more of an
   interest of being along through the system with kids in a lot of ways.
   The kids feel a lot of support, and mixed messages come out that
   way. Parents come in and are very supportive of the child, not of the
   crime. Sometimes the support is misinterpreted as validation or encouragement for committing crimes. Like, 'See I was right, distrust-
   ing the police and the system; so do my parents and they're not really
   upset about the way I'm being mistreated by the system that's mistreated my family too.' Sometimes that does the kids a disservice
   when that's the perception, whether it's accurate or not.
2. The minority kids are more suspicious. I don't know if that equates
   into having a bad attitude or not. It all goes back then to the family,
   to the parents . . . if you have a mom or dad or parents that are supportive of what the system is attempting to do with their children,
   then you will normally see that same type of attitude in the child. If
   you have parents that are very hostile to the system, feel as though

the system is prejudiced or biased or racist, that attitude then goes over onto the kids. That's very difficult to deal with. . . . The problems in this city come from the Native Americans.

The influx of different racial/ethnic groups into the area was seen as causing problems in the community. Decision-makers were asked if African Americans, Hispanics, and Native Americans have different needs and what, if any, consequences or implications these have for the juvenile court. Most felt that minorities have needs that may be different than those of whites, and most believed that underlying the needs of minorities is a better understanding of the U.S. culture and language. A number of the respondents also indicated that it is not necessarily their responsibility to change or accommodate the needs of the varying racial/ethnic groups. Some suggested that these differences not only have affected the likelihood of delinquency and contact with the system but have also led to problems within the schools.

1. There may be different needs . . . but I don't think that requires any higher degree of attention. . . . The tool needs to be a little bit different. I don't know what programs would be best. There's without a doubt that programs set up for Hispanic kids would be beneficial. . . . programs could help kids understand the U.S. culture, the white culture, the other culture. That's where you get a lot of clash. I've run into a couple of confrontational situations with a mother who says that we need to be more culturally aware of the Hispanic, Mexican, . . . [Native American] or black kids. I commonly respond to that, 'So you want me to treat them differently.' I generally get a silent response to that. . . . The needs of the black population is probably so much different than the Asians or the Hispanics because of the culture. You've got fifth-generation black families here. Boat people and others coming into the country don't even speak our language.

    Q. Do you think the economic structure, [and] lack of opportunity, is a cause of delinquency?

    A. I don't want to play toward society not giving them, black or any other population, opportunity. America is the land of opportunity. . . . Do you go out and get the opportunity, or do you wait for the opportunity to come to you? You know, . . . every kid goes into kindergarten on the same page. . . .

2. The . . . [Native American] and the Hispanic children have very special needs. We have a terrible language problem. We have to

have interpreters for a lot of these kids. We don't have any residential treatment centers to help understand the Hispanic culture. . . .
How are you going to get these people to come in and understand
our culture? They have to learn to respond to the dominant culture,
too. People have to understand the different cultures, but at the
same point in time they're going to have to understand what's
going on culturally here just like you and I.

As discussed earlier, according to Blalock's (1967) threat thesis, under
certain circumstances minority group immigration into a community leads to
economic and social conflict with the majority or dominant group and increases the likelihood of social control. Using data on Pennsylvania criminal
sentencing outcomes, Steffensmeier and Demuth found that Hispanic defendants received more severe outcomes than whites and African Americans.
They conclude that these findings are the result of a number of factors that
include the growing number of Hispanic immigrants and the threats they
pose stemming from perceived and actual competition for "jobs, the primacy
of the English language and Anglo-American Culture. . . . ." (2001:
152–153).

   Bortner, in his study of a juvenile court, also discovered cultural differences
between white decision-makers and African American youth and noted that
these differences generated an "atmosphere of mistrust" and that many court
personnel were "uncomprehending and unsympathetic to the life situations and
value systems of minority children" (1982: 157–158). In Jackson, the respondents also appear to be affected by the immigration of minorities into their
community and in response adhere to a strong ethnocentric view of how things
are to be, and values, attitudes, language, demeanor, dress, and behaviors that
are contrary to those expectations are wrong and justify intervention.

EXPLANATIONS FOR THE QUANTITATIVE FINDINGS

The main findings regarding the intake stage from the quantitative analysis for
Jackson are white youth with a history of prior contact with the system who are
referred to petition; white youth not attending school are likely to be released,
while those involved with property crimes are more likely to be diverted at intake; younger Native Americans or those charged with serious delinquent activity tend to be released; and Native American youth already under the
authority of the court are diverted rather than released. The respondents were
asked about the differential treatment provided to Native Americans at this
stage in the proceedings. The comments shed light on the treatment given to
both African Americans and whites. The decision-makers' views revolve around

a correctional policy of nonintervention and a formal agreement between the court and an agency that specializes in handling Native Americans.

Some decision-makers indicated that their case management orientation revolves around initial leniency in the form of release or participation in diversion. This orientation is tied to their overall philosophy of nonintervention and according to the officers is applied to all racial groups. "We've done the same things with the . . . [Native Americans] that we've done with blacks and whites. In terms of not doing anything with them when they first come in the first couple of times. Turning them over to their parents and when they do come in the third time we pound them. . . ." Most of the decision-makers, however, indicated that the findings specific to Native American youth are not surprising and, if anything, reflect current practices in the juvenile court office. The explanation for these findings rest with an agreement between the juvenile court office and an agency called Indian Youth of America (IYA).

1. Well, I guess I don't have an . . . [good] explanation. Other than I know we have, the . . . [Native Americans] have another diversion program or another agency that we use a great deal (IYA). That is specifically set up to work with them and we cooperate with them. I mean it's a cooperative type effort between the two agencies. It's been a nice marriage.
2. That doesn't surprise me about the . . . [Native Americans] because they are almost always referred to Indian Youth of America. . . .
3. The . . . [Native American] findings are not surprising. I just think that people don't know how to deal with the Native Americans so they shuffle them off into that program. I think they feel like their hands are tied in what they can do with Native American children.

Because of the acknowledgment that Native Americans are diverted to IYA, decision-makers were asked why and for elaboration on what the agency does with referred youth. The agreement between the two agencies is motivated by a belief that Native American youth may be more likely to respond to tribal authority than to the "white dominant culture." There appears to be some confusion as to how IYA handles referred youth. Some decision-makers seem informed, while others lack a clear idea of what occurs at IYA.

1. . . . I have no idea what goes on at Indian Youth. They just tell us that they were referred there, and we don't know if they do community serviceor if they receive individual or family counseling, or if the school system is tutoring, or what they do. We have no idea. . . .
2. I've gotten a written referral back on every kid I've ever sent there. But whether or not, I mean I don't follow up on those kids, so I really

don't know how in depth they go, . . . I'm not real familiar with their services other than they do go out to the homes and visit with the kids and the family, if the family will let them.

In response to the finding that both Native Americans and African Americans were less likely than whites to be petitioned, juvenile court personnel and the district attorney's office cited a breakdown in coordination between the two parties as a possible explanation.

I know the intake officers down there and it wouldn't surprise me if there is race bias going on down in that office. I'm not sure if it would necessarily be intentional but it would not surprise me at all.

Q. Explain to me why you feel that way.

A. Because I see from some intake officers more of an almost revenge type attitude for non-compliance. Things like, they set up an intake conference, and these people didn't come in, therefore [the officers] file a petition. Or, they came in and they didn't like the mother's attitude. Mom was questioning on every little thing. So it will come up to me with this statement that mom had a real attitude problem, and I don't think she will be supportive in any kind of informal adjustment. Therefore, file a petition . . . I can think of a particular case where the officer met with a black mother and her child over a theft of some Jolly Rancher candy, two cents a piece, and I think the kid had five of them. And it ended up coming up here for a petition request because this mother's attitude really rubbed this particular intake officer the wrong way. . . .

The lack of coordination between the juvenile court personnel and the county attorney's office is made more evident by the belief that intake officers are seen by the county prosecutors as filing "elevated charges," which ultimately lack legal sufficiency and result in dismissals. In some instances, the elevated charges may be tied to the over concern on part of some juvenile court officers with gangs.

There is some thought that anybody who looks or claims any gang knowledge is going to be referred by certain entities in the intake office. Whether or not there is a real basis for filing a petition. The crime may be fairly minor but the elements seem to be there. He was wearing a Raiders hat at the time of the crime so perhaps this is a gang child and someone should be looking closer at him. I know that the county attorney's office may be less concerned with that than others in the office . . . I'm not a full believer in our gang problem.

Thus decision-makers at one stage in the proceedings appear to be correcting for biases that occurred at intake. This is consistent with past study in both the criminal (e.g., Hepburn, 1978) and the juvenile justice systems (e.g., Dannefer and Schutt, 1982).

The respondents were not asked specifically about African American youths' participation in diversion at the initial appearance hearing relative to the other two racial groups. While speculative, it could be that an offer by the state to participate in diversion had not been offered to this point or the court and African American youth and the family were unable to reach an agreement until this stage in the proceedings.

SUGGESTIONS FOR REDUCING MINORITY OVERREPRESENTATION IN THE JUVENILE COURT

A majority of the decision-makers did not believe that the overrepresentation of minority youth in secure facilities was their concern. A number of the decision-makers argued that they provide fair treatment toward all racial groups. Differential offending is seen as the primary reason for minority youth involvement in the system. Consequently, most of these individuals viewed the hiring of minorities to the all-white staff as having little to no effect on their relations with youth. One person contended that "A minority will never work here." Some indicated that even if they wanted to hire minority staff, no qualified minorities have applied for positions within the office or in other positions of authority in general.

Rather than diversifying the staff, some suggested that there was a greater need on the part of minorities to adapt to our culture and they themselves establish programs of their own.

A good example is the Native Americans. They have their own system, and they try to really work with their children. I mean they'll try to have some kind of program to not have their child involved with the system. For instance, the youth program that they have and I think that if the blacks, and the Asians, and the Laos population developed something like that . . . I know the blacks are intelligent people; they need to come up with those kinds of programs.

Some decision-makers did indicate that there was need for alternative programming, especially those that focus on the family and provide positive role models. "We need more positive role models for their culture. . . . We don't have a lot of strong minority workers in treatment areas. . . ." A few of the respondents recognized the need to diversify the staff and to provide cultural sensitivity training.

SUMMARY

Two themes emerge from the interviews that provide a context for understanding race and social control in juvenile justice proceedings and in decision making in general in Jackson. The first theme concerns rehabilitation, diversion, and the protection of society. The second and interrelated theme is the emphasis placed on the adherence to white middle-class standards and values. The perception is that youth and their parents who fail to abide by these standards warrant differential treatment than those who conform. Inappropriate style of dress, perceived lack of respect for the law and the court, suspected or actual gang affiliation, lack of morals and religious guidance, and youth and parental lack of cooperation appear to be factors indicative of defiance of these standards. Images of violence believed to be associated with rap music and with other forms of media are also sources of nonconformity.

Native Americans are not necessarily expected to meet these standards. They are seen as different and as part of an organizational policy and formal agreement are often released or participate in diversion at intake under the guidance of an agency representing Native Americans. African Americans and other minorities, and to a degree whites, are expected to abide to white middle-class standards but are seen as unlikely of doing so.

A number of factors appear to influence decision making in Jackson, specifically, a historical precedent of practicing diversion coupled with an organizational ideology emphasizing rehabilitation of offenders and the protection of society. The organizational ideology is fostered or complemented by concerns of moral decay, evidenced by a decline in parental responsibility and in respect for authority. The perceived need for rehabilitation and for the protection of society is fueled further by beliefs that these factors are worse for minorities. Recent immigration of diverse minority groups into the community and the parochial background of the decision-makers appear to intensify these concerns. Most of the race effects seem to be indirect and operate through abidance to middle-class standards and assumptions of participation in gang activity, but many are also overt.

Decision-makers' commitment to respect and adherence to the dominant culture (beyond avoidance of delinquent activity) is not shared by all. The strongest emphasis on this ideological position is evident at intake and least emphasized by those representing the prosecution and the judiciary. Although a working relationship exists, the schism, especially between intake officers and prosecutors, appears to have resulted in some tension that has implications for youth. For example, both African Americans and Native Americans are less likely than other youth to be petitioned. Explanations for this occurrence are tied to the breakdown in relations between these decision-makers. Cases appear to be dismissed due to legal insufficiency that is the result of elevated charges and intake decision-makers' concern with middle-class norms and gang activity, a concern not necessarily as strongly shared by the district attorneys in Jackson.

The results also revealed that African American youth are likely to participate in diversion at the initial appearance hearing even after controlling for legally relevant factors. This finding appears to be the result of the involvement of the prosecutor's office at this stage in the proceedings. Perhaps, a change of heart on the part of the juvenile court staff occurs that results in an offer to participate in diversion. Or, African American youth and the family finally agree to accept the offer.

Because most of the interviewees believe that they themselves do not act in a biased manner and that minorities commit more crime, come from dysfunctional families, and may be uncooperative, suggestions to reduce minority over-representation focus on methods to reduce crime. Some decision-makers argued that there was a greater need on the part of minorities to adapt to the culture of white middle-class America and to establish programs on their own. A small number of the juvenile justice personnel indicated a need for alternative programming, such as family support and sessions on cultural sensitivity. These same people also saw a need to recruit minorities to diversify the all-white staff.

Chapter 9

Formal Rationalized Justice
and Nonintervention

Twenty-two juvenile court probation officers, 2 judges, 2 prosecutors, and 2 public defenders were interviewed in King. Of the 28 decision-makers, 19 are male, and 2 are African American. The mean age of the respondents is 42, and the average length of time on the job is ten years. King has the following characteristics:

- Relative to the other three jurisdictions, King has the largest population and is the wealthiest and most urban setting but has low rates of racial concentration, poverty, racial inequality, sexual promiscuity, crime, and criminal justice expenditures.
- The juvenile court has a high caseload consisting of cases involving delinquency and Children in Need of Supervision.
- It has a bureaucratic court that emphasizes the maintenance of order and the protection of society in a legalistic manner through a non-intervention approach.
- At intake, youth are released more often than in any other jurisdiction. Only 17 percent of youth at intake were referred for further court proceedings. The jurisdiction evidenced the lowest amount of social control as measured by the probability of a youth referred to intake ultimately receiving a change of placement/transfer to adult court. Relative to the other three jurisdictions, the racial gap, however, is quite significant in terms of the probability of being referred to intake and receiving a severe outcome as judicial disposition.
- African Americans are more likely than whites to be referred for further proceedings at intake once legal factors are controlled.
- Prior record is predictive of decision making at every stage.

In general, decision-makers from King adhere to a legalistic orientation with an emphasis on speed, efficiency, and minimal intervention. The court appears to practice a form of rationalized justice. If the court is to intervene, the response should be strict with the intention of holding youth accountable for their behavior. Furthermore, decision-makers believe that youth choose to engage in delinquent activity. A significant percentage of the respondents feel that African Americans are involved in crime more frequently, especially assaults and drug offenses than whites. Minority overrepresentation in the system and secure facilities is seen as a result of differential offending due to impoverished conditions, dysfunctional families, and affiliation with gangs. Other identified sources for overrepresentation are police discrimination, police deployment practices, and, to a lesser degree, African American youth and their families' unwillingness to cooperate with court proceedings. A heavy reliance by decision-makers on the youth's history of prior contact with the system also appears to be a significant factor in decision making and results in greater movement into the system for African Americans than whites. This finding is consistent with a bureaucratic court (e.g., Bridges et al., 1987; Zatz, 1987).

PERCEIVED ROLE OF THE JUVENILE COURT AND VIEWS OF THE SYSTEM

Almost all of the respondents indicated that the maintenance of social order and the protection of society are most important in interacting with youth. These goals can be attained through nonintervention and through the use of harsher outcomes if the needs of the child and the community justify such responses. Juvenile court personnel indicated that they would like to be more involved in rehabilitation but have found themselves "stretched in too many directions." Also, some of the decision-makers felt pressure from the legislators and from the community at large to handle cases in a legalistic rather than a rehabilitative manner. ". . . we have always done a pretty good job of trying to weigh the best interests of the community against the best interests of [the] child, but at times the community screams louder to be protected." Similar to decision-makers in the other jurisdictions, they also feel their role has changed from one of a social worker emphasis from the earlier years to one of legalities and punitiveness.

> When I started, the basic philosophy in juvenile court nationwide was *parens patriae* in regard to helping them and trying to assess and assist families as a wise parent would do . . . that system is disappearing from juvenile court work, and the juvenile justice system is moving more toward a junior criminal justice system with the accent on due process.

High caseloads and an insufficient number of case workers appear to have placed a strain on juvenile court officers causing stress, burnout, and even feelings of hopelessness. The lack of time to deal with youth was stressed by a number of the respondents.

1. As a juvenile court officer, I spend much more time now doing paperwork and investigating whether the case meets the criteria of the code rather than actually spending the time with kids and their families.

2. What I worry about is whether or not I can sustain that kind of commitment that is necessary to this job, both with dealing with delinquents and with children in need of supervision (CHINA's).

3. With the budget restraints . . . it's not business as usual anymore. Sometimes I feel that we're also insurance agents because in order to get a service provided, we have to fill out forms, contact insurance companies, making sure the people are not covered by any additional insurance. There's a lot of things that's been brought into play that takes away from the time that we can spend with our delinquent youth and follow them in the community. . . . It's [come] to the point where there's a problem even having them come in on a weekly basis or getting into the community. . . . That's pretty non-existent with me personally because we're tied up with so many other things in particular dealing with CHINA cases.

A lack of treatment alternatives and placements for youth were also seen as factors hindering the ability of the juvenile justice decision-makers to effectively treat youth. Placement opportunities in general and in particular for female youth were viewed as scarce. The lack of placement options may explain why female youth are less often referred to diversion at intake than male youth (table 6.6).

1. There just isn't enough space out there. So, the only kids that really get detained are the ones that are so bad that they probably belong in adult court.

2. The number of beds available for a teenage female are preposterously low. . . .

3. Females are hard to place. Basically, we have the state training school and a few other placements.

4. Immediate consequences for a child are sometimes not possible to do. It can be months before they are seen at intake, and by that time the kid has sort of forgotten what he did. Things that cause the system to slow down so bad are lack of placements.

The perceived causes of delinquency are personal choice, the family, and the school. Peer pressure and "hanging around with the wrong crowd" are seen as additional factors that influence the likelihood of delinquency. Those respondents who believe that environmental factors play a role in delinquent behavior link the lack of economic opportunities to youth involvement in drug offending. "What teenager wants to go out and get a job at Burger King making $4 per hour when they can stand on a street corner and sell crack for $350 per hour?" (see also Hagedorn, 1994; Anderson, 1999).

Both the institutions of the family and the schools are seen as problematic in jurisdiction 3. Family values are seen as lacking, but it is the school system that received the most attention as failing to prevent and deter delinquent behavior. The schools were described as intolerant and pushing youth out who do not conform to the ideal model student. The schools were also seen as ineffective in providing alternative educational programs for problematic students. Some decision-makers argued for an increase in the hiring of minorities within the school system. It is believed that a more racially/ethnic diversified teaching force could provide needed role models for minority youth. "Schools don't have enough minority role models within the system, particularly at the elementary level. I think that if we have more black people in education, in the roles of teaching, . . . it would really help a lot." In summary, the juvenile court in King adheres to a legal orientation that emphasizes accountability and the protection of society. These goals can be attained through nonintervention and if necessary, through a heavy-handed approach for dealing with youth. Personal choice is seen as the primary cause of delinquency. The belief that delinquency is the result of individual choice is in line with the juvenile court's due process approach for dealing with youth. To a lesser degree, a decline in family values, a lack of tolerance on the part of the schools toward nonconforming youth, and a lack of alternative educational programming are also seen as contributing factors to delinquency.

RACE, CRIME, FAMILY, AND DISTRUST OF THE SYSTEM

Juvenile justice decision-makers expressed a wide range of opinions regarding what factors may account for the overrepresentation of minority youth in the juvenile court. Compared to the other three jurisdictions, the respondents were often indifferent and provided responses that were guarded, usually short, nonrevealing, and generally, "catchall" statements to explain disproportionate minority confinement (DMC). Jurisdiction 3 was also the least willing of the jurisdictions to participate in the study. The court is suspicious of "outsiders" and is driven by concerns with maintaining an image of being efficient and a "fair" court. The indifference on the part of the personnel in King toward the study and in particular, questions that focused on race, fits with the bureaucratic nature of the court.

Notwithstanding the court's lack of enthusiasm for the study, and the brevity and lack of insightful responses, the decision-makers did provide some information that sheds light on their views regarding race differences in crime, family, and distrust of the system. A majority of the respondents did not believe that African American youth commit more crime, commit more serious, crime, or are involved in different crimes than white youth.

Some of the personnel, however, indicated that African Americans participate more often in gangs and drug offenses than whites.

1. The main problem now is the gang influx in the community and how that is related to the drug dealing. There are more weapons in the minority community, and I think that there is a greater likelihood of the violent types of crimes.
2. The majority of the crimes that black youths get into is usually possession with intent to deliver narcotics, controlled substances.
3. The majority of the gang members and gang activity . . . [consists of] minorities.

Although the decision-makers cited problems between being African American and participation in drugs and gangs, the concerns are not as prominent and driving sources for intervention as in Jackson.

Decision-makers believed that one reason why there are differences in referrals to the system is that African Americans get caught more often and are more likely to be turned in than whites. A majority of the decision-makers also argued that minority overrepresentation in the system may be the result of law enforcement practices and bias among police officers at the arrest stage of the process.

1. There is a lot more discrimination on the part of the police in this town.
2. The police are more likely to get upset with and arrest a black youth than a white youth.
3. I don't think there's any doubt that as a group the police are pretty prejudiced against blacks.
4. Law enforcement is where the most blatant discrimination occurs.

Two explanations emerged as to why police are more likely to respond differently toward African Americans than whites. The first explanation cites a lack of education on the part of the police officers as a cause for the perceived differential treatment. "The police force is not made up of college graduates, and studies show that the more education you have, the more you view things with an open mind and that would allow you to be less prejudiced." The second explanation provided to account for the different treatment given African Americans by police centered on deployment patterns. "The police are concentrating in areas where most of the people . . . are minorities. So, if that is where they are concentrating their effort, that is who they are going to arrest." A few of the respondents recognized the possibility of race selection bias on a broader and more general level as a cause of overrepresentation and were quite frank concerning the issue.

1. I think that society tends to deal with their minority youth much more harshly for the same crimes as non-minority persons. . . . Society has chosen to deal with . . . minorities and the problems they have by locking them up.
2. There is still, in our society, a perpetuation of the racist philosophy and the gender thing, the old values of society . . . that males and females are treated differently and that blacks and whites are treated differently . . . those persist.

Some of the personnel denied the possibility of racial bias in society at large and at any stage in the system, including the police, as an explanation for minority overrepresentation in the system. There were a number of the respondents who would not even respond to inquiries into the topic. Similar to some of the respondents in Jackson, there were those who disagreed that minority overrepresentation exists in the system and in secure facilities: "I don't believe it." Many individuals operated with a view of race bias as overt and intentional, ignoring the possible existence of subtle, unintentional forms.

1. I don't see any race bias in the system. We are professionals, trained and selected among several candidates. We [were] asked to make a decision based on the facts of the case and the needs of the individual. If we weren't doing our job properly we wouldn't be employed very long.
2. When an individual is detained, at no point and time is there information given as to his race. He is detained on the basis of the crime he has committed.

Eighty-two percent of the juvenile justice personnel indicated that African Americans are less trustful of the system than whites. Yet only 42 percent viewed African American youth and the family as problematic or uncooperative with the juvenile court proceedings. A few respondents believed that the lack of respect on the part of African Americans toward the juvenile court worked to their disadvantage.

1.   As a group, they [blacks] present themselves less respectfully than whites. I think that works against them. I think that is unfortunate but that is just the way, as a group, the blacks tend to react and in the long run it does hurt them.

2.   They force us into a corner a lot of the times; often they flunk the attitude test.

Interestingly, some of the decision-makers argued just the opposite claiming that it is white youth, not African American youth, who are uncooperative. This view is highlighted in the following statement: "I see the upper-class kids . . . who think that they have the world by the tail because they have money and they don't give a damn what the heck they have done. So, I would have to say that I see more inner-city kids being more remorseful for what they have done." In short, juvenile justice decision-makers in King provided guarded responses regarding explanations for minority youth overrepresentation in the system. By denying the existence of race bias, race differences in delinquent offending, and cooperation with the juvenile court proceedings, the respondents, for the most part, were at a loss to offer explanations for the overwhelming presence of minority youth in the juvenile justice system. The juvenile justice decision-makers' belief that the police respond differently to African Americans is an exception.

Another exception is the belief by some decision-makers that African Americans are more likely to be involved in gangs and drug offenses than whites. A lack of education and deployment patterns that focus on the neighborhoods of African Americans and the poor are also cited as reasons for the differential handling of African American youth by the police. While the explanation of the police disproportionately arresting and referring African American youth may result in overrepresentation at the front end of the system, it provides little insight into the dynamics of decision making once the youth has entered the juvenile court.

EXPLANATIONS FOR THE QUANTITATIVE FINDINGS

The most significant results from the quantitative analysis are as follows: (1) African American youth are more likely than white youth to be referred from intake to petition, (2) a large number of youth are either released or diverted at the stage of intake and initial appearance, (3) most youth who reach the stage of petition and adjudication receive the more severe outcome, and (4) the youth's history of prior referrals is heavily relied upon by decision-makers in determining case outcomes. Unfortunately, decision-makers were not asked for their interpretations concerning either the finding that African Americans are more likely than whites to receive recommendations for further court proceedings at intake or the court's reliance on the prior record of youth. In the original study, race was a statistically insignificant predictor of intake decision making and the effects of prior record at every decision-making stage were not present (Leiber, 1993). The presence of a statistically significant race effect at intake and prior record at every stage in the present research can be attributed to sample weighting that was not used in the initial research.

While there is no direct input from decision-makers regarding the effects of race and prior record and the relationship between the two on case outcomes, insights into these associations can be derived from the structural and organizational characteristics of King and the results from the quantitative findings. An examination of the zero-order correlation results (4A.3.), for example, indicates a statistically significant association between race and the number of prior referrals ($r = .15, p < .01$). That is, African American youth have greater past contact with the system than white youth. The regression results revealed that African Americans were more likely to be referred at intake to petition and prior record was predictive of decision making at every stage. Together, these relationships suggest that prior record is relied upon to legitimately justify the use of more severe sanctions and further court processing of youth, especially African Americans since they as a group have a greater history of prior referrals than whites in King. The effect of prior record on decision making is exasperated by the bureaucratic nature of the court. The findings suggest that prior record is used as a "shorthand cue" to indicate case seriousness and the need for intervention. This occurrence also suggests that prior record is racially tainted (e.g., Hagan, 1974; Farrell and Swigert, 1978; Pope and Feyerherm, 1992) and works to the disadvantage of African Americans compared to whites in King. At a minimum, these findings also raise questions concerning the extent prior record should be used to differentiate and produce the kinds of outcomes that contribute to minority overrepresentation in King.

Results from the interviews indicate that the use of release in King appears to be tied to a number of factors that include an orientation toward nonintervention for nonserious cases, heavy caseloads, and the lack of programming alternatives.

1. We don't have the time to deal with the minor crimes. We don't have the manpower. We just don't have the time.
2. If you get a kid that has normal court involvement, you're apt to give the young man and lady a break. Kids need a break. Who's . . . going to give it to them, if we don't.
3. What is bad is that in other counties, they have more diversionary programs than we do.
4. Money is the number one problem. We're not able to provide the programming we need.

The juvenile court also uses formal adjustments frequently at the initial appearance stage, preferring a formal adjustment over an informal adjustment at intake. The rationale for this preference lies with the belief that formal adjustment provides a stronger message to youth and the family regarding the severity of the situation. Recall that an informal adjustment occurs at intake, prior to the petition stage or the point that begins formal court proceedings.

1. Lots of kids do one stupid thing in their life. If it is just one stupid thing, I am willing to do a formal adjustment.
2. We really try to keep the kids from having a permanent record and these kids can walk in there with a lot of negatives and still get a consent decree [formal adjustment]. We make a conscious effort to do that here.
3. If there are no additional problems, I will give a formal adjustment. I prefer formal adjustments over informal adjustments. With the former, formal proceedings are initiated.
4. I see a consent decree [formal adjustment], as being a second chance, . . . To me, a second chance is not just a slap on the wrist and say don't do it again. That is not a second chance; that doesn't do anything for a kid. If a kid is processed through the system and at a pretrial conference the judge recommends that the child be put on a consent decree and if successfully completed, that case is closed and that individual does not receive a criminal record. Okay, there is no adjudication shown on the record; to me that is a second chance.

Thus, it appears that release is the option of choice. However, if a case warrants intervention, the decision-makers prefer a formal adjustment which, in part, may account for the increased likelihood of being petitioned for those who reach that stage. The decision-makers also believe that in their jurisdiction only the more serious cases typically go further into the system, and consequently, if an agreement cannot be worked out at the initial appearance, an adjudication would most likely follow. Some respondents also believe that the prosecuting attorneys adhere to a "get tough" philosophy that may explain decision making at petition and adjudication.

SUGGESTIONS FOR REDUCING MINORITY OVERREPRESENTATION IN THE JUVENILE COURT

Most of the suggestions provided by the decision-makers for addressing minority youth overrepresentation in the system focused on means to prevent and deter delinquency and to improve the overall life opportunities for the poor and minorities. The underlying assumption driving these suggestions is that these groups commit more crime.

1. Some of these kids . . . need to be given more job training and to be given that advantage to be able to go out and find a job.
2. I think recreational kinds of opportunities need to be constantly developed.
3. The community falls short in job opportunities.

Some of the respondents also cited the need for community-based programming designed specifically for minority youth. Within this context, African American personnel should be hired to fill needs not met by the family; namely, support and mentoring.

1. We need more programs that are in the community . . . but are right there where the kids are living in order to keep an eye on things and strengthen the family structure and help them to make it at home. We also need treatment facilities that are in the inner city.
2. Programs with a very strong black male role model which a lot of black youth are lacking in their environment. Role models that will tell them to do as they do and set an example. This is what a lot of young black male youth are missing.
3. Mentoring programs would be good. . . . If we could see a real assertive effort on the part of those minorities to set examples and be more visible, that would be very positive.

A few of the decision-makers extended the expressed need for greater racial diversification to their own court. All of these respondents felt that there should be more than two minority officers on staff.

SUMMARY

In King, juvenile court decision-makers seem to have a dual philosophy for dealing with youth. The court emphasizes minimal intervention in the form of release and participation in informal and formal adjustments. If the situation does not warrant a release at intake, formal adjustments are preferred over informal adjustments because the former is seen as sending a stronger message to youth and to the family. The court also adheres to a legalistic orientation. The two approaches appear to be linked and are complementary rather than in opposition to one another. Underlying the dual philosophy is the notion that young offenders must be held accountable for their behavior. Crime is seen as the result of personal choice.

The large size of the community, a heavy caseload, and a lack of resources, especially diversionary programs and placement facilities, appear to drive the court's philosophy for dealing with delinquent youth. Decision making appears to be very bureaucratic with an emphasis on expediency. Rehabilitation is viewed as important, but has a secondary role due to the lack of time, money, and diversionary alternatives. In place of rehabilitation, court personnel focus instead on the protection of society. This is in contrast to Jackson, where the protection of society is also emphasized, but the factors fostering this orientation are quite different. In Jackson, the focus on the protection of society is driven by a rehabilitative orientation due to the movement of minorities into the community and a perceived failure on the part of some to abide by middle-class values pertaining to moral behavior and respect for authority. The impact for youth is that although both communities advocate the protection of society, the circumstances or contexts influencing the adoption of this philosophy differ. Still, both communities exert lower levels of social control relative to the other two jurisdictions.

Explanations for minority overrepresentation in the juvenile justice system and in secure facilities focus on alleged police discrimination and police deployment patterns. Other explanations include impoverishment, the lack of job opportunities, and to a lesser extent, dysfunctional families. The majority of the decision-makers do not feel that African American youth engage in crime more frequently, in more serious crime, or in different kinds of crime. For those who do believe that differences exist, African American youth are believed to commit more crime, and participate more often than white youth in drug offenses, assaults, and gang activity. Most of the respondents indicated that African American youth and their families are suspicious of the court, yet a slight majority of the decision-makers perceive no differences in the extent to which they cooperate with the court proceedings relative to their white counterparts.

African American youth were more likely to be referred to petition than white youth and legal and extralegal factors do not account for this occurrence. However, while the race effect at intake resulted in a significant increase in the size of the African American composition making up the cohort continuing through the system, legal and extralegal factors appear to explain decision making at subsequent stages. Prior record is a statistically significant determinant of decision making at all four stages and appears to be used to type-script youth to justify the need for intervention. Prior record is a racially tainted legal criterion and contributes to the overrepresentation of minority youth in King's juvenile court.

Most of the suggestions for addressing minority overrepresentation in the system and in secure facilities involved the development and use of programs to prevent delinquent behavior and to improve the overall life chances of African Americans and the poor. The employment of more minorities was also cited as a possible solution. The racial diversification of the juvenile court and other agencies that handle minority youth is seen as a method for providing positive role models for African Americans.

Chapter 10

Dysfunctional Family, Subcultural Values, Lack of Resources, and Rehabilitation

Twelve juvenile court officers, 1 judge, and 1 referee were interviewed in the jurisdiction of Parks. Of the 14 respondents, 7 are male. All of the subjects are white. The mean age of the personnel is 41 and the average length of time on the job is 12 years. The structural characteristics of the community, the organizational features of the juvenile court, and the results from the quantitative analyses are as follows:

- Parks has the second largest community of the four studied and evidences the highest racial inequality, percent of babies born out-of-wedlock to teenage mothers, and criminal justice expenditures.
- The juvenile court has a relatively high caseload, and the stated organizational ideologies center around accountability and intervention.
- Youth referred to intake have a greater probability of receiving a change of placement/transfer to adult court than youth in Jackson and King.
- At intake, African American youth who come from single-parent households are more likely than other youth to be referred for further court proceedings.
- African Americans are less likely than whites to be petitioned and adjudicated delinquent.

An understanding of these findings can be found in the interrelationships among the structural characteristics of the community (i.e., racial inequality, and percent of babies born out-of-wedlock to teenage mothers) and the organizational ideologies of the court (i.e., correctional orientations consisting of accountability, intervention, and rehabilitation). Decision-makers' beliefs and

133

stereotypes that African Americans are more delinquent due to dysfunctional families and subcultural values and in general, are distrustful of the system, also impact decision making. For the first time, the inability to secure private counsel and to pay for private treatment emerge as additional sources that influence the handling of youth. Together, these factors provide insights into case outcomes especially the disproportionate overrepresentation of African Americans in Parks' juvenile justice system.

PERCEIVED ROLE OF THE JUVENILE COURT AND VIEWS OF THE SYSTEM

Although only a few of the decision-makers actually stated in the interviews that the main goal of the juvenile justice system is rehabilitation, it was clear from their responses that rehabilitation is the guiding philosophy for dealing with youth. The emphasis placed on rehabilitation is evident in the decision-makers' desire to counsel, oversee probation, and protect the community. Personnel indicated that it was especially important to keep probationers from becoming recidivists and "growing up" in the system. According to one respondent, philosophies of how to deal with recidivists within their court have recently changed. The old philosophy was that if a youth re-offended after two successful probation periods, a new strategy was needed, and an automatic placement would be sought. The new philosophy, however, is that youth who did well on probation before, should be given another chance on probation. Rehabilitation, not punishment, is seen as the method best suited to prevent recidivism. "The purpose of the juvenile court system is to rehabilitate the people."

The rehabilitation of youth was seen as attainable through intervention and through a stern response for the purpose of accountability. A lack of services and treatment alternatives were believed to hinder the decision-makers' ability to fully accomplish this goal.

1. There's a lack of resources and programs.
2. More and more kids are referred, more cases but less services available.
3. ... The ability to initiate services and follow through with services that are needed are lacking. After you identify the problem, being able to deal with that immediately and have some kind of services for them would be nice.

Another factor that was cited as blocking the effectiveness of rehabilitative efforts is the change from a *parens patriae* approach to a more legalistic orientation. Most of the decision-makers felt this orientation restricted their ability to "change the youth." "I have gone from more of a social work belief to more of a, 'you do the crime, you do the time' attitude. I would like to think I am more realistic now." Some decision-makers believed that the emphasis on legalistic concerns has resulted in an increased ability to be effective in their job. These individuals contend they are now able to take into account such things as the needs of the child and society. According to the respondents, they are able to look more closely at youths' background to justify requirements as stipulated by state statute. Thus, the decision-makers believe they are getting more at the root of the youth's problem(s).

The primary causes of juvenile delinquency, as discussed by the respondents, are being poor, living in high-crime neighborhoods, gangs, poor parental supervision, and living in a single-parent family. Overall, most of the personnel maintain that if youth were given a proper upbringing, including economic, psychological, emotional, and physical support, they would be law-abiding citizens. The belief is that most of the juvenile's problems begin at home. "Parents need to take a lot of control back from their kids and spend time with their kids. We need to get the family unit back in this country. I don't think it is there like it used to be." The peer group, however, is also seen as very influential in the participation of delinquency. Those interviewed do not believe that there are race differences in gang participation or the kinds of behaviors in which gang members are involved. Most of the decision-makers believe gang membership increases participation in violent crime and drugs.

1. (The gang situation) has gone from bad to worse. Twelve years ago there was nothing noticeable, nothing specific, then we had the gangs but no big problems. Then came the drugs and then the shootings.
2. We are seeing the kids involved in crack cocaine, and we never saw that before. We are starting to see a lot more turf battles, shootings, . . . We have a lot more senseless community violence, a lot more graffiti, a lot more intimidation.

In short, the juvenile court is concerned with rehabilitation, accountability, and intervention. Youth need rehabilitation due to poverty, single-parent homes, and gang affiliation. The use of diversion alternatives to achieve rehabilitation, however, appears to be lacking.

RACE, CRIME, FAMILY, AND DISTRUST OF THE SYSTEM

Most of the decision-makers (64%) did not believe that African American youth participate in different types of delinquent behavior than white youth. Over half indicated that African American youth commit more crime and more serious crime. Most of the decision-makers argued that if race differences do exist in delinquent offending it is most likely because African Americans disproportionately live in impoverished communities.

1. Being at the lower end of the economic spectrum, they probably don't have the coping skills that a lot of whites who come from a more middle-class background have. I think that if you look at low-income whites, you probably find that they too are overrepresented in crime.
2. The blacks with the more extensive prior record, the charges have a tendency to be more serious than whites and that could be perhaps that whites are not in the economic situation that the majority of the minorities are in. I think that blacks have a tendency to have more violent crimes whereas whites have more of a tendency to shoplift or things like that.
3. Yes, they commit more crime. They don't have money; they don't have jobs; they come from single-parent homes.

The overall sentiment of the respondents concerned the relationship between impoverishment and single-parent households. In general, it is believed that a single parent may have a more difficult time effectively supervising his or her child.

1. It is because of the breakup of the family and the high incidence of poverty.
2. . . . What you find is the poverty, the poor parental supervision, the single parent, the inner city, all of those factors contribute to juvenile delinquency. What we find in this community, I think, is that, especially African American youngsters are more highly represented in all those risk factors. It just goes to show that if all African American kids in this community were from two-parent families, living in middle-class areas, and were employed, we wouldn't see them.
3. (They are) unable to secure a job at a young age or having no jobs available for them with their lack of skills, then they fill that void in any way they possibly can. I think that that's probably one of the biggest reasons . . . why a lot goes on in juvenile court. The kids are taking care of needs that aren't being taken care of by parents.

Many of the personnel also believe that certain families adhere to subcultural values that contribute to their children's participation in crime. According to some respondents, in some families, particularly African Americans, youth are brought up to believe that it is okay to steal, so basically, ". . . they learn delinquency at home."

The black community right now is undergoing a very difficult time in terms of family structure . . . and it seems like when we take a look at the case, we assess how the family can help deal with the problem. . . . The white kids that are in placement, . . . the parents are having a difficult time dealing with the kid. It's certainly true that there are some white kids who commit the same crimes that the black kids do, that the white kids aren't as prone to get put into placement. That's true, when you're talking about the severity of the crime. But, when we're looking at everything overall, how things are going with that kid in his family and his schoolwork, and the community, it seems like the black families that have been referred for delinquencies are having a more difficult time dealing with those kids.

Some of the decision-makers also argue that many of the African Americans are related to each other and are recidivists. Therefore, because many people in the same family seem to be involved in crime, it is assumed that they all learn it from their family; they are "taught to commit crime."

1. A lot of our re-offenders are black kids that we have already been working with. I think that sometimes it comes down to a cultural thing with them and they are trying to establish who they are, or it comes down to the black-and-white thing and they just allow that unresolved anger to stay there.

2. The Hispanic culture seems to take care of each other better or more so than the other cultures do. But [in] the black culture, I think that sometimes violence is an accepted norm or accepted way of living, and if they want something and that is their means to get it then that is what they do.

3. A lot of it has to do with the fact that they don't have money; they don't have jobs; they come from single-parent families; the way they are brought up that it is okay to steal; their role models are terrible. Kids learn all of that behavior, and they learn it at home, and that is why we have a problem.

4. . . . We have had a few minority families that comprise one clan and they are all related and interrelated, and the parents do not keep control of their kids, and so their kids are probably involved in a horrendous amount of crime themselves. . . .

The decision-makers in Parks generally felt that attitude plays an important factor in the decision-making process. Both African American youth and the family are seen as having negative attitudes and an overall distrust of authority.

1. They have a lack of respect for the system because they think it is discriminatory. And the purpose of the juvenile court system is to rehabilitate the people . . . [who] come before it, and if you don't get cooperation with the rehabilitation efforts, you are likely to get recidivism.

2. An uncooperative attitude, maintained long enough, will get them [African Americans] arrested, past intake as opposed to diversion, on the way up, including Eldora [the state training school for boys]. If you're maintaining an attitude of 'Screw you, I'm not going to do it, and I don't care, and I'm not going to change, and you're wasting my time.' Those, no matter who they are, are going to end up going further in the system.

Some officers also believe that African American families often use the system to excuse their children's behavior. That is, they see it as a "white system," a system "out to get them." For others, according to the respondents, defiance is a symbol of status among African Americans. "I think some of them have to prove themselves in their own little community; they see who is the toughest and the meanest and I think it is just for show, status among themselves." When discussing the importance of attitude, the decision-makers stated that the parent's attitude is often more important than the child's because it is seen as an indication of the family's willingness to cooperate. "Their parents are the biggest impediment. I think because the kids who make it are the kids who have parents who love them and are supportive and are not just trying to cover up and minimize." The respondents' portrayal of African American involvement in crime and the role of impoverishment and the family in fostering such behavior and disrespect toward the court parallels the accounts provided by studies of life in structurally disorganized communities (e.g., Clark, 1965; Liebow, 1967; Suttles, 1968; Massey and Denton, 1993; Jones and Newman, 1997). Anderson, for example, notes that "many young blacks sometimes . . . find it difficult to take white people or even conventional black people seriously, and they actively live their lives in opposition to them and everything they are taken to represent" (1999: 109). Sampson and Wilson and others (e.g., Clark, 1965) contend that such cultural adaptations arise from discrimination, lack of employment, urban poverty, and social isolation that deprive individuals "not only of resources and conventional role models, but also of cultural learning from mainstream social networks that facilitate social and economic advancement. . . . (Sampson and Wilson, 1995: 50–51 cite omitted). Other researchers, such as Hagan and Palloni (1990) also acknowledge the existence of a subculture that includes oppositional values, but find that criminal justice responses and past labeling of parents and sons as *criminal* affect future delinquency above and beyond cultural factors (see also Nagin and Patternoster, 1991).

Some decision-makers did not necessarily view African American families as less cooperative than white families. These individuals, however, did indicate that African Americans often either expect the system to do nothing or to do everything.

The respondents also stated that the police and the lack of financial resources in terms of the ability to secure private counsel and to pay for private treatment play significant roles in minority youth involvement in the juvenile justice system. Most of the juvenile justice decision-makers indicate that the police watch and patrol African American communities more than white communities. Many of the respondents admitted that they believe there is some discrimination or bias by the police at the arrest stage. Reasons for this belief focused on outright racial bias and reliance on stereotypes.

1. I've heard the word nigger, both here in our office and at the police, and I guess I consider that blatant racism, when blacks weren't present and also when they were.
2. You like to think that all of the police are fair, but when I talk to the kids I realize that they do discriminate. They stop blacks a lot quicker than they would whites and check them out, especially the juveniles, and after awhile, you just realize that black kids will face police scrutiny more than the average white kid and even Hispanics unless they are in a neighborhood that is middle class.
3. Young black males don't feel part of the community because as soon as two or three of them are seen together, they're assumed to be a gang or delinquents of some kind.

Some decision-makers also believe that the police expect a great deal of respect, and when it is not forthcoming, they get upset and may over-arrest.

We asked about the black kids, especially responding to white authority. And I don't think they have much respect for white authority, and I think they tend to shoot off their mouths at the police officers as they drive by. Whereas, a white kid out in another neighborhood will tend to be sort of sneaky about it, maybe saying it under his breath, but he won't say it out loud. But these black kids will have the chip right there on their shoulder in full view. Police officers aren't very good at dodging that or ignoring that.

There were quite a few decision-makers who believe that it is possible for whites to get better outcomes and less severe sentences than African Americans because they can retain private attorneys as opposed to court-appointed attorneys. "I don't know why it happens. But we have real good court-appointed attorneys so I don't know. Maybe it has more to do with the family and their ability to pay." Although limited research exists on the topic, it has been found that most youth in the juvenile justice system are not represented by legal counsel and when representation is present, the majority of youth have a public defender or a court-appointed attorney (e.g., Feld, 1988). Research has also shown that irrespective of the severity of the offense, youth with counsel receive more severe sanctions than those without an attorney (e.g., Bortner, 1982; Feld, 1988, 1989). A number of explanations have been offered to explain the relationship between having an attorney and the application of a more severe outcome. These explanations range from the competency of defense counsel to the appearance the presence of legal representation may have for the court (i.e., serious and/or a more formal case) (e.g., Duffee and Siegel, 1971; American Bar Association, 1995). For a detailed review of the topic refer to Feld (1999: 109–165).

Decision-makers also felt that case outcomes can be affected by a youth's access to resources that go beyond the ability to secure private counsel. According to this view, the system will not intervene as much if the youth can afford private treatment. That is, if a youth's family has the financial resources necessary for private treatment, the court may allow the family to take care of the matter privately, without being forced to do so by court order.

1. Sometimes juveniles might be able to have access to better treatment as a result of having money and therefore maybe having another alternative available for a court disposition that otherwise wouldn't be available under normal circumstances.

2. When a family has resources, you are more likely to do less with them than an individual who has no resources whatsoever. As far as I am concerned, if the court can keep out of someone's life, I think that we owe that to that individual to let them show the court that they do have the resources, and if they don't follow through with it, then the court should get involved. Parents need to take action and get involved.

The inability to secure private legal representation and private treatment has significant class and race implications as to how youth are responded to within the juvenile court (see also, Bortner et al., 1993). Because African Americans are more likely to be poor than whites they are also more likely to be unable to afford private counsel and private treatment. Consequently, the likelihood that African American youth will enter the system and receive more severe outcomes relative to white youth is increased.

A small number of the respondents saw prejudice and racial discrimination as a possible explanation for the overrepresentation of minority youth in the juvenile justice system. The following statement captures this sentiment:

I think there's institutionalized racism in America. There's lots of reasons; I kind of attribute it to white people not understanding black people. I don't think they mean to. I think it's ignorance, not a lot of studying or understanding, not living around black people, listening to what they were told, believing in myths and other hypocrisies or stories. It's unfortunate, but I really attribute it to a lack of understanding on the part of white people. . . . And not enough white people have been in a situation where they've been around black people until later in life, and then sometimes their ideas are formulated and then they have to work at changing themselves. That's kind of where I believe a lot of the problem lies.

Racial inequality and children born out-of-wedlock to teenagers are significant social problems in Parks. These were prominent issues that also emerged from the interviews with the juvenile justice personnel. African Americans are seen as differentially involved in crime due to impoverishment, single-parent households, and subcultural values. Crime is also seen by the decision-makers as generational among some families, particularly, African Americans. African American youth and the family are also believed to be more distrustful than their white counterparts, which could play a role in the likelihood of arrest and receiving more severe outcomes in juvenile justice proceedings. Police bias toward minorities and the inability to secure private counsel and to pay for private treatment are additional factors contributing to minority overrepresentation in the juvenile justice system. The shortage of diversionary treatment programs in Parks provide added weight to the significance to the contention that financial resources determine case processing and outcomes.

EXPLANATIONS FOR THE QUANTITATIVE FINDINGS

In Parks, decision-makers exercise greater social control than in Jackson and King. African American youth are responded differently at intake, petition, and adjudication. At intake, African American youth who come from single-parent households are more likely than other youth to be referred for further court proceedings. African Americans are less likely than whites to be petitioned and adjudicated delinquent. Other than at intake to petition, the disproportionate overrepresentation of African Americans appears to be accounted for by factors other than race (i.e., problems at school, prior record, and number of charges). The juvenile court decision-makers were asked for their interpretations of the race effect at the petition stage. Insights into the other findings are drawn from responses to questions focusing on race and court processing in general. My initial research did not find evidence of race effects at intake or adjudication (Leiber, 1992b). The discrepancies from that research and the present study are most likely due to the employment of weighting that was not used in the initial examination of decision making in Parks.

As stated previously in the section concerning the philosophy of the juvenile court, decision-makers emphasize the protection of society through accountability and the rehabilitation of youth. To attain this "balanced approach," as described by one respondent, the court utilizes informal adjustments and, with an equal vigor, formal adjustments and community-based alternatives at judicial disposition. The latter two methods are seen as adding "more bite" than the informal adjustment because the court is formally involved.

Explanations for the finding that African American youth who come from single-parent households are more likely to be referred at intake for further court proceedings rest on two viewpoints. The first is that African American youth are generally given several chances and then it comes to the point where "enough is enough" and more severe outcomes are sought.

> . . . Black kids come in with a series of minor offenses, and it's kind of slap, slap, slap on the hand. And then all of a sudden it's like on the fifth or sixth one, we've said, "That's it, we've had it!" We hit them with a hammer. But they aren't maybe diverted out as much, the diversion programs are looked upon as more white. And I . . . [must] think there's some truth to that. . . . But I don't know that we don't go on minor offenses, "Well, gosh, he's 12 years old, he lives in the inner-city, of course he'd have 1, 2, or 3 shoplifts." It's just [that] crime is so acceptable and let's not do anything with this one. We almost excuse it.

The second viewpoint concerning the race finding at intake stresses African Americans' lack of cooperation, support, and resources to effectively supervise and control youth. The belief that the African American family is dysfunctional has already been discussed and will not be elaborated upon.

Most of the respondents were somewhat surprised that African Americans were petitioned less than whites because they expected just the opposite. The explanations provided for understanding why African American youth are less likely to be petitioned than whites centered on reverse racism, or giving African Americans too many "breaks" due to guilt or trying to be nonracist. The following interviews illustrate these explanations:

1. I know that sometimes I bend over backward to make damn sure I am not doing anything to a kid just based on the color of his skin, and maybe sometimes I am trying to be so fair that I give kids a

break when they really don't deserve one. I would rather have it be that way though than the other way around.

2. I think probably it would be that we got to make sure we're giving them a fair shake, that we aren't being prejudiced. So it would go totally opposite, to bend over backwards to make sure we aren't.

3. The (finding) about blacks being less likely to be petitioned than whites, that one strikes me as odd although there may be a feeling on the part of the juvenile court officers or the county attorney that blacks are likely to have more legal problems than whites, and therefore they overlook more of them for black youths than they do for whites.

4. I've got to think that it's probably that our expectations are lower, sort of a watering down. I think that's kind of insulting to them. Giving them a second chance, or a third, or a fourth. saying, "We will look where they live, look what they've got going for them." And I'm not sure that does them any favors.

A less frequent explanation for the finding, but one that was mentioned by a number of the personnel, focused on the familiarity of the juvenile court with the youth and the youth's family. This explanation is tied to the view that there are many youth, siblings, and parents who have extensive prior contacts with the court. Consequently, the familiarity allows for the use of options other than petition. Conversely, it could be that African Americans are not petitioned because the county attorney does not believe legal justification merits formal court proceedings (see Jackson; chapter 8 in this volume).

No information was obtained from the respondents regarding the finding that African American youth are less likely than whites to be adjudicated delinquent. It is at the adjudication stage where most of the juvenile's rights apply and a determination of a finding of delinquency must be based on proof beyond a reasonable doubt. Although speculative, like at petition, African Americans could receive the less severe outcome due to the judge's decision that the state lacks sufficient cause to warrant further court involvement.

SUGGESTIONS FOR REDUCING MINORITY OVERREPRESENTATION IN THE JUVENILE COURT

The suggestions offered by decision-makers in Parks for addressing minority overrepresentation focused on ways to prevent delinquent behavior, including employment opportunities and family parenting classes. "I think that family preservation is one of the best sorts of programs that we have going, where people actually go into the home and work with people to try and adjust basic attitudes about relationships. Effective and better job training would also be good." Respondents also cited the need to provide positive male role models for adolescent males, especially for African American youth. Other strategies for reducing minority youth contact with the system involved improvements in retaining youth in the school system.

> It has to be the community that does that [a need for community services], and it has to be programs that the community will get involved in, like Big Brother and Big Sister, and churches providing programs. Helping these kids to develop social skills and working with kids that are struggling with school and are discouraged and ready to drop out and trying to help them on a more one-to-one basis is important.

While most of the respondents' recommendations focused on ways to deal with the prevention of crime, a few expressed a need for greater cultural sensitivity training and the employment of minorities within the juvenile court. Sensitivity training is believed to be a mechanism to educate whites of possible cultural differences between racial groups that may result in improved communication between people, and more effective responses for handling minority youth.

Recall that there are no minority juvenile court decision-makers in Parks. The lack of minority juvenile court personnel was seen as problematic by a small number of the decision-makers, but even those who believed minorities should be hired stated that qualified minority candidates were not available. "We've not been able to recruit minority applicants who have either the experience or the education."

SUMMARY

In Parks, juvenile court personnel emphasize rehabilitation of young offenders through accountability and intervention. Poverty, the lack of employment opportunities, and dysfunctional families are seen as causes of youth involvement in delinquent behavior. African Americans are generally believed to be more impoverished and more likely to come from dysfunctional families. Family distrust, police deployment patterns that target minority communities and police bias, and adherence to subcultural values that involve nonconformity are additional factors believed to contribute to differential minority participation in crime and to disproportionate overrepresentation of African American youth in the juvenile justice system.

Racial inequality and pregnancies among single teenage mothers are significant social problems in Parks and appear to influence the perceptions and reactions of decision-makers toward youth, especially African American youth.

While legal and extralegal factors at least partially explain decision making at all stages, race is a determinant at intake, petition, and adjudication. Being African American and from a single-parent household increases the likelihood of going further into the system at intake. Respondent explanations centered on the inability of these families to ensure youths' abidance to the orders of the court and/or to attain private counsel and/or treatment services. A lack of co-operation on the part of minority youth and their families, and the belief that after receiving leniency in the past the court decided "enough is enough" were also offered as reasons for the observed finding.

Reverse discrimination was cited by the decision-makers as an explanation for the finding that African Americans were less likely than whites to be released at petition and could possibly also explain similar decision making at adjudication. Although not offered as a reason by the respondents in Parks, previous research (e.g., Hepburn, 1978; Miller, 1996) and comments by personnel in Jackson (chapter 8 in this volume) suggest that a lack of legal sufficiency may account for the results at petition and adjudication.

As in the other three jurisdictions, suggestions for the reduction of minority youth overrepresentation in the system were directed at crime prevention efforts, such as parental skill-building and better education and employment opportunities for both youth and their families. Some decision-makers argued for the implementation of more and new treatment and diversion programs, while others stated that cultural sensitivity training was needed as well as the hiring of minorities in the juvenile court.

In short, decision making in Parks takes place in a community evidencing high racial inequality and pregnancies among single teenage mothers. The court operates under a philosophy of rehabilitation through accountability and, intervention is to some degree influenced by being African American and residing in a single-female household. Decision-makers' beliefs that these family types and African Americans in general, espouse subcultural values that are passed on from generation to generation seem to shape case outcomes. Class issues pertaining to legal representation and to the ability to access private treatment alternatives also explain minority youth overrepresentation in the juvenile justice system.

Chapter 11

Summary and Conclusions

Efforts have recently begun to refine theory and to conduct studies of court processing by paying greater attention to the conditions and circumstances when race matters. The search for the contexts of decision making has resulted in an emphasis on the structural and/or the organizational characteristics of communities and courts (e.g., Ulmer, 1997; Crawford et al., 1998) and to a less extent, sociopsychological contingencies (e.g., Tittle, 1994; Bridges and Steen, 1998). Some have also included within the contextual framework the relationship between adherence to various types of correctional orientations and decision-makers' perceptions of minorities (e.g., Albonetti and Hepburn, 1996). More specifically, these contextual perspectives have emphasized structural and organizational contingencies, ideologies focused on punishment, and the conceptualization of minorities as threats to community safety or symbolic threats to middle-class standards (e.g., Sampson and Laub, 1993; Steffensmeier et al., 1998).

The objective of the present study was to build upon previous contextual analyses to account for the presence of race effects in four homogeneous juvenile courts in Iowa where the structural and organizational characteristics are more limited than varied. The contextual framework employed represents a refinement conceptually and in application. Although predominately white, Iowa has a minority presence and is disproportionately overrepresented in both the juvenile justice system and the criminal justice system.

The focus of inquiry moved beyond punishment-focused ideologies and beyond the association between race and drugs to encompass multiple correctional orientations and decision-makers' views concerning race, crime, family, and respect for authority. Theory and prior research suggest that these factors influence decision making, have race implications, and result in advantage and disadvantage (e.g., Cicourel, 1968; Pope and Feyerherm, 1990; Frazier and Bishop, 1995; Feld, 1999). Both quantitative and qualitative techniques were employed to provide a more direct examination of the interrelationships among race, crime, family, respect for authority, correctional orientations, and characteristics of the community and court and their effects on decision making than conducted by previous research (cf., Myers and Talarico, 1987). This analytic strategy was utilized to discover decision-makers' perceptions of minorities and how these perceptions may interact to explain race differences in case processing and outcomes in four juvenile courts.

SUMMARY OF RESULTS

The analysis was conducted in three stages. The first stage of the research examined the extent of social control exercised in each of the four jurisdictions. This stage involved the examination of the case processing and outcomes of youth, differentiated first by jurisdiction then race. Logistic regression was used in the next stage to determine if the observed associations and patterns in the movement of youth in each court remained once controls were employed. The third and final stage of the analysis entailed the use of semistructured interviews with juvenile court personnel regarding their views on correctional orientations, race, crime, family, and respect for authority. The respondents were also asked for their explanations of the quantitative findings and suggestions to reduce disproportionate minority confinement (DMC). This stage in the analysis was driven by the belief that the effects of race are subtle and often conditioned by factors used by decision-makers to legally justify case processing and outcomes. Table 11.1 presents a summary of the findings, the community and organizational characteristics of the four jurisdictions, and the themes that emerged from the interviews with the decision-makers.

In terms of social control, youth have the greatest probability of moving through the system and receiving a change of placement/transfer to adult court in Bond, followed by Parks, then Jackson, and finally King. Increased social control was also greatest for minority youth in Bond and Parks, relationships consistent with theory and prior research (e.g., Sampson and Laub, 1993). Still, African American youth are subjected to greater social control in Jackson and King than whites. In fact, the racial gap is greater in these jurisdictions than in Bond. These findings are contrary to expectations.

Results from the multivariate analysis reveal the presence of race effects in all four jurisdictions that are not accounted for solely by legal and relevant extralegal factors. The race effects vary by stage and involve both more severe and more lenient outcomes, sometimes in the same jurisdiction. Race effects, however, were found at the intake stage in all four jurisdictions. The examination of the community characteristics, organizational features of the juvenile court, and the themes from the interviews with the court personnel provided added

TABLE 11.1

Summary of Findings, Community and Organizational Characteristics, and Emerging
Themes from Interviews with Decision-Makers Differentiated by Jurisdiction

		Jurisdiction		
	Bond	Jackson	King	Parks
Youth & Social Control (probability)[1]	.14	.03	.02	.08
Race & Social Control (probability)[1] W.[2]	.14	.03	.02	.07
B.	.15	.06	.04	.11
I.		.02		
Race Effects Intake	B. referred on	W./prior record referred on[3] W./property diversion W./not attend school release I./court authority diversion I./younger release I./serious crime release	B. referred on	B./family status referred on
Petition		B. no petition I. no petition		B. no petition
Initial Appearance			B. diversion	
Adjudication				B. no adj.

(continued)

TABLE 11.1 (cont.)

Summary of Findings, Community and Organizational Characteristics, and Emerging Themes from Interviews with Decision-Makers Differentiated by Jurisdiction

	Jurisdiction			
	Bond	Jackson	King	Parks
Other Notable Effects	Legal/Extralegal	Legal/Extralegal	Legal/Extralegal Relationship b/B. & prior record	Legal/Extralegal
Community Characteristics	Poorest Greatest Race Inequality Greatest Black Presence Highest Crime Rate	Smallest pop. Greatest race diversification	Wealthy Largest pop. Lowest crime rate	High on race inequality Highest on babies born to unwed teens Most spent on CJ resources
Organizational Characteristics			Heaviest caseload	
Stated Court Ideology	Accountability Intervention	Rehabilitation Protection of society	Maintain order Protection of society	Accountability Intervention

TABLE 11.1 (cont.)

Themes from Interviews				
Correctional Orientations	Accountability Intervention Rehabilitation	*Parens patriae* Protection of society Diversion	Legalistic Minimal intervention	Accountability Rehabilitation Early intervention
Source of Orientations	History—Judge Multiproblem youth Younger youth Single-parent families	History—Judge Adherence to middle-class values Immigration Decline in morals	Population Caseload Community pressures Lack of treatment alternatives	Crime as result of poverty & single-parent Subcultural values
Race, Crime, Family, & Respect for Authority	Dysfunctional families Kids having kids Distrustful but not uncooperative	More crime Family & youth lack respect indicated by dress, demeanor, behavior Gangs	Distrustful Crime individual choice	More crime Dysfunctional families & single-parent Subcultural values generational Distrustful Uncooperative Unable to secure private counsel & treatment

(continued)

TABLE 11.1 *(cont.)*
Summary of Findings, Community and Organizational Characteristics, and Emerging
Themes from Interviews with Decision-Makers Differentiated by Jurisdiction

	Jurisdiction			
	Bond	*Jackson*	*King*	*Parks*
Explanations for Findings	Correctional orientations At intake, failure to abide to stipulations & appear for meetings	At intake, formal policy agreement w/ Indian Youth of America At petition, breakdown in coordination w/prosecutors & elevated charges	Correctional orientations No race information	At intake, youth given enough chances & family unable to supervise At petition, give break
Suggestions for Reducing DMC	Prevention of delinquency Cultural sensitivity	Adapt to white culture Family support	Prevention of delinquency Mentoring	Parenting classes Role models Employment

[1]Probability from initial referral to change of placement/transfer adult court.

[2]W. (white), B. (African American), I. (Native American).

[3]W./ or B./ or I./ represents interaction effect.

insights into the contexts of decision making and the role that race plays in the process in each jurisdiction.

The court ideology of Bond centers on offender accountability, intervention, and rehabilitation that may account, in part, for the willingness to exercise social control. The sources of this ideology are rooted in history at the level of the court and the community in general, as well as beliefs that the court is dealing with youth who have multiple problems, are younger, and come from single-parent families. These characteristics are seen to be most acute among African American families. African Americans are also viewed as more distrustful though not necessarily less cooperative with representatives of the court. The last depiction of African Americans is noteworthy, as it in some ways contradicts decision-makers' explanation for the finding that African Americans were more likely to be referred at intake than whites. Decision-makers believed this to be the result of African Americans either failing to agree to participate in the conditions of diversion or not appearing for intake meetings. The suggestions for reducing DMC focused on the prevention of delinquency and to a less degree increased cultural sensitivity among court personnel.

In summary, the increased social control of youth, especially African Americans, in Bond appears to be fostered by historical practices that involve a strong emphasis on intervention and the implementation and use of diversionary programs. Failure to abide to intake procedures and perceptions that youth are troubled also contribute to the overrepresentation of African Americans in the juvenile justice system. Bond is a poor community with racial inequality, and has a strong African American presence and high crime rates relative to the other three jurisdictions. The jurisdiction has also high levels of babies born to unwed teens, ranking second to Parks.

Jackson has the smallest population of the four jurisdictions but is the most racially diversified. The correctional orientations of this court emphasize *parens patriae*, the protection of society, and diversion. The court ideologies are driven by history and, by a strong commitment to middle-class values. With increased minority immigration into the community and increased concern over a "moral decline" in society, adherence to middle-class standards appear to have taken on increased importance. Minorities in general are believed to be in greater need of rehabilitation, since they are allegedly more likely to be involved in gangs, commit crime, listen to rap music, and dress, and act "inappropriately."

Race effects are quite evident in Jackson, especially at intake and to a lesser degree, in petition. Whites and Native Americans receive either the more lenient or the more severe outcomes at intake, depending on the circumstances. Native Americans and African Americans are less likely to be petitioned than whites. At intake, decision making appears to be guided by the concerns for *parens patriae* and by the protection of society and an organizational policy that entails the diversion of Native Americans to an agency. Underlying the policy is the belief that Native American youth can be best handled by other Native Americans. At petition, decision-makers cited organizational breakdowns or a lack of coordination between intake officers and prosecutors in the kinds of cases to be referred for further court proceedings. Suggestions for reducing DMC focused on family support and minorities adopting the values and norms of the white culture.

King has the largest population and caseload, is also the wealthiest, and has the lowest crime rate of the four jurisdictions. The court can be characterized as bureaucratic with an emphasis on speed and efficiency, and it operates from a legalistic orientation that espouses minimal intervention. The size of the community's population, community pressures, caseload, and the lack of treatment alternatives seem to foster adherence to these correctional orientations. Little information was provided by the decision-makers regarding their views on race, crime, family, and respect for authority, with the exception that African Americans were seen as more distrustful than whites.

African American youth were found to be more likely to be referred for further court proceedings at intake than white youth in King. Few explanations can be offered for this finding. Prior record is a statistically significant determinant of decision making at every stage and a positive association exists between being African American and having a prior record. These associations may provide some possible insights into the relationships between race and decision making. First, a reliance on prior record by decision-makers appears to account, to some degree, for the greater likelihood of African American youth moving through the system than whites.

A second and related explanation is that the reliance on prior record by decision-makers represents a shorthand script, clue, or stereotype to gather information and to arrive at decisions in a quick and efficient manner (e.g., Farrell and Swigert, 1978). Concomitantly, it could be that African Americans, and not whites, are subject to similar categorizations that involve stereotyping and other evaluations of character at intake (e.g., Cicourel, 1968; Albonetti and Hepburn, 1996; Bridges and Steen, 1998). The results from the interviews, however, do not reveal evidence that decision-makers employ such classifications as they pertain to race, crime, family, and respect for authority.

Parks is very similar in terms of community and organizational characteristics to Bond. The jurisdiction ranks high on racial inequality, unwed teenage pregnancies, and criminal justice expenditures. The size of the community and average caseload is somewhat higher than Bond, but the stated court ideology is similar. Both jurisdictions espouse a philosophy of accountability and intervention and practice greater social control than the other two jurisdictions. Despite these similarities, differences are evident in decision making, the case processing of African American youth, and the factors that account for the differences.

In Parks, the correctional orientation of rehabilitation is more pronounced than in Bond and appears to be the result of views that crime is due to impoverishment, dysfunctional families, and subcultural values. African Americans are seen as more likely to be poor, participate in crime, and reside with a single-parent mother. Juvenile court personnel also believe that generations of problematic families exist in the community, families that are predominately African American. Rehabilitation is sought through intervention and through holding youth and families accountable.

The relatively high levels of racial inequality and babies born to unwed teens, coupled with beliefs that crime is due to poverty, dysfunctional families, and subcultural values and adherence to rehabilitation, intervention, and accountability provide a context for understanding decision making and the finding of race effects in Parks. For example, Bond exerts greater social control over youth in general than Parks, but the racial gap is larger in Parks. In addition, African American youth from single-parent homes are more likely than other youth to be referred from intake to petition. African Americans are also less likely to be petitioned and adjudicated delinquent than whites.

Decision-makers cite the inability of African American families to follow through on the conditions of diversion and to secure private counsel and private treatment as explanations for the finding of the interaction between race and family at intake. The explanation for the discovery of being released at petition rests on African American youth receiving "a break." While speculative, it is also possible that there is a breakdown in coordination between persons making decisions at intake and decision-makers at later stages in the proceedings, in this case the prosecutor at petition and the judge or referee at adjudication. Suggestions for reducing DMC focused on parenting classes, positive role models, and employment opportunities for African Americans.

In short, decision making within each of the four jurisdictions is multifaceted and more complex than often portrayed by theory and prior research. History, structural characteristics of the community and organizational features of the court, legal criteria, lack of individual resources, and ideas and perceptions of decision-makers concerning race, crime, family, and respect for authority also impact decision making and the treatment of minority youth and youth in general, to varying degrees. The effect that these factors have on decision making may differ by jurisdiction, the stage in the proceedings, and the racial group. The findings support the view that an analytic framework must be used that allows for the discovery of the multiple contexts involved in juvenile justice decision making and the confinement of minority youth.

THEORETICAL SIGNIFICANCE

The present research did not formally test any single theoretical perspective because traditional consensus, labeling, and conflict models are insufficient to understand the complexities of juvenile justice decision making. Weber's theory of bureaucracy, formalization, and the urban/rural differentiation; Blalock's minority group-threat thesis of minority concentration and wealth; and Sampson and Laub's conflict macrolevel structural theory are subject to similar criticisms (chapter 2 in this volume). These perspectives are also unable to explain the presence of race effects in communities and courts that are more similar than varied on structural and organizational characteristics. These theoretical limitations served as the impetus for the study.

Conflict theory could be a viable perspective for understanding race and decision making but revisions are needed. Traditional interpretations of conflict theory, for example, have argued that the poor and African Americans are more likely to be subject to social control than whites (Chambliss and Seidman, 1971), with social control evidenced in the form of the poor and minorities receiving more severe outcomes. Those in power are more likely to label the powerless as *delinquent* and subject them to greater control because the poor and minorities are potential threats to the interests of the majority group (Quinney, 1970). Anything less than a more severe outcome, such as receiving a more lenient outcome, is seen by many as discrediting conflict theory (e.g., Wilbanks, 1987; see chapter 2 in this volume).

As noted by Tittle and Curran, "[I]t is hard to imagine that adult whites actually fear that racial minorities or youth will overthrow them politically or submerge them economically" (1988:53). Rather, the emphasis should be on what minorities symbolize to decision-makers, how decision-makers respond to these perceptions, and what factors give birth to these perceptions. By placing the focus more on the symbolic qualities of minorities and the social-psychological reactions of decision-makers to minorities, interpretations of conflict theory can expand to include the meanings underlying differential treatment (e.g., Bell and Lang, 1985). A focus on the equitable treatment of youth who have characteristics that are more alike than different place one in a better position to understand a youth receiving both the more severe and less severe outcomes as he or she moves through the system and the reasons for the outcomes.

As the results from the research reveal, in some situations, differential treatment may be the result of race bias, while in others it may be due to corrections for bias and/or lack of sufficient evidence. Differences in the way in which African Americans are treated relative to Hispanics, Native Americans, and other minority groups could be also better understood. Revisions of this sort to the conflict perspective could allow for greater attention to decision-makers' perceptions of minorities and how, when, and under what conditions these perceptions result in differential treatment.

Concomitantly, it may be that rather than relying just on conflict theory, an integrative approach may have to be developed that incorporates a number of perspectives to improve upon our understanding of the intricacies involved in decision making. Myers and Talarico stated that the challenge is to "integrate attitudinal, role, and social theories in decision making models" (1987: 179). Sampson and Laub (1993) incorporated the symbolic threat thesis within their conflict structural model. Results from Albonetti (1991) and Bridges and Steen (1998) provide support for the inclusion of structural organizational theory and attribution theory into a theoretical model to explain decision making. Similarly, borrowing a term from Miller (1958), Steffensmeier and his colleagues (1998) espouse a "focal concerns" theory of sentencing that emphasizes the offender's blameworthiness and the degree of harm caused to the victim, protection of the community, and practical implications of sentencing decisions.

As the findings reported here illustrate, an integrative approach could prove to be fruitful if the social construction of race stereotypes and social problems in general were developed beyond the notions of "powerlessness" and "racial threat," crime and drugs, and the interrelationships with punitiveness. Such an approach would be more in line with juvenile justice decision making and the factors that influence decision-makers as well as allowing for changes in correctional movements or philosophies that impact social control.

Whether the choice is theoretical refinement or integration, a theory is needed that recognizes and explains the contingent nature of race and juvenile justice decision making. The theory would provide a clearer and more complete picture of decision making than offered by traditional and more recent versions of the consensus, conflict, and labeling perspectives.

RESEARCH SIGNIFICANCE

The results from the present study provide support for the call by Myers and Talarico (1987), Sampson and Lauritsen (1997), Hagan (1989), and others (e.g., Pope, 1976) for the identification of the conditions and circumstances when race makes a significant difference. A better understanding of decision making can be attained by the examination of structural and organizational contexts. The findings also show that neither one of these contexts alone nor in conjunction may fully capture the complexities involved between race and decision making. This point is especially true in settings that are more alike on these contingencies than different.

Research is needed that recognizes the significance of the "justice by geography" concept (Pope, 1976; Feld, 1991). There is also the need to push the inquiry beyond an emphasis on economics, the urban versus rural categorization, and the size or concentration of the minority population. These factors are important considerations, but the results from the present research and other previous research (e.g., Bridges et al., 1995) suggest that other characteristics of the community and the court must be incorporated into the contextual framework.

Further research, for example, is needed that incorporates greater awareness as to how historical factors initiate and sustain working relationships among different actors and agencies and practices within the juvenile justice system, decision making, the creation and implementation of treatment programs, and stereotypical notions of minorities and racism. The present research did not provide a historical context for understanding the settlement or migration of minorities into the jurisdictions, the presence or absence of segregation, and race relations in general.[1] This is a critical omission since prior research has discussed the importance of the historical contexts of youth and social control (e.g., Platt, 1969; Sutton, 1988) and race and punishment (e.g., Adamson, 1983; Peterson and Hagan, 1984). Results from the interviews indicate that history has significant importance in the correctional orientations and in the case processing of whites and minorities in at least three of the four juvenile courts.

A contextual analysis can also benefit from a consideration of the relationships between various institutions of control within a jurisdiction. We often think of formal institutions as separate entities, but as Sutton points out, "we must compare patterns of development across institutional sectors. Courts, prisons, welfare agencies, mental hospitals, and reformatories are in varying degrees administratively and politically interdependent; so, then, are the relative official rates of crime, poverty, mental illness, and delinquency" (1994: 240). The view that agencies of social control may be bounded and influenced by shared concerns is not new.

The interrelationships between agencies and social control have been addressed by Erickson (1966) in his study of "crime waves" and by the stability of punishment in the tradition of Emile Durkheim (1938), by Piven and Cloward (1971) in their discussion of the relationship between welfare and fluctuations in the capitalist labor market, and by Foucault in his explorations of the history of the prison (1977) and the asylum (1965). Research has also shown relationships between the mental health system and the criminal justice system (e.g., Dickey, 1980) and the lesser known method of social control, protective services (Leiber, 1988, 1992c).[2] Linkages have also been cited between the mental health system and the juvenile justice system.

Schwartz (1989), for example, reports on youth placed in psychiatric and chemical dependency treatment where admissions are "voluntary" and the services provided are largely paid for by third-party health care insurance providers and by parents. The incentives to pursue the use of private care are that public funds, for the most part, are not expended and private agencies often are not subject to the same federal restrictions as are public facilities. Issues arise concerning the extent the association between payment and private and public treatment impacts youth and minorities in terms of the amount of social control, the avoidance of being labeled, the conditions and quality of the care, and the length of intervention (Schwartz, 1989).

Despite the concept of human agency and the potential implications for the treatment of youth, the development of this concept within a contextual analysis of juvenile justice decision making has been relatively ignored (cf. Emerson, 1969; Platt, 1969; Hagan and McCarthy, 1994). The results from the present research suggest that relations exist between agencies of social control in Jackson and Parks. In Jackson, the juvenile court and the agency Indian Youth of America (IYA) were engaged in a formal agreement that had consequences for the treatment of Native Americans while some kind of associations seemed to exist between private and public agencies of control in Parks. The extent the juvenile court has relationships with other agencies and impacted decision making any further in these two jurisdictions and in general in Bond and King is not known and needs to be explored.

The ability or inability to pay for private treatment services provides additional avenues for future inquiry. Since financial resources are important determinants of treatment and social control research is needed that employs better measures of expenditures than the criminal justice variable used in the present study. Research should examine not only the amount of money available to a juvenile court for providing services but also the kinds of services provided (e.g., tutoring and mentoring), and the role(s) of third-party agencies, public or private, in the placement of youth in these services. Research in this area could provide added insight into the intricacies involved in the relationships that might exist between the juvenile court and other agencies of control and the possible organizational pressures that lead to the formation of these associations and the use of private rather than public care.

The present research attempted to use a refined contextual framework that also expanded the sociopsychological processes of decision making beyond the focus on punitiveness and drugs. This refinement expanded the focus to include adherence to multiple correctional orientations and to decision-makers' perceptions of minorities as criminal, residing in dysfunctional families, and lacking respect for authority. Consistent with prior research on attitudes (e.g., Cullen et al., 1985; Bridges et al., 1995; Leiber, 2000; Moon et al., 2000), juvenile justice decision-makers support an array of correctional orientations that to varying degrees include accountability, the protection of society, rehabilitation, and the social welfare of youth.

Results from both the quantitative and qualitative analyses also reveal no evidence of an association between race, drug offending, and social control. The race interaction with drug offending and increased social control is a key component of Sampson and Laub's (1993) macrolevel structural perspective. As these findings suggest, the scope of a contextual framework needs to be broadened to include not only concerns with drugs but additional factors that decision-makers encounter with youth and families on a day-to-day basis. The results indicate that concerns about crime, the ability of the family to ensure the youth follows the conditions of diversion, and so forth, and a willingness of youth and their families to cooperate, and respect authority are some factors that influence decision-makers and have race implications.

The present research also provided a more direct and in-depth inquiry into the effects these factors have in shaping decision making and the case processing and outcomes by using both quantitative and qualitative methodologies. The results from this effort provide clearer insights into how, when, and to what extent structure, the organization of the court, and the orientations and views of decision-makers interact and produce more lenient and severe outcomes for youth in general and minorities in particular. For example, information obtained from interviews with decision-makers revealed that assessments about the family, especially for minority youth, are much more important than the results suggest from the quantitative analyses. At a minimum, the findings indicate that attempts to capture inquiries into assessments about the family need to go beyond the simple measure of family structure.

Despite these advancements, there is still a need for an even more in-depth inquiry into the factors that influence the perceptions of decision-makers and how these perceptions result in responses that affect whites and minorities. One strategy is to augment the use of quantitative and qualitative techniques in the form of interviews with observations. On-site observations may indicate whether inconsistencies exist between responses provided by decision-makers to interviews and their actual reactions to minority youth who may or may not dress, talk, or act according to white middle-class standards or expectations (Conley, 1994). Another strategy is to conduct more research in-line with the work of Bridges and Steen (1998) who focused on the subjective qualities of decision making and the construction of recognizable, but racially tainted, images of offenders.

The use of multiple research methods that include observations and/or content analysis of case records has the potential to capture the dynamics involved in the interactions between the juvenile court, the youth and family, and the development of a youth's court record. In the present study, race effects were evident at intake in all four jurisdictions, and intake is the point in the juvenile justice system where race bias is most likely to be found (Pope and Feyerherm, 1990; Hamparian and Leiber, 1997). Next to arrest, intake is in most states the gatekeeper to the juvenile justice system. It is also the stage in the proceedings where discretion is most widespread; most of the due process rights and legal criteria that constrain decision making apply at the adjudication and dispositional stages. Yet detailed information is lacking concerning intake decision making and what role contextual factors play in youth being recommended for further court involvement, the use of diversionary options, and the kind of diversion that may be most suitable for youth (Leiber and Stairs, 1999).

Observational studies and the examination of case records would allow for the assessment of the processes involved and the extent race, dress, demeanor, and the family influence how the encounter(s) is recorded and responded to. Questions that could be explored are as follows: Are minority youth more likely to miss an intake meeting than whites? Are minority youth given the same chances to reschedule a missed intake meeting as whites? Are there cultural differences in the perceived importance of the meeting? Are minority youth given the same opportunities to agree to participate in diversion as whites? Are minority youth and the family less willing to cooperate than whites? What kind of legal counsel is secured and what kind of services (quality) are provided?

A few of the respondents in one jurisdiction point out that the construction of a prior record needs to be examined more closely. Individuals in academia have also questioned the reliance on prior record by decision-makers on several grounds (Hagan, 1974; Kleck, 1981; Sampson, 1986). In their discussion of the creation of offender and the criminal record as a self-fulfilling prophecy, Farrell and Swigert summarize these views.

> Reliance on prior record . . . overlooks the possibility that a criminal history may, in fact, be a product of prior differential justice. This possibility becomes even more apparent when we consider that criminal records reflect earlier definitions of situations. . . . Such records, therefore, may not be measures of criminal events but of subjective decisions within the legal system and the community at large. . . . A criminal record, once constructed, becomes an important determinant of subsequent legal involvement. Persons with criminal histories are more likely to be suspected of crime. If arrested, they are more likely to be found guilty. (1982:78–79)

Farrell and Swigert (1982) further point out that minorities and the poor are more likely to conform to popular conceptions of criminals, and therefore, these groups are more likely to be arrested (see also, Miller, 1996; Mann and Zatz, 1998).

In the present study, prior record was found to be a consistent predictor of case processing and outcomes in King. An association was also evident between being African American and having a greater history of contact with the juvenile court. Consequently, African American youth were more likely than whites to move through the system on the basis of a legally justifiable criterion. Court observations and intensive examinations of case files need to be conducted to shed more light into the social construction of the prior record by looking at the reasons for the referrals and the classification of those reasons as crimes and the severity of the crime. The real question, however, is whether a prior record should produce such race differentials in outcomes. The answer is no. A prior record is an important source of information but that information too often can become an easy mechanism to stereotype and typecast youth to justify the handling of cases in a quick and nonjudicious manner.

POLICY SIGNIFICANCE

This research was initially conducted to address the overrepresentation of minority youth in disproportionate minority confinement (DMC) in Iowa. There are two general strategies to reduce the overrepresentation of minority youth in secure facilities. The first strategy focuses on efforts to affect decision-makers and the juvenile justice system. Underlying this first strategy is the belief that racial bias is a cause of DMC. The second strategy emphasizes approaches for the prevention of delinquency. This strategy is driven by views that minority overrepresentation is the result of disproportionate involvement in crime. The results from the present research indicate that both are relevant. Minorities appear to disproportionately commit crime or at least be disproportionately arrested, and once in the system, minorities are at times and under certain conditions subject to racial bias. Accordingly, the initiatives could vary by the circumstances, the court, and the community.

For the purpose of clarity, the forthcoming discussion, however, focuses on general recommendations to reduce racial bias and to prevent delinquency within the context of the DMC mandate. I primarily draw upon recommendations and strategies cited by Devine and his colleagues (1998), Hamparian and Leiber (1997), Pope and Leiber (2003), Rubin (2001), and the DMC Technical Assistance Manual (2000).

The first part of the discussion centers on coalition building, public education, funding, and legislation. The second part and the heart of the discussion represents activities that are system related and those associated with youth and involvement in delinquency. The topics covered in the discussion on interventions are diversification, training and education, prevention services, diversion alternatives to secure confinement, and policies and procedures. Although each of these areas is treated separately, they are interrelated, and efforts to reduce DMC must encompass the implementation of multiple intervention strategies.

Coalition Building

A coalition is an alliance of individuals and organizations sharing a common interest in succeeding to change specific practices in a short period of time by harnessing the goals and resources of many and focusing their energy on a specific issue. Coalitions provide individuals and organizations greater power and influence over an issue than any single effort would have working alone. The driving force behind having a coalition guide and fuel efforts to address DMC is that reversing DMC trends will require dramatic, yet constructive, results based upon the involvement of stakeholders that are both within and outside the juvenile justice system. Disproportionate minority youth involvement in the juvenile justice system is the result of both system factors and nonsystem factors, and therefore cannot be adequately remedied by the juvenile justice system alone.

The membership of the coalitions must include representatives from the state level and from those in the local community who either work in the field of juvenile justice or are especially affected by juvenile crime and justice practices. A coalition consisting of a diversified group that includes local representatives will establish ownership of the DMC issue or at least be seen as the authority on the topic and thus gain creditability in the community. A coalition group needs to work with other entities involved with DMC (e.g., the State Advisory Group and the juvenile court) and share in the planning of strategies. It is recommended that standing committees be used at the state and the community level and together coordinate planning efforts.

A DMC coordinator can play a pivotal role in providing linkage between committees and coalitions at the community and state levels as well as disseminating DMC information (Devine et al., 1998). In Iowa, a DMC coordinator had been funded by the Office of Juvenile Justice and Delinquency Prevention (OJJDP) Formula Grants funds and had many responsibilities that included training and program development involving DMC issues and working to implement programs at the local level. More recently, a DMC Resource Center has been created, displacing the coordinator, and acts as the main conduit, along with the DMC subcommittee, for the DMC initiative.

Public Education

Organizations, coalitions, committees, and individuals at both the state and local level need to be active participants in educating the public about the DMC issue. Plans should be developed that entail a number of tasks and activities that include

- public dissemination of written findings with a comment period;
- public hearings, town hall meetings, and focus groups to receive input from the community and invested individuals;
- presentation of DMC results before agency governing boards and legislative committees;
- scheduling of a yearly conference on the DMC issue; and
- distribution of brochures on DMC and activities to deal with DMC.

Potential benefits from educating the public are the dissemination of information highlighting the problem of minority overrepresentation along the two dimensions of race bias and differential involvement in crime and citizen input.

Funding

A funding plan should be developed that covers several fiscal years and addresses the costs for the completion of objectives set out by coalition groups and others involved in DMC. Funding sources for the implementation of programs and services may come from the State Advisory Group, Challenge Grants, Juvenile Accountability and Incentive Block Grants, State appropriations, Formula Grants allocations, and so forth. Funding may be also obtained from a pooling of interagency dollars dedicated to reducing crime (e.g., Violent Offender and Truth-In-Sentencing Block Grants). The use of funds can be the incentive for local communities to develop, implement, and sustain strategies to reduce DMC.

Some states require as part of the funding process that agencies and communities indicate how the proposed activities will reduce DMC. In Iowa, for example, applicants requesting funds from the state to develop and/or maintain programs must address how the project involves DMC. Funds are made available to the state from Formula grants money and Title V funding or from Juvenile Crime Prevention grants.

Legislation

The issue of disproportionate confinement of youth of color needs to be brought to the attention of legislators and if possible, inserted into the legislative process if major change is to take place. During legislative sessions a critical eye should be kept on bills that involve juvenile justice issues and children and families in general. Attention to legislation or proposals of these types assures they do not fuel further overrepresentation or result in statutes that bias decision making or reporting by justice officials (e.g., how a gang is defined, mandatory sentencing guidelines for juveniles, and building more secure facilities). Interested legislators should be also kept informed of the committee's plans, work, and findings.

Intervention Activities

Interventions should represent efforts to deal with the system and with minority involvement with crime since factors associated with both contribute to DMC. Multiple interventions are also needed and should involve the modification and enhancement of existing programs and the development of new programs. The intervention activities discussed are organized into five categories: diversification, training and education, prevention services, diversion, and policies and procedures.

Diversification

Diversification can be defined in two ways. The first definition involves efforts to develop hiring policies and practices to increase the number of minority and bilingual staff employed in the juvenile justice system and to increase opportunities for career advancement for minorities. In Iowa, internship programs and volunteer programs have been instituted as methods to provide employment experience for minorities. Recall that only four nonwhite decision-makers were employed (out of eighty-four) in the four jurisdictions studied, and there were no minority officers in Jackson and Parks. A similar idea has been implemented in Pennsylvania (DMC Technical Assistance Manual, 2000). A program has been developed by the Center for Juvenile Justice Research and Training at Shippensburg University to place minority students in juvenile justice agencies.

The second definition of diversification entails advocacy. Advocacy strategies attempt to improve the ability of juveniles and their families to understand the system and the ability of the system to meet the needs of minorities and youth in general (Leiber et al., 1997; Devine et al., 1998; Puritz and Wan Long Shang, 1998; Pope and Leiber, 2003). The use of an advocate, for example, could be useful in dismissing or reducing distrust and tension that may exist between the juvenile court officers, the youth, and the parents and possibly, the community. The advocacy strategy can also include sensitizing juvenile justice personnel of policies and practices that lead to DMC and methods to better meet the needs of minority youth and their families, such as relevant services for minority youth that may exist in the community.

In Oregon, Marion County, for example, has used advocates in the form of interns who may rely on a resource list of culturally appropriate service providers to aid with the case management of minority youth, translate documents, and help implement bilingual foster homes (DMC Technical Assistance Manual, 2000). In Iowa, innovative advocacy approaches could prove to be fruitful for youth and families at intake proceedings. An advocacy program that involves advocates, community liaisons, or lawyers could be especially beneficial in Parks to offset concerns that intake decision making is influenced by the inability to secure private counsel and private care.

Training and Education

This intervention strategy includes efforts to support and provide training for juvenile justice practitioners, appropriate elected officials, and the general public regarding issues related to the disproportionate confinement of minority youth in secure facilities and in the juvenile justice system in general. The concept of training and education can also involve enhancing collaboration between the juvenile justice system, community organizations, and individual community representatives.

California, for example, has included cultural enhancement training for the State Advisory Group and for top officials in the juvenile justice system. Iowa has included the development, improvement, support, and institutionalization of cultural competency training designed to reduce unintentional bias on the part of juvenile justice decision-makers. In the three-year plan submitted to OJJDP, the state of Washington urged the development and implementation of an ethnic and cultural diversity curriculum for all superior court judges, commissioners, and other court personnel. The plan also calls for interpreters to enable non-English speaking youth and families to better understand the procedures in the juvenile court as well as sensitivity or cultural diversity training for staff to help them better understand the clients they serve (see also, Leiber et al., 1997). In Marion County, an organizational self-assessment tool has been developed that measures cultural competency at the organizational level (DMC Technical Assistance Manual, 2000).

The use of cultural sensitivity curriculum and annual training sessions can be useful as a method for addressing DMC and probably is the strategy most often adopted by states to confront racial bias. However, the effectiveness of such a strategy is questionable if not implemented properly. Kurt Lewin (1943), a pioneer in the area of planned change, for example, argues that before any change can take place, the change target's environment needs to be assessed in order to understand the interplay of resisting and driving forces that will affect the promotion of change. In other words, before change can occur, there is a need to understand why factors influence persons and/or organizations in deciding case processing and outcomes. There is also a need on the part of the decision-makers to be made *aware* of and *believe* that they may be acting in ways that may result in bias treatment of minority youth. Alternatives must also be provided. Thus, the task to introduce change is threefold.

The first step is to identify what factors may be indicative of blatant and the more common form of bias, subtle, unintentional bias. Recurring themes from the present research are adherence to traditional middle-class values and norms, that racial bias does not exist, and that solution or interventions for DMC should focus on crime prevention and family parenting. For the purpose of illustrations, I will focus on the first theme.

Decision-makers' attitudes toward perceived deviations from middle-class values and norms are likely to be manifest in biased treatment toward African Americans and Native Americans and others relative to whites. Examples of deviation to these standards include lack of individual responsibility, alternative styles of dress and demeanor, listening to rap music, perceived or actual affiliation with gangs, nontraditional family structure, and interaction patterns with juvenile court officials or agencies of social control. Similarly, beliefs in the existence of minority subcultures that are believed to de-emphasize education and respect for the law or authority, and to encourage sexual promiscuity, as evident by unwed childbearing, are also indicative of defiance to middle-class norms and values. Results from the present research suggest that youth who fail to abide to middle-class standards are responded to differently than those who meet or are perceived to meet these expectations. Thus, decision-makers would have to be made aware that these factors may result in racial disparity and indirect bias.

The second stage in Lewin's change strategy is to develop a belief in the need to change those sources of bias. To accomplish this task, decision-makers and society in general, need to recognize that racism can take many forms. Most people do not see themselves as racist or capable of treating someone differently because of her skin color, ethnicity, or culture because she operates from images of blatant racism or intentional racism. Most people are not willing to recognize or accept the notion of subtle, unintentional bias. The results from the present research confirm this statement. Many of the juvenile court personnel in all four jurisdictions had a difficult time even acknowledging the presence of DMC, let alone the existence of subtle bias.

Thus, efforts are not only needed to have juvenile court decision-makers become aware of unintentional expressions of bias; they also need to recognize that they themselves may practice subtle racism. Cultural sensitivity initiatives seem to have a difficult task especially when decision-makers might attend such programs once a year for a day or two or as in the case of Iowa, a few hours. For change to occur there must be recognition and acceptance of the duality of racism. Even if this occurs, efforts are needed to provide decision-makers with alternative choices or options for responding to minority youth (e.g., structured decision making). A DMC coordinator can help in the overall process.

Prevention Services
Activities to prevent delinquency entail a wide range of services that most often include efforts to increase parenting skills, developing the employment skills of youth, providing mentoring services, and enhancing and strengthening community organization (Leiber and Mawhorr, 1995; Sherman et al., 1997; Devine et al., 1998). For example, Georgia plans to increase the number of early intervention and prevention programs serving minority youth as the primary vehicle to address minority overrepresentation.

North Carolina's three-year plan indicates that efforts will be made to provide family resource centers, structured after school programs, and an array of classes such as conflict resolution and parenting classes for minorities. In Pennsylvania, programs have been developed that emphasize positive choices including the value of staying in school (Hsia and Hamparian, 1998; Pope and Leiber,

2003). In Cedar Rapids, Iowa, the Jane Boyd House provides counseling, mentoring, access to social services, and other activities and interventions to minority youth and families to prevent delinquency and involvement with the juvenile justice system (Rhoden, 1994). The Jane Boyd House is also involved in case management by coordinating services provided to youth and family from multiple agencies (referred to as PATCH). Iowa has also funded other community crime prevention programs such as those that emphasize life skills, school-based liaisons, day treatment, tracking and monitoring, and "rights of passage" programs. Rights of passage programs are culturally based, serve African American youth, and among other things involve recognition of phases into adulthood.

More specific examples of programs and information on approaches to prevent delinquency can be found elsewhere (e.g., Montgomery et al., 1994; Krisberg et al., 1995; Pope, 1995; Welsh et al., 1996; Hsia and Hamparian, 1998; Pope et al., 2001). Sherman et al.'s (1997), "Preventing Crime" is a comprehensive document that provides great detail of programs and evaluations of effectiveness.

Diversion

The concept of diversion includes strategies that result in providing alternatives to youth prior to entering the juvenile justice system and the use of less severe sanctions and interventions within the court, such as alternatives to detention and other forms of secure confinement. For example, Florida has implemented a Civil Citation Program in Hillsborough County that allows law enforcement officers to avoid taking youth into custody for involvement in nonserious delinquency. Police officers can issue a sanction of up to forty hours of community service. In 1994–1995, there was a 5 percent decrease in the number of judicially handled cases involving African American youth and a 30 percent increase in the number of cases handled nonjudicially (DMC Technical Assistance Manual, 2000).

Alternatives to secure corrections include the development and use of day treatment programs, intensive probation, and staff-secure residential treatment programs. In Wayne County, Michigan, a central component of the Intensive Probation Program is the In-Home Care Program. This program allows youth who might otherwise be held in a secure facility to remain at home. Supervision, family-focused treatment services, counseling, and employment training are provided by a private agency. Staff meet with youth and families up to five times a week for period no longer than twelve months (DMC Technical Assistance Manual, 2000).

In the jurisdiction of Bond in Iowa, a diversionary program has been implemented that targets male African American youth who are one step away from placement in the state training school. Second Chance involves sixteen weekly group meetings aimed at developing certain social skills, along with a pre-employment-training component that includes how to conduct a job search, interview for a job, and practice good work habits. Through an arrangement with the Juvenile Court Services and a regional job training program called Area VII Job Training (referred to as JTPA by juvenile court officials) youth in the program participate in work experience. JTPA provides the costs for training and the wages of the youth for the first 130 hours of employment. If the youth performs her job satisfactorily, the agency is expected to, and most often does, retain the employee after the 130-hour period. During the tryout employment period, the employer is required to submit biweekly reports to the JTPA employment/training specialist. Although the overall effectiveness of Second Chance in reducing recidivism is questionable, the program has resulted in the reduction of involvement in more serious delinquency and confinement in secure facilities (Leiber and Mawhorr, 1995).

Policies and Procedures

Policies and procedures may contribute to racial bias and overrepresentation in secure confinement. As pointed out by the authors of the revised DMC Technical Assistance Manual (2000), existing sentencing guidelines, detention procedures, risk assessments, probation classification systems, release criteria, factors considered in judicial waiver cases, and other methods to transfer youth to adult proceedings need to be evaluated to determine if they contribute to DMC.

As the results from the present research show, decision making based on objective legally justifiable factors, such as prior record and family supervision can result in minority overrepresentation. Similarly and as found in Parks, participation in diversion and less secure interventions may be based upon payment and if youth and the family are unable to pay, the youth is excluded from participation in the program.

The results from the present research also reveal that intake lacks specific criteria to guide decision making and it is at this stage that race effects are most prominent (see also, Pope and Feyerherm, 1990). Although not a focus of inquiry in the present research, detention admission procedures lack similar specificity (Orlando, 1998) and African American youth are more likely to be held in detention than whites (McCarthy and Smith, 1986). The involvement of multiple decision-makers, review panels, and the development of race-neutral decision-making guidelines could help rectify these occurrences. The development of alternatives to detention could also lessen DMC.

Pope (1995), for example, has argued for a "checks-and-balance" approach to intake and detention decision making where responsibility and accountability could be shared by a number of personnel, including advocates and community liaisons rather than just one, possibly two decision-makers. A review panel would serve the same function.

Pope also calls for the development of guidelines to aid decision-makers in reaching outcome decisions. If properly constructed, guidelines can reduce discretion and ensure greater equity in processing for minorities and youth in general. As correctly discussed by Pope, "[T]he overall emphasis should be the development of guidelines leading to the 'least restrictive' alternative. For example, detention guidelines should focus on keeping youths out of confinement rather than brining them into confinement" (1995: 212). Orlando (1998) found that the implementation of specific, objective screening criteria reduced the use of detention and closed the racial gap in admissions.

In Baltimore, a Detention Response Unit (DRU) has been created to provide services to detained youth and was implemented with the specific purpose of reducing the presence of minorities in detention by locating community alternatives and by having shorter lengths of stay in detention. A social worker performs assessments of referred youth and identifies appropriate alternatives to detention while an attorney is responsible for the legal aspects of the case. The DRU initiative has resulted in a reduction in the number of African Americans held in detention (DMC Technical Assistance Manual, 2000).

For the last decade, the Annie E. Casey Foundation's Juvenile Detention Alternatives Initiative (JDAI) has worked with Multnomah County, Oregon, and others across the nation to combine strategies to make detention more efficient in only detaining youth who truly represent a risk to public safety, and moving youth quickly through the system to other kinds of treatment and punishment. To make detention more efficient and to detain fewer youth, four core strategies were recommended and implemented in Multnomah County and these are (1) objective admissions screening instruments, (2) new or enhanced alternatives to detention programs, (3) expedite case processing to reduce lengths of stay, and (4) new policies and practices for probation violations, warrants and "awaiting placement" cases (Justice Policy Institute, 2002).

It is important to note that in the implementation of the first core strategy the objective instruments were based on criteria that are more race neutral. For example, instead of criteria like "good family structure" that that be biased toward intact, nuclear families and, therefore, against minority youth, the instruments asks whether there is an adult willing to be responsible for assuring the youth's appearance in court (Justice Policy Institute, 2002). Results from an evaluation of the detention project indicate that only 12% of African Americans, 11% of Latinos, and 9% of whites brought to intake ended up being detained, and the average daily population of the detention center dropped from 60 in 1995 to 33 in 2000 (12).

CONCLUSION

Minorities are overrepresented in both the juvenile justice and the criminal justice systems. To explain this occurrence, recent research have emphasized quantitative contextual analyses that focus on the interactions between the structural characteristics of the community and the attributes of the court with punitively oriented ideologies and the stereotyping of African Americans as drug offenders. However, this type of contextual framework appears to be unable to explain the presence of race effects in more homogeneous court environments and therefore, provides only a partial picture of the contingent nature of decision making. The present research utilized a contextual analysis that expanded the focus of the inquiry and relied upon both quantitative and qualitative methodologies.

The findings suggest that differential involvement in crime and racial bias, influenced by decision-makers' views of minorities as criminal, residing in dysfunctional families, and lacking respect for authority, and adherence to multiple correctional ideologies impact the case processing and outcomes of youth and in particular, minority youth. Historical contexts and the characteristics of the community and the court also played prominent roles in the process. The extent these factors individually or in some combination explain decision making, however, vary by the court. Strategies and interventions should be implemented to address both delinquency causation and race bias and yet be sensitive to contexts. Further developments in theory and research are also needed that build upon the analytic framework and the findings presented here to increase our understanding of decision making and the conditions when race matters.

Appendixes

Zero-Order Correlations, Means, Standard Deviations, and Range of Social Characteristics
and Legal Variables and Decision-Making Stages (N = 2,020)
Bond

Variable	1	2	3	4	5	6	7	8
Social Characteristics								
1. Race	1.00							
2. Gender	.09**	1.00						
3. Age	−.07**	−.02	1.00					
4. Family status	.19**	.05*	−.08**	1.00				
School								
5. Attending, but problems	−.01	−.04	−.01	.07**	1.00			
6. Not attending	.01	.02	.20**	.04	−.16**	1.00		
Legal								
7. Number of prior referrals	.04*	−.17**	.23**	.02	.12**	.17**	1.00	
8. Court authority	−.01	−.12**	.14**	.01	.14**	.08**	.50**	1.00
9. Number of current charges	−.02	−.08**	.09**	.01	.10**	.09**	.13**	.09**
10. Crime severity	.00	−.11**	.03	.01	.02	.10**	.12**	.13**
11. Property	.07**	.03	−.06**	.06**	.01	.02	.02	.06**
12. Person	.06**	−.02	−.04	.00	.04	−.04	.01	.00
13. Drugs	−.10**	−.03	.17**	−.05*	−.00	.02	.03	.00
Stages								
14. Release/ adjustment vs. further court processing	.06**	−.09	.17**	.03	.08**	.17**	.40**	.41**
15. Release vs. adjustment/ further court processing	−.02	−.01	−.01	−.01	.01	.03	−.01	.05*
16. Petition	−.04	−.09*	.10**	−.01	−.02	−.02	.07	.02
17. Initial appearance	.04	.10*	.08	.03	.02	−.02	.25**	.20**
18. Adjudication	−.00	.04	.02	−.03	.02	−.06	.06	.16**
19. Judicial disposition	−.05	−.03	.26**	−.09*	.06	.18**	.34**	.11**

*p < .05. **p < .01.

(continued)

Zero-Order Correlations, Means, Standard Deviations, and Range of Social Characteristics
and Legal Variables and Decision-Making Stages (N = 2,020)

Bond

9	10	11	12	13	14	15	16	17	18
1.00									
.21**	1.00								
.08**	.37	1.00							
−.00	−.07**	−.39**	1.00						
−.01	−.18**	−.42**	−.16**	1.00					
.19**	.36**	.12**	.03	−.04	1.00				
.07**	.10**	.12**	−.09**	.02	.27**	1.00			
.10**	.06	.15**	−.08*	−.05	—	—	1.00		
.00	.01	.04	.01	−.01	—	—	—	1.00	
.04	.08	.10*	−.05	−.10*	—	—	—	—	1.00
.03	−.01	−.11*	.03	−.01	—	—	—	—	—

$^*p < .05.$ $^{**}p < .01.$

Zero–Order Correlations, Means, Standard Deviations, and Range of Social Characteristics
and Legal Variables and Decision Making Stages (N = 2,020)
Bond

Variable	19	Mean	SD	Range
Social Characteristics				
1. Race		.10	.30	0–1
2. Gender		.19	.39	1–2
3. Age		15.45	1.82	6–18
4. Family status		.41	.49	0–1
School				
5. Attending, but problems		.19	.40	0–1
6. Not attending		.09	.29	0–1
Legal				
7. Number of prior referrals		1.59	2.62	0–22
8. Court authority		.24	.44	0–1
9. Number of current charges		1.30	.80	1–9
10. Crime severity		.23	.42	0–1
11. Property		.51	.50	0–1
12. Person		.13	.34	0–1
13. Drugs		.14	.35	0–1
Stages				
14. Release/ adjustment vs. further court processing		.34	.47	0–1
15. Release vs. adjustment/ further court processing		.88	.32	0–1
16. Petition		.94	.24	0–1
17. Initial appearance		.78	.41	0–1
18. Adjudication		.87	.33	0–1
19. Judicial disposition	1.00	.60	.49	0–1

*p < .05. **p < .01.

Zero–Order Correlations, Means, Standard Deviations, and Range of Social Characteristics and Legal Variables and Decision Making Stages (N = 1,966)

Jackson

Variable	1	2	3	4	5	6	7	8
Social Characteristics								
1. African American	1.00							
2. Native American	−.09**	1.00						
3. Gender	−.03	.07**	1.00					
4. Age	−.07**	−.16**	.06**	1.00				
5. Family status	.07**	.25**	−.07**	−1.7**	1.00			
School								
6. Attending, but problems	.08**	.13**	−.14**	−2.0	.10**	1.00		
7. Not attending	−.02	.04*	−.00	.24**	.10**	−.14**	1.00	
Legal								
8. Number of prior referrals	.02	.31**	−.11**	.05*	.20**	.21**	.14**	1.00
9. Court authority	.10**	.11**	−.08**	.04	.08**	.23**	.03	.29**
10. Number of current charges	.02	.07**	.04	.08**	.01	−.01	.05*	.09**
11. Crime severity	.03	−.01	−.13**	.11*	.02	.12**	.15**	.08**
12. Property	.01	−.02	.01	−.11**	−.05**	−.05**	.06**	−.08**
13. Person	.07**	.00	−.07**	.06**	.05*	.08**	.04	.07**
14. Drugs								
Stages								
15. Release/ adjustment vs. further court processing	.03	−.04	−.13**	.15**	.00	.15**	.11**	.09**
16. Release vs. adjustment/ further court processing	−.05*	−.02	−.00	−.02	−.04	.01	−.04*	−.04
17. Petition	−.10	−.07	−.02	−.00	.04	.12	.15*	−.00
18. Initial appearance	−.07	.03	−.14*	−.00	.08	.09	.17*	.18**
19. Adjudication	−.01	.01	.05	.17*	.12	.13	.05	.12
20. Judicial disposition	.15*	.08	−.13	.23**	.16*	−.02	.08	.28**

*p < .05. **p < .01.

Zero–Order Correlations, Means, Standard Deviations, and Range of Social Characteristics
and Legal Variables and Decision Making Stages (N = 1,966)

Jackson

Variables	9	10	11	12	13	14	15
Social Characteristics							
1. African American							
2. Native American							
3. Gender							
4. Age							
5. Family status							
School							
6. Attending, but problems							
7. Not attending							
Legal							
8. Number of prior referrals							
9. Court authority	1.00						
10. Number of current charges	.08**	1.00					
11. Crime severity	.10**	.00	1.00				
12. Property	−.01	−.12**	.17**	1.00			
13. Person	.06**	.02	.07**	−.33**	1.00		
14. Drugs	−.05	.08**	−.14**	−.44**	−.11**	1.00	
Stages							
15. Release/ adjustment vs. further court processing	.05*	.03	.40**	.05*	.08**	−.08**	1.00
16. Release vs. adjustment/ further court processing	−.01	−.03	−.00	.13**	−.13**	−.09**	.18**
17. Petition	.05	.06	−.05	.01	−.01	.06	—
18. Initial appearance	.09	−.17*	−.12	−.11	.13	−.26**	—
19. Adjudication	.05	.03	.10	−.12	.05	.03	—
20. Judicial disposition	.23**	.12	.14	.08	−.15*	−.16*	—

*p < .05.   **p < .01.

Zero–Order Correlations, Means, Standard Deviations, and Range of Social
Characteristics and Legal Variables and Decision Making Stages (N = 1,966)
Jackson

16	17	18	19	20	Mean	SD	Range
					.05	.22	0–1
					.14	.35	0–1
					.26	.44	1–2
					14.30	2.60	4–18
					.38	.49	0–1
					.18	.39	0–1
					.08	.28	0–1
					1.33	3.16	0–54
					.07	.25	0–1
					1.08	.38	1–7
					.14	.35	0–1
					.56	.50	0–1
					.08	.27	0–1
					.13	.34	0–1
					.12	.33	0–1
1.00					.81	.39	0–1
—	1.00				.86	.35	0–1
—	—	1.00			.83	.37	0–1
—	—	—	1.00		.98	.15	0–1
—	—	—	—	1.00	.29	.45	0–1

*p < .05. **p < .01.

Zero–Order Correlations, Means, Standard Deviations, and Range of Social Characteristics
and Legal Variables and Decision Making Stages (N = 1,798)[a]

King

Variable	1	2	3	4	5	6	7	8
Social Characteristics								
1. Race	1.00							
2. Gender	.09**	1.00						
3. Age	−.12**	−.03	1.00					
4. Family status	.15**	.04	−.10**	1.00				
School								
5. Attending, but problems	.02	−.06**	−.01	−.03	1.00			
6. Not attending	−.03	.07**	.16**	−.00	−.09**	1.00		
Legal								
7. Number of prior referrals	.15**	−.11**	.06**	.10**	.02	.14**	1.00	
8. Court authority	.05*	−.06**	.03	.02	.06**	.06**	.39**	1.00
9. Number of current charges	.00	−.05*	.09**	−.05*	.02	.08**	.05*	−.00
10. Crime severity	−.04*	−.15**	−.01	−.01	.06**	.09**	.06**	.04
11. Property	.03	.08**	.00	.06**	.02	.06**	.00	.03**
12. Person	.07**	−.04	−.02	.01	.01	−.03	.08**	.03
13. Drugs	−.10**	−.01	.11**	−.03*	.01	.02	−.01	.00
Stages								
14. Release/ adjustment vs. further court processing	.05*	−.08**	.08**	.01	.18**	.20**	.20**	.17**
15. Release vs. adjustment/ further court processing	−.04	−.10**	.06**	−.00	.15**	.10**	.14**	.13**
16. Petition	—	—	—	—	—	—	—	—
17. Initial appearance	.02	−.02	.02	.09	.08	.17**	.24**	.20**
18. Adjudication	—	—	—	—	—	—	—	—
19. Judicial disposition	.13	−.18	−.03	−.08	−.08	.07	.35**	.14

*p < .05. **p < .01.

[a]Too few cases in categories of petition and adjudication.

Zero–Order Correlations, Means, Standard Deviations, and Range of Social Characteristics
and Legal Variables and Decision Making Stages (N = 1,798)[a]

King

9	10	11	12	13	14	15	16	17	18
1.00									
.02	1.00								
−.03	.19**	1.00							
.08**	.04	−.51*	1.00						
−.02	−.11**	−.33**	−.14**	1.00					
.07**	.36**	.06**	.08**	−.04	1.00				
.05*	.25**	.07**	−.00	−.00	.45**	1.00			
—	—	—	—	—	—	—	1.00		
−.01	.15*	.11	.05	−.10	—	—	—	1.00	
—	—	—	—	—	—	—	—	—	1.00
−.05	−.02	.06	−.05	−.03	—	—	—	—	—

*p < .05. **p < .01.

[a]Too few cases in categories of petition and adjudication.

Zero–Order Correlations, Means, Standard Deviations, and Range of Social
Characteristics and Legal Variables and Decision Making Stages (N = 1,798)[a]
King

Variable	19	Mean	SD	Range
Social Characteristics				
1. Race		.18	.38	0–1
2. Gender		.22	.41	1–2
3. Age		15.29	1.81	4–18
4. Family status		.52	.50	0–1
School				
5. Attending, but problems		.07	.25	0–1
6. Not attending		.11	.31	0–1
Legal				
7. Number of prior referrals		.92	2.02	0–54
8. Court authority		.09	.29	0–1
9. Number of current charges		1.14	.50	1–7
10. Crime severity		.23	.42	0–1
11. Property		.54	.50	0–1
12. Person		.18	.38	0–1
13. Drugs		.08	.28	**0–1**
Stages				
14. Release/ adjustment vs. further court processing		.15	.36	0–1
15. Release vs. adjustment/ further court processing		.47	.50	0–1
16. Petition		.96	.21	0–1
17. Initial appearance		.38	.49	0–1
18. Adjudication		.94	.24	0–1
19. Judicial disposition	1.00	.45	.50	0–1

*p < .05.   **p < .01.

[a]Too few cases in categories of petition and adjudication.

182

Zero–Order Correlations, Means, Standard Deviations, and Range of Social Characteristics
and Legal Variables and Decision Making Stages (N = 1,423)

Parks

Variable	1	2	3	4	5	6	7	8
Social Characteristics								
1. Race	1.00							
2. Gender	.07**	1.00						
3. Age	−.13**	−.01	1.00					
4. Family status	.27**	.03	−.08**	1.00				
School								
5. Attending, but problems	−.00	−.06*	−.02	.06*	1.00			
6. Not attending	.04	.00	.17**	.10**	−.11**	1.00		
Legal								
7. Number of prior referrals	.18**	−.16**	.23**	.15**	.07**	.12**	1.00	
8. Court authority	.05*	−.08**	.14**	.09**	.06*	.11**	.46**	1.00
9. Number of current charges	−.03	−.05	.11**	.04	.05*	.05*	.08**	.04
10. Crime severity	−.03	−.11**	.05*	.05*	.10**	.04	.04	.04
11. Property	.01	.11**	−.04	.02	.08**	.04	−.06**	−.01
12. Person	.12**	−.05*	.03	.03	−.00	.00	.08**	.04
13. Drugs	−.11**	−.05*	.20**	−.05*	−.04	.03	.01	.01
Stages								
14. Release/ adjustment vs. further court processing	.03	−.11**	.29**	.12**	.05	.15**	.35**	.26**
15. Release vs. adjustment/ further court processing	−.00	.07**	.06*	.06**	.15**	.07**	.01	−.01
16. Petition	−.15**	−.03	.08	−.05	.01	−.04	−.03	.04
17. Initial appearance	.24**	−.01	−.02	.15**	.09	.06	.36**	.32**
18. Adjudication	−.08	.04	.14*	−.04	.07	.01	.12	.14
19. Judicial disposition	.14**	−.01	.27**	.14*	.04	.06	.33**	.09

*p < .05. **p < .01.

183

Zero–Order Correlations, Means, Standard Deviations, and Range of Social Characteristics
and Legal Variables and Decision Making Stages (N = 1,423)

Parks

Variable	9	10	11	12	13	14	15
Social Characteristics							
1. Race							
2. Gender							
3. Age							
4. Family status							
School							
5. Attending, but problems							
6. Not attending							
Legal							
7. Number of prior referrals							
8. Court authority							
9. Number of current charges	1.00						
10. Crime severity	.16**	1.00					
11. Property	.03	.24**	1.00				
12. Person	.03	−.08**	−.53**	1.00			
13. Drugs	−.01	−.08**	−.29**	−.12	1.00		
Stages							
14. Release/ adjustment vs. further court processing	.23**	.30**	−.02**	.08**	.12**	1.00	
15. Release vs. adjustment/ further court processing	.04	.05	.05*	−.00	.01	.25**	1.00
16. Petition	.11*	.01	.03	.00	.02	—	—
17. Initial appearance	.05	−.12*	−.10	.22**	−.21**	—	—
18. Adjudication	.16*	.17*	−.04	.05	.10	—	—
19. Judicial disposition	−.04	−.06	−.01	−.08	.04	—	—

*p < .05.   **p < .01.

Zero–Order Correlations, Means, Standard Deviations, and Range of Social
Characteristics and Legal Variables and Decision Making Stages (N = 1,423)
Parks

16	17	18	19	Mean	SD	Range
				.30	.46	0–1
				.19	.40	1–2
				14.29	2.35	4–18
				.46	.50	0–1
				.18	.39	0–1
				.06	.23	0–1
				.82	1.52	0–54
				.11	.32	0–1
				1.28	.79	1–7
				.29	.46	0–1
				.57	.50	0–1
				.17	.38	0–1
				.06	.24	0–1
				.29	.45	0–1
				.87	.34	0–1
1.00				.94	.24	0–1
—	1.00			.63	.48	0–1
—	—	1.00		.85	.36	0–1
—	—	—	1.00	.36	.47	0–1

*p < .05. **p < .01.

Notes

1. There is debate concerning the definitions of race and ethnicity (Hawkins, 1995). While recognizing that the definition of *race* is socially constructed and possibly arbitrary, the term generally refers to skin color, while ethnicity refers to place of origin or the countries from which ancestors can be traced. In the present research, I rely upon the classification of the youth's race as provided by the juvenile justice decision-makers in the case files. The term *minority* is used to reflect social groups that lack political, economic, and social power relative to the majority (Mann, 1993).

2. The Formula Grants Program functions somewhat as a federal financial incentive for states that want to comply with the Office of Juvenile Justice and Delinquency Prevention (OJJDP) mandates although states may opt to not participate. The amount of money is based on the number of persons age seventeen and younger in a given state and the amount awarded to an individual state can be significant. For example, in 1998 California received $7,839,000, Florida $3,026,000, Michigan $2,243,000, and Oklahoma $779,000 (OJJDP, 1998). If a state is found to be in compliance with a particular mandate, the money can be then used for the continuation of compliance with that mandate, used to comply with the other mandates, and/or to further other juvenile justice efforts.

3. All identification stage information should distinguish between white youth versus youth of other specific racial and ethnic groups. Originally, data were also to be provided for the state as a whole and for Metropolitan Statistical Areas (MSAs). More recently, OJJDP has encouraged states to use the county as the unit of analysis instead of the MSA (DMC Technical Assistance Manual, 2000). Should quantifiable documentation not be available, the state must provide a time-limited plan of action, not to exceed six months, to develop and implement a system for the ongoing collection, analysis, and dissemination of information to determine whether minority youth are disproportionately confined.

4. States could provide information on at least three MSAs in the state where minorities represented at least 1 percent of the youth population at risk. Counties or jurisdictions within each state could be used to satisfy this requirement if finances were a concern. In addition, if there were more than one minority group that represented at least 1 percent of the statewide population, separate data should have been presented on each group. If a completed assessment was not available, the state had to submit a plan of action indicating how and when the assessment would be completed.

5. As a result of a 1990 national training workshop, attended by researchers and practitioners, a technical assistance manual was developed (DMC Technical Assistance Manual, 1990) and in 2000 a more detailed manual was created to provide further guidance to research and address the overrepresentation of minority youth in the juvenile justice system (DMC Technical Assistance Manual, 2000). In addition, the Office of Juvenile Justice and Delinquency Prevention was to focus on minority overrepresentation in its grant activities, and the National Institute for Juvenile Justice and Delinquency Prevention was required to support research on this issue (Coalition for Juvenile Justice, 1993). OJJDP also contracted with Community Research Associates (Champaign, IL) to provide training and technical assistance on all aspects of the mandate to states upon request through the Formula Grants Training and Technical Assistance Program (Roscoe and Morton, 1994). Recently, OJJDP awarded the Formula Grants Training and Technical Assistance Program contract to Development Services Group (Bethesda, MD). The intervention strategies that were implemented in each of the five pilot states were evaluated by Caliber (Devine et al., 1998). In 2000, Research and Evaluation Associates (Chapel Hill, NC) entered into a cooperative agreement with OJJDP to develop instruments, design training and technical assistance manuals, and to provide intensive technical assistance to help selected jurisdictions reduce minority overrepresentation.

6. The information provided by Iowa on DMC as part of the identification phase of the requirement does not comply with requests by OJJDP to differentiate among minority youth and to provide index values for at least three counties. These shortcomings also plague reporting by other states (Hamparian and Leiber, 1997; DMC Technical Assistance Manual, 2000; Pope and Leiber, 2003).

7. In late 2002, the OJJDP Act was re-authorized. The DMC mandate was changed to disproportionate minority contact.

NOTES TO CHAPTER 2

1. It is important to note that labeling theory has been applied to not only understand the differential application of sanctions but the consequences of labeling including the alteration of personal identity and greater involvement in delinquent behavior (e.g., Lemert, 1967; Patternoster and Iovanni, 1989). Some researchers have also used a Marxist perspective to guide research on status characteristics and juvenile justice decision making (e.g., Carter and Celland, 1979). Although there are some overlaps between conflict theory and Marxist theory, the primary distinction between the two is that the former is more pluralistic and not as class or economic-bounded as the latter (Lynch and Groves, 1989).

2. Robert Sampson's (1986) findings also reveal an ecological bias with respect to arrest decisions and the compilation of a prior record. Lower-class neighborhoods and the people who reside within these areas were found to be stereotyped as criminogenic and subject to increased police control. This social class bias at the neighborhood level increased the probability of arrest and the accumulation of more serious criminal histories for poor youth.

3. Findings of leniency for minorities is seen by some as a weakness of the labeling and conflict approaches, especially the latter. Both perspectives typically argue that minorities and other disadvantaged groups will receive harsher rather than more lenient outcomes (e.g., Chambliss and Seidman, 1971; Patternoster and Iovanni, 1989). This is a rather narrow interpretation of what constitutes racial bias. "Lenient" outcomes may simply be the result of prejudicial attitudes and beliefs that devalue the life and property of minorities, including minority victims of crime. For example, African Americans who victimize whites will receive harsher punishments than African Americans who victimize other African Americans (e.g., LaFree, 1989). Similar processes may be at work that involve stereotypes concerning the suitability for rehabilitation of minorities relative to whites (Pope, 1978; Spohn et al., 1980–1981; Fisher and Doyle-Martin, 1981; Leiber and Stairs, 1999). Bell and Lang have argued that

> . . . if black juveniles are labeled as criminals, they are likely to be labeled as unreceptive to the benefits of diversion. . . . White juveniles, on the other hand, because they are not labeled as criminals, may be perceived as more responsive to such treatment. Hence, in cases where the choice is between release and diversion, whites may receive the harsher treatment. (1985: 311)

The appearance of leniency may also represent a correction for biases that occurred at previous stages in the proceedings (Hepburn, 1978; ; Dannefer and Schutt, 1982; Leiber, 1994).

4. Much of the debate concerning race and the purpose and objectives of the criminal and juvenile justice systems revolves around philosophical assumptions (Zatz, 1990). Sampson and Lauritsen summarize this point succinctly by stating:

> For some, *any* evidence of differential treatment, whether anecdotal or empirical, direct or indirect, or at the individual or jurisdictional level, is indicative of a discriminatory system. For those at the other end of the continuum, the term is reserved for widespread and consistent differentials in processing unaccounted for by relevant legal factors. Recognizing these differences in the use of terms implies that the assessment of racial discrimination is not simply a matter of empirical debate. (1997: 351–352, cite omitted and emphasis added)

Thus, we have on one end of the continuum the conflict orientation of Mann who views the law and the legal system as perpetuating "an ingrained system of injustice for people of color" (1993: 160). On the other end, there is the consensus approach of Wilbanks who argues that the belief of the criminal justice system as racist is a "myth" and at best, discrimination should be viewed as a random occurrence (1987: 5–6).

5. Although Tittle and Curran (1988) did not directly examine how decision-makers felt, they found some support for their reformulation of conflict theory in an examination of juvenile court dispositions in thirty-one jurisdictions in Florida. They found that a selection bias in dispositions was influenced by the type of crime and two contextual variables: the size of the nonwhite population and the age of the population. A larger nonwhite population and a younger population overall resulted in different case outcomes of minority youth charged with status offenses, drug offenses, and sex offenses.

6. The research results from Leiber and Jamieson (1995) may be questioned since they included aggregate-level variables in the same equations with individual-level variables. This kind of estimation procedure may result in model misspecification (Bryk and Raudenbush, 1992).

7. Quillian points out that the effect of economic conditions on the perceived threat should be seen in absolute rather than relative terms. He argues that economic prosperity reduces "the feeling that racial groups are locked in a zero-sum game over resources. As a result, prejudice and other anti-black attitudes increase among whites when the group economic situations worsens" (1996: 821 note 6). Some have also argued that the interaction between economic conditions and the percentage of African Americans as representing a threat is curvilinear (Jackson and Carroll, 1981; Nalla et al., 1997).

8. Most of the research that employed the structural characteristics of communities as explanatory factors focused on the police and social control (Jackson and Carroll, 1981; Lizotte et al., 1982; Jackson, 1989; Chamlin, 1990). Increased police strength appears to be the result of nonwhite population levels rather than solely crime levels (Nalla et al., 1997). That is, the larger the percent minority of a population, the greater the spending for police protection. Liska and his colleagues (1984, 1985, 1992) also found that the probability of contact with minority populations influenced whites' fear of crime and their reliance on police for social control. The power-threat thesis has also been applied to explain the lynching of African Americans in the South (Tolnay et al., 1989).

9. Recent research of the courts from an organizational contingency perspective has adopted a "local court community" approach to understand case strategies and sentencing patterns. The concept of the "local court community" is a metaphor for community and the characteristics associated with a community such as legal culture, politics, members' shared workplace, and other organizational arrangements (Eisenstein et al., 1988). Eisenstein, Flemming, and their colleagues (1977, 1988, 1992) have developed this concept by emphasizing the importance of loose coupling (see also Hagan et al., 1979; Stapleton et al., 1982) and the interdependent relations that exists between sponsoring agencies (e.g., prosecutor's office, judicial branch, and the defense bar) and the court actors. The philosophies, norms, and traditions of the courtroom workgroup play pivotal roles in the administration of justice. Because of the breadth of the court community framework, a variety of interrelated contexts both external and internal to the court are seen as important determinants of decision making. Examples of contexts stemming from this perspective are (1) size of the community; (2) court community stability and familiarity; (3) local party politics; (4) character (morale) of the sponsoring agencies and the balance of power between them; (5) attitudes toward punishment, rehabilitation, and due process; (6) organizational type and leadership style; and (7) informal sentencing norms (Eisenstein et al., 1988; Ulmer, 1997).

10. In a series of articles, Ulmer (1995), Ulmer and Kramer (1996), and Steffensmeier and his colleagues (1998) found that county court differences in personal relationships among the court room work groups and sponsoring agencies interacted with ideologies about case processing and sentencing that resulted in racial differences in case outcomes. In comparison to the other two county courts, the Rich (pseudonym) County

court community shared personal, professional, and political relationships that covered many years. Ulmer illustrates this point by stating,

> Most of the major players in this medium-sized suburban court community shared social relationships outside the courthouse, playing golf at the same clubs, attending the same social events, and participating in activities with the county's powerful Republican Party. Not only did the DA's office, public and private defense bar, and judges' bench exhibit . . . stability . . . the three sponsoring agencies also exchanged personnel . . . a pattern described as "incestuous". . . . (1995:592)

In addition to the personal and working relationships, the Rich county court community shared a common ideological "get tough" orientation to sentencing emphasizing punishment and deterrence. The shared relationships and ideological agreements produced and environment where cooperative negotiation in case processing was emphasized and expected. Consequently, Rich County had fewer trials than the other two county courts (Ulmer and Kramer, 1996). Jury trial convictions, however, resulted in a greater likelihood of incarceration. African Americans were more likely to be incarcerated in Rich County relative to the other two county courts and women defendants were less likely to be imprisoned. These findings were evident despite the presence of sentencing guidelines (Ulmer and Kramer, 1996).

NOTES TO CHAPTER 3

1. Both the Uniform Crime Reports and the National Crime Victimization Survey indicate that African Americans differentially offend relative to whites that may account for minority overrepresentation in the system (Hindelang, 1978; O'Brien, 1985; Sampson and Lauritsen, 1997; Pope and Snyder, 2003). The results from self-report surveys have been inconclusive (Elliott and Ageton, 1980; Hindelang et al., 1981; Huizinga and Elliot, 1987; Farrington et al., 1996). All three measurements of crime have been criticized. For a discussion in general on the validity and reliability of the three measurements of crime see Blumstein and his colleagues (1991, 1992); Farnworth and her colleagues (1994); Gove and his colleagues (1985); McDowall and Loftin (1992); Mann (1993); McCleary and his colleagues (1982); Pope (1979, 1984); and McNeely and Pope (1978, 1981).

2. Wilson (1987, 1996) and West (1993) point out that following the criticisms of Moynihan's 1965 controversial report, *The Negro Family*, many liberals including African Americans have been reluctant to discuss, research, and write about crime and the other social pathologies of the ghetto. Moynihan gave a negative depiction of the African American family and emphasized the rise in the rates of broken marriages, female-headed homes, out-of-wedlock births, and welfare dependency. According to Moynihan (1965) the key to black equality was a stable family. The problems of the black family, however, could be traced to slavery and to other forms of racial and economic discrimination and to the adaptations to these barriers. Critiques of Moynihan's report focused on the portrayal of black matriarchy as a cause of social pathology (Bailey, 1996). Moynihan's report was

viewed as "blaming the victim" or a "cultural deviant" perspective (Johnson, 1988). Scholars focused on the positive aspects of the black family among the lower class (Willie, 1991) and the lack of opportunities to improve one's position in life (Morton, 1991). Consequently, the "devastating effects of the inner-city environment were either ignored, played down, or denied" (Wilson, 1996: xvii). Conservatives, on the other hand, downplayed racism and the lack of opportunities and instead focused on the African American culture, liberal social policies, and individual character (Murray, 1984; Herrnstein and Murray, 1994).

It has not been until recently that some liberals have begun to emphasize the interplay between both structure and culture in accounting for crime, impoverishment, family disruption and other social problems. Sampson and Wilson's statements illustrate this position:

> [W]e advance . . . a theoretical strategy that incorporates both structural and cultural arguments regarding race, crime, and inequality in American cities. . . . [W]e view the race and crime linkage from contextual lenses that highlight the very different ecological contexts that black and whites reside in—regardless of individual character. The basic thesis is that macro-social patterns of residential inequality give rise to the social isolation and ecological concentration of the truly disadvantaged, which in turn leads to structural barriers and cultural adaptations that undermine social organization and hence control of crime. (1995:38)

Wilson (1996) has further developed this theoretical perspective by teasing out the consequences of unemployment and the lack of employment opportunities for African Americans living in the urban ghetto. For a slightly different explanation—one that focuses on segregation—refer to Massey and Denton (1993).

NOTES TO CHAPTER 4

1. Information in the case files did not allow for a breakdown of the various Native American tribal groups, and Hispanic Americans were not included in the analysis because the small number (n = 350) precluded jurisdictional comparisons. Leiber (1995) conducted a study of juvenile justice case processing comparing Hispanic youth to whites and African Americans without controlling for court jurisdiction and found that Latinos received similar outcomes as whites at intake. African Americans received both the more lenient (release) and severe (recommendation for further proceedings) outcomes at this stage. Both African American and Latino youth were less likely to be petitioned than white youth. No information was provided in the case files differentiating Hispanics from Cubans, Dominicans, Puerto Ricans, Mexican Americans, Colombians, and so forth.

2. The names of the counties have been changed to protect the confidentiality of the court and the respondents.

3. In Iowa, juvenile justice courts make up judicial districts. There are eight judicial districts. A number of counties comprise a judicial district, and the county courts focused on in the present research represent the largest, most populated, and most racially

diversified. It is also important to note that almost a decade has passed since the collection of the data. It is possible that the findings reported in the text no longer apply to decision-makers or explain how youth are currently processed. While these are valid concerns, confidence in the results are warranted for several reasons. First, little turnover has occurred in juvenile court personnel in the four jurisdictions and continued overrepresentation of African American youth in Iowa is evident in detention, secure corrections, and waiver to adult court (Division of Criminal and Juvenile Justice Planning and Statistics Analysis, 2000). Second, the four jurisdictions comprising the focus of inquiry in the present research still contribute the most to the minority overrepresentation. The third and final reason why the study and the findings should not be dismissed due to concerns regarding the applicability to explain current decision making or the views of decision-makers rest with the value obtained from using a contextual analysis that represents a refinement both in theory and in application.

4. The percentage of persons in poverty, the percentage of persons age sixteen and older employed, and the measures for racial inequality and wealth were calculated for each county from 1980 and 1990 census figures and represent an average of the two time frames. The rate of unemployment, the percentage of babies born out-of-wedlock to teenage mothers, and the percentage of juvenile arrests reflect an average in each county for each year during the twelve-year time span. The criminal justice resource measure is based on an average for the years 1981–1982 and 1986–1987.

5. Information on the organizational characteristics were obtained from the chief juvenile court officer of each juvenile court jurisdiction at the start of the initial assessment study and from the State Court Administrator's Office.

6. Leiber (1993) did not examine police decision making in the four jurisdictions. This is a critical omission (Conley, 1994) since the police are the first contact the youth will have with the juvenile justice system and possibly, the agency with the greatest impact on them. Youth were administered self-report surveys (n = 419) and semistructured interviews (n = 190) asking for their opinions and experiences with the police in their respective communities. Overall, no jurisdictional differences were discovered (Leiber, 1993). Leiber and his colleagues (1998a), in a more thorough analysis, found that minority youth held more negative views of the police and believed that police discriminated more against minorities than whites.

7. The intake variable may be seen as ordinal (i.e., release, diversion, and recommendation for further court processing). An examination of the proportional odds results within PROC LOGISTIC in SAS, however, indicated that the variable's effects on the odds of a response equal to or above category k is not the same for all k when k is the cutpoint parameter of the model (Agresti, 1989). The violation of the proportional odds assumption necessitates the estimate of two equations (one using the lower cut point as the reference point-release and another that used the upper cut point-referral for further court proceedings).

8. The discrepancy in the number of youth petitioned and youth at the initial appearance hearing is the result of those transferred to adult proceedings.

9. Prior to the early 1990s, Iowa employed a discretionary waiver system (Iowa Code Sec. 232.45) where the upper age was seventeen. In cases involving a youth of at

least age fourteen who has been accused of any criminal offense, the youth, the district attorney, or the juvenile court may motion a waiver hearing. The court may waive jurisdiction if it finds (1) there is probable cause that the youth committed the crime and (2) there are no reasonable opportunities for rehabilitation within the juvenile court system and the waiver is in the best interests of the youth and the community (Iowa Code Sec. 232.45). In addition to the discretionary waiver, Iowa enacted a statutory exclusion waiver (Iowa Code Sec. 232.8), a reverse waiver (Iowa Code Sec. 232.8), and "once an adult, always an adult waiver" (Iowa Code Sec. 232.45A) in the 1990s. A detailed discussion of the waiver process in Iowa can be found in Leiber and his colleagues (1996) and in Griffin and his colleagues (1998). The relatively few number of youth transferred to adult court (n = 257) prevented jurisdictional comparisons. Slightly over 8.5% of youth in the sample were recommended for waiver to adult court, and only 4% of youth in the sample were transferred to adult court. Thirty-eight percent of youth at the disposition stage received a sanction involving just a change of placement.

10. Equations were reestimated without controlling for sample selection bias or lambda. For the most part the results confirmed those using the hazard rate. Exceptions will be noted.

11. Severity of the most recent disposition and detention status have been found in previous research to be strong predictors of decision making and tied to race (e.g., Bortner and Reed, 1985; Hamparian and Leiber, 1997) but were not included in the analysis. Relatively few youth in the sample were adjudicated delinquent at the most recent disposition (7%) and/or held in detention (3%). Because of limited variation, the severity of the prior disposition and detention status are not employed as variables. Models were reestimated with detention status included as an independent variable and the overall results paralleled those presented in the text.

Notes to Chapter 6

1. The models for judicial disposition were reestimated with transfer to adult court omitted as part of the dependent variable. The results were the same, with the exception that age was no longer a statistically significant predictor. Also, the model was reestimated with the hazard rate consisting of youth who reached the petition stage rather than adjudication. The results were the same, with the exception that youth not attending school was a statistically significant determinant of a change of placement/transfer to adult court ($p < .01$). Last, the models were reestimated without the hazard rate. Some changes were evident. Gender had an inverse statistically significant effect at petition ($p < .05$). At judicial disposition, not attending school had a positive statistically significant effect ($p < .01$).

2. Results from initial estimations with the two dummy variables representing race—African American and Native American—revealed statistically significant interaction effects between the reference category white and three independent variables with intake decision making. For the purpose of clarity, the models were reestimated with African American the reference category.

3. The models for judicial disposition were reestimated with transfer to adult court omitted as part of the dependent variable. The results were the same, with the exception that age was no longer a statistically significant predictor and family status had a positive statistically significant effect on the dependent variable ($p < .01$). Also, the model was reestimated with the hazard rate consisting of youth who reached the petition stage rather than adjudication. The results were the same. Last, the models were reestimated without the hazard rate. At judicial disposition, crimes against persons increased the likelihood of receiving community-based treatment ($p < .05$).

4. The models for judicial disposition were reestimated with transfer to adult court omitted as part of the dependent variable. The results were the same, with the exception that family status had a statistically significant inverse effect on the dependent variable ($p < .05$). Also, the model was reestimated with the hazard rate consisting of youth who reached the petition stage rather adjudication. The results were the same. The models were reestimated without the hazard rate and no differences in the results were apparent.

5. The models for judicial disposition were reestimated with transfer to adult court omitted as part of the dependent variable. The results were the same, with the exception that age now has a positive statistically significant effect on the dependent variable ($p < .01$). Also, the model was reestimated with the hazard rate consisting of youth who reached the petition stage rather adjudication. The results were the same. Last, the models were reestimated without the hazard rate. At adjudication, race is no longer predictive of decision making.

NOTES TO CHAPTER 11

1. An attempt was made to trace the history of each jurisdiction in terms of settlement, industry, immigration, and race relations. At the time of the writing of the book, information was lacking on the subject.

2. Protective services can apply to a number of social services offered by public or private agencies to assist persons with personal, financial, and health problems. Generally, protective services involve voluntary support services. However, many courts conduct hearings for the protection of individuals having difficulty coping with life. Social agencies can provide emergency services, involuntary protective services, and protective placement. In short, protective services legislation lacks procedural safeguards and suffers from vague and inappropriate standards for identifying who shall receive such services (Leiber, 1988, 1992c).

Bibliography

Adamson, C. (1983) "Punishment after Slavery: Southern State Penal Systems, 1865–1880." *Social Problems* 30: 555–569.

Aday, D. (1986) "Court Structure, Defense Attorney Use, and Juvenile Court Decisions." *Sociological Quarterly* 27: 107–119.

Agresti, A. (1989) "Tutorial on Modeling Ordered Categorical Response Data." *Psychologist Bulletin* 105: 290–301.

Akers, R. (1994) *Criminological Theories: Introduction and Evaluation.* Los Angeles: Roxbury Publishing Company.

Albonetti, C. (1991) "An Integration of Theories to Explain Judicial Discretion." *Social Problems* 38: 247–266.

Albonetti, C. and J. Hepburn (1996) "Prosecutorial Discretion to Defer Criminalization: The Effects of Defendant's Ascribed and Achieved Status Characteristics." *Journal of Quantitative Criminology* 12: 63–81.

American Bar Association (ABA) (1995) *A Call for Justice: An Assessment of Access to Counsel and Quality of Representation in Delinquency Proceedings.* Washington, DC: ABA Juvenile Justice Center.

Anderson, E. (1990) *Street Wise: Race, Class, and Change in an Urban Community.* Chicago: University of Chicago Press.

———. (1995) "The Code of the Streets." *Atlantic Monthly* 273: 82.

———. (1999) *Code of the Street: Decency, Violence, and the Mmoral Life of the Inner City.* New York: Norton.

Applegate, B., F. Cullen, B. Fisher, and T. VanderVen (2000) "Forgiveness and Fundamentalism: Reconsidering the Relationship between Correctional Attitudes and Religion." *Criminology* 38: 719–753.

Arnold, W. R. 1971. "Race and Ethnicity Relative to Other Factors in Juvenile Court Dispositions." *American Journal of Sociology* 77: 211–227.

Austin, T. (1981) "The Influence of Court Location on Type of Criminal Sentence: The Rural-Urban Factor." *Journal of Criminal Justice* 9: 305–316.

Bailey, F. (1996) "The 'Tangle of Pathology' and the Lower Class African American Family: Historical and Social Science Perspectives." In Lynch, M. and E. B. Patterson (eds.) *Justice with Prejudice: Race and Criminal Justice in America.* Albany: Harrow and Heston. Pgs. 49–71.

Barak, G. (1994) "Between the Waves: Mass-Mediated Themes of Crime and Justice. *Social Justice* 21: 133–147.

Becker, H. (1963) *Outsiders: Studies in the Sociology of Deviance.* New York: Free Press.

Beckett, K. (1995) "Fetal Rights and 'Crack Moms': Pregnant Women in the War on Drugs." *Contemporary Drug Problems* 22: 587–612.

Beckett, K. and T. Sasson (1998) "The Media and the Construction of the Drug Crisis in America." In Jensen, E. and J. Gerber (eds.) *The New War on Drugs: Symbolic Politics and Criminal Justice Policy.* Cincinnati: Anderson Publishing. Pgs. 25–43.

Beckett, K. and T. Sasson (2000) *The Politics of Injustice: Crime and Punishment in America.* Thousand Oaks, CA: Pine Forge Press.

Bell, D. and K. Lang (1985) "The Intake Dispositions of Juvenile Offenders." *Journal of Research in Crime and Delinquency* 22: 309–328.

Belsley, D., E. Kuhn, and R. Welsch (1980) *Regression Diagnostics Identifying Influential Data and Source of Collinearity.* New York: Wiley.

Bennett, W., J. Dilulio, and J. Walters. (1996) *Body Count: Moral Poverty and How to Win America's War Against Crime and Drugs.* New York: Simon & Schuster.

Berk, R. A. (1983) "An Introduction to Sample Selection Bias in Sociological Data." *American Sociological Review* 48: 386–398.

Bernard, T. (1992) *The Cycle of Juvenile Justice.* New York: Oxford University Press.

Bilchik, S. (1999) "Minorities in the Juvenile Justice System." 1999 National Report Series Juvenile Justice Bulletin. Washington, DC: U.S. Department of Justice, Office of Juvenile Justice and Delinquency Prevention.

Bishop, D. and C. Frazier (1988) "The Influence of Race in Juvenile Justice Processing." *Journal of Research in Crime and Delinquency* 22: 309–328.

Bishop, D. (2003). "The Role of Race and Ethnicity in Juvenile Justice Processing. In Hawkins, D. and K. Kempf-Leonard (eds.) *Race, Development and Juvenile Justice.* The John T. and Catherine Macarthur Foundation. Chicago: University of Chicago Press.

Blalock, H. (1967) *Toward a Theory of Minority-Group Relations.* New York: Wiley.

Blumstein, A. (1982) "On the Racial Disproportionality of United States' Prison Populations." *Journal of Criminal Law and Criminology* 73: 1259–1281.

Blumstein, A., J. Cohen, J. Roth, and C. Visher (eds.) (1986) *Criminal Careers and "Career Criminals."* Washington, DC: National Academy Press.

———. (1993) "Making Rationality Relevant." *Criminology* 31: 1–16.

Blumstein, A., J. Cohen, and R. Rosenfeld (1991) "Trend and Deviation in Crime Rates: A Comparison of UCR and NCS Data for Burglary and Robbery." *Criminology* 29: 237–263.

Blumstein, A., J. Cohen, and R. Rosenfeld (1992) "The UCR-NCS Relationship Revisited: A Reply to Menard." *Criminology* 30: 114–124.

Bortner, M. and W. Reed (1985) "Race and the Impact of Juvenile Deinstitutionalization." *Crime & Delinquency* 31: 35–46.

Bortner, M., M. Zatz, and D. Hawkins. (2000) "Race and Transfer: Empirical Research and Social Context." In Fagan, J. and F. Zimring (eds.) *The Changing Borders of Juvenile Justice: Transfer to the Criminal Court.* Chicago: University of Chicago Press. Pgs. 277–320.

Bortner, M.A., C. Burgess, A. Schneideo and A. Hall. (1993) Equitable Treatment of Minority Youth: A Report on the Overrepresentation of Minority Youth in Arizona's Juvenile Justice Systems. Phoenix, AZ: Governor's Office for Children.

Bortner, M. A. (1982) *Inside a Juvenile Court.* New York: New York University Press.

Bray, J. H. and E. M. Hetherington (1993) "Families in Transition: Introduction and Overview." *Journal of Family Psychology* 7: 3–8.

Bridges, G. and M. Myers (1994) "Problems and Prospects in the Study of Inequality, Crime, and Social Control." In Bridges, G. and M. Myers (eds.) *Inequality, Crime, and Social Control.* Boulder: Westview Press. Pgs. 3–18.

Bridges, G. and R. Crutchfield (1988) "Law, Social Standing, and Racial Disparities in Imprisonment." *Social Forces* 66: 699–724.

Bridges, G. and S. Steen (1998) "Racial Disparities in Official Assessments of Juvenile Offenders: Attributional Stereotypes as Mediating Mechanisms." *American Sociological Review* 63: 554–570.

Bridges, G., D. Conley, R. Engen, and T. Price-Spratlen (1995) "Racial Disparities in the Confinement of Juveniles: Effects of Crime and Community Social Structure on Punishment." In Kempf-Leonard, K., C. E. Pope, and W. Feyerherm (eds.) *Minorities in Juvenile Justice.* Thousand Oaks, CA: Sage. Pgs. 128–152.

Bridges, G., R. Crutchfield, and E. Simpson (1987) "Crime, Social Structure and Criminal Punishment: White and Nonwhite Rates of Imprisonment." *Social Problems* 34: 345–361.

Brown, M. E., R. Sagan, and E. Greenblatt (1980) "Juvenile Bindovers: 1979." Prepared for the Office of the Commissioner of Probation.

Bryk, A. and S. Raudenbush (1992) *Hierarchical Linear Models.* Newbury Park: Sage.

Bureau of the Census. (1990) 1990 Census of Population: General Population Characteristics.

Bureau of Justice Statistics (1998) "National Crime Victim Survey." In *Criminal Victimization 1997: Changes 1996–97 with Trends 1993–97*. Washington, DC: U.S. Department of Justice.

Butts, J. and H. Snyder (1997) "The Youngest Delinquents: Offenders under Age 15." *Juvenile Justice Bulletin*. U.S. Department of Justice. Office of Juvenile Justice and Delinquency Prevention (OJJDP), September.

Carroll, J. (1978) "Causal Attributions in Expert Parole Decisions." *Journal of Personality and Social Psychology* 36: 1501–1511.

Carter, T. J. and D. Celland (1979) "A Neo-Marxian Critique: Formulation and Test of Juvenile Dispositions as a Function of Social Class." *Social Problems* 27: 96.

Chambliss, W. (1995) "Crime Control and Ethnic Minorities: Legitimizing Racial Oppression by Creating Moral Panics." In Hawkins, D. (ed.) *Ethnicity, Race, and Crime: Perspectives across Time and Place*. Albany: State University of New York Press. Pgs. 235–258.

Chambliss, W. and R. Seidman (1971) *Law, Order and Power*. Reading: Addison-Wesley.

Chamlin, M. B. (1990) "Determinants of Police Expenditures in Chicago, 1940–1958." *Sociological Quarterly* 31: 485–494.

Champion, D. (1994). *Measuring Offender Risk: A Criminal Justice Sourcebook*. Westport, CT: Greenwood Press.

———. (1998) *The Juvenile Justice System: Delinquency, Processing, and the Law*. 2d ed. Upper Saddle River, NJ: Prentice-Hall.

Chiricos, T. (1996) "Moral Panic as Ideology: Drugs, Violence, Race and Punishment in America." In Lynch, M. and E. B. Patterson (eds.) *Justice with Prejudice: Race and Criminal Justice in Amercia*. Pgs. 19–48.

Chiricos, T. and C. Crawford (1995) "Race and Imprisonment: A Contextual Assessment of the Evidence." In Hawkins, D. (ed.) *Ethnicity, Race and Crime*. Albany: State University of New York Press. Pgs. 281–309.

Church, V. (1994) "Juveniles: A Generation at Risk: Meeting Disproportionate Minority Confinement Mandates." *Corrections Today*. Pgs. 70–72.

Cicourel, A. (1968) *The Social Organization of Juvenile Justice*. New York: Wiley.

Clark, K. B. (1965) *Dark Ghetto: Dilemmas of Social Power*. New York: Harper.

Clear, T. (1994) *Harm in American Penology: Offenders, Victims, and Their Communities*. Albany: State University of New York Press.

Coalition for Juvenile Justice (1987) *An Act of Empowerment*. 1987 Annual Report. Washington, DC: Coalition for Juvenile Justice.

———. (1989) *A Delicate Balance*. 1989 Annual Report. Washington, DC: Coalition for Juvenile Justice.

———. (1993) *Pursuing the Promise: Equal Justice for All Juveniles.* 1993 Annual Report. Washington, DC: Coalition for Juvenile Justice.

Cohen, L. and J. Kluegel (1978) "Determinants of Juvenile Court Dispositions: Ascriptive and Achieved Factors in Two Metropolitan Courts." *American Sociological Review* 43: 162–176.

Cohen, L. and J. Kluegel (1979) "Selecting Delinquents for Adjudication: An Analysis of Intake Screening Decisions in Two Metropolitan Juvenile Courts." *Journal of Research in Crime and Delinquency* 10: 143–163.

Conley, D. (1994) "Adding Color to a Black and White Picture: Using Qualitative Data to Explain Racial Disproportionality in the Juvenile Justice System." *Journal of Research in Crime and Delinquency* 31: 135–148.

Crawford, C. (2000) "Race and Pretextual Stops: Noise Enforcement in Midwest City." *Social Pathology* 6: 213–227.

Crawford, C., T. Chiricos, and G. Kleck (1998) "Race, Racial Threat, and Sentencing of Habitual Offenders." *Criminology* 36: 481–512.

Crew, B. K. (1991) "Race Differences in Felony Charging and Sentencing: Toward an Integration of Decision Making and Negotiation Models." *Journal of Crime and Justice* 14: 99–122.

Cullen, F. T., B. Applegate, and B. S. Fisher (1997) "Public Support for Correctional Treatment: The Continuing Appeal of the Rehabilitative Ideal." *Prison Journal* 77: 237–258.

Cullen, F. T., S. Levrant, B. Fulton, and J. F. Wozniak (1999) "Reconsidering Restorative Justice: The Corruption of Benevolence Revisited?" *Crime and Delinquency* 45: 3–27.

Cullen, F. T., G. Park, J. Cullen, and R. Mathers (1985) "Attribution, Salience, and Attitudes Toward Criminal Sanctioning." *Criminal Justice and Behavior* 12: 305–331.

Daly, K. and M. Tonry (1997) "Gender, Race, and Sentencing." In Tonry, M. (ed.) *Crime and Justice: A Review of Research.* Vol. 22. Chicago: University of Chicago Press. Pgs. 201–252.

Dannefer, D. and R. Schutt (1982) "Race and Juvenile Justice Processing in Court and Police Agencies." *American Journal of Sociology* 87: 1113–1132.

Davis, T., L. Severy, and S. Kraus (1993) "Predictors of Sentencing Decisions: The Beliefs, Personality Variables, and Demographic Factors of Juvenile Justice Personnel." *Journal of Applied Social Psychology* 23: 451–477.

DeJong, C. and K. Jackson (1998) "Putting Race Into Context: Race, Juvenile Justice Processing, and Urbanization." *Justice Quarterly* 15: 487–504.

DeKeseredy, W. and B. MacLean (1990) "Discrimination against Native Peoples in the Canadian Parole Process." In MacLean, B. and D. Milovanovic (eds.) *Racism, Empiricism and Criminal Justice.* Vancouver: Collective Press. Pgs. 61–68.

Delisi, M. and B. Regoli (1999) "Race, Conventional Crime, and Criminal Justice: The Decline Importance of Skin Color." *Journal of Criminal Justice* 27: 549–557.

Des Moines Register (2000) "A Generation in Prison." Editorial. December 30.

Devine, P., K. Coolbaugh, and S. Jenkins (1998) "Disproportionate Minority Confinement: Lessons Learned from Five States." Juvenile Justice Bulletin, Office of Juvenile Justice and Delinquency Prevention, December.

Dickey, W. (1980) "Incompetency and the Nondangerous Mentally Ill Client." *Criminal Law Bulletin* 16: 22–30.

Disproportionate Minority Confinement Technical Assistance Manual (1990). U.S. Department Of Justice. Office of Juvenile Justice and Delinquency Prevention.

———. (2000). U.S. Department of Justice. Office of Juvenile Justice and Delinquency Prevention.

Division of Criminal and Juvenile Planning and Statistical Analysis (2000) " Youth Development Approach for Iowa's Children and Families." Formula Grant Application and Three-Year Comprehensive Plan, April.

Dixon, J. (1995) "The Organizational Context of Criminal Sentencing." *American Journal of Sociology* 100: 1157–1198.

Dorfman, L. and V. Schiraldi (2001) *Off Balance: Youth, Race & Crime in the News.* Berkeley Media Studies Group and the Justice Policy Institute. Washington, DC: Building Blocks for Youth.

Drass, K. and J. W. Spencer (1987) "Accounting for Pre-Sentencing Recommendations: Typologies and Probation Officers' Theory of Office." *Social Problems* 24: 277–293.

Duffee, D. and L. Siegel (1971) "The Organization Man: Legal Counsel in the Juvenile Court." *Criminal Law Bulletin* 7: 544–553.

Duneier, M. (1992) *Slim's Table: Race, Respectability, and Masculinity.* Chicago: University of Chicago Press.

Durkheim, E. (1938) *The Rules of the Sociological Method.* New York: Free Press.

———. (1964) *The Division of Labor in Society.* New York: Free Press.

Eby, C. (2001) "Black Hawk Sentences among the State's Toughest" Waterloo Courier, February 25. Pgs. A1, A7.

Eisenstein, J. and H. Jacobs (1977) *Felony Justice: An Organizational Analysis of Criminal Courts.* Boston: Little, Brown.

Eisenstein, J., R. Flemming, and p. Nardulli (1988) The Contours of Justice: Communities and Their Courts. Boston: Little, Brown.

Elliott, D. and S. Ageton (1980) "Reconciling Race and Class Differences in Self-Reported and Official Estimates of Delinquency." *American Sociological Review* 45: 95–110.

Emerson, R. (1969) *Judging Delinquents: Context and Process in Juvenile Court.* Chicago: Aldine.

Equality in the Courts Task Force (1993) "Final Report of the Equality in the Courts Task Force." Paper prepared by the Supreme Court of Iowa, Des Moines.

Engen, R., S. Steen, and G. Bridges (2002) "Racial Disparities in the Punishment of Youth: A Theoretical and Empirical Assessment of the Literature." *Social Problems* 49(2): 194–220.

Erikson, K. T. (1966) *Wayward Puritans: A Study in the Sociology of Deviance.* New York: Wiley.

Esbensen, F. and L. T. Winfree (1998) "Race and Gender Differences between Gang and Nongang Youths: Results from a Multisite Survey." *Justice Quarterly* 15: 505–525.

Everett, R. (1998) "The Evolution of the Federal Sentencing Guidelines for Crack Cocaine: Social Construction and Social Control." In Jensen, E. and J. Gerber (eds.) *The New War on Drugs: Symbolic Politics and Criminal Justice Policy.* Cincinnati: Anderson Publishing. Pgs. 91–106.

Fagan, J., E. Slaughter, and E. Harstone (1987) "Blind Justice? The Impact of Race on the Juvenile Justice Process." *Crime and Delinquency* 33: 224–254.

Fagan, J. and F. Zimring. (eds.) 2000. *The Changing Borders of Juvenile Justice: Transfer of Adolescents to the Criminal Court.* Chicago: University of Chicago Press.

Farnworth, M. and P. Horan (1980) "Separate Justice: An Analysis of Race Differences in Court Processes." *Social Science Research* 9: 381–399.

Farnworth, M., R. Teske, and G. Thurman (1991) "Ethnic, Racial, and Minority Disparity in Felony Court Processing." In Lynch, M. and E. B. Patterson (eds.) *Race and Criminal Justice.* Albany: Harrow and Keston. Pgs. 54–70.

Farnworth, M., T. Thornberry, M. Krohn, and A. Lizotte (1994) "Measurement in the Study of Class and Delinquency: Integrating Theory and Research." *Journal of Research in Crime and Delinquency* 31: 32–61.

Farrell R. and V. Swigert (1982) *Deviance and Social Control.* Glenview, IL: Scott, Foresman and Company.

Farrell, R. and M. Holmes (1991) "The Social and Cognitive Structure of Legal Decision-Making." *Sociological Quarterly* 32: 529–542.

Farrell, R. and V. Swigert (1978) "Prior Offense Record as a Self-Fulfilling Prophecy." *Law and Society Review* 12 (Spring): 437–453.

Farrington, D. (1986) "Age and Crime." In *Crime and Justice: An Annual Review of Research* 7: 189–250.

Farrington, D., R. Loeber, M. Stouthamer-Loeber, W. Van Kammen, and L. Schmidt (1996) "Self-Reported Delinquency and a Combined Delinquency Seriousness Scale Based on Boys, Mothers, and Teachers: Concurrent and Predictive Validity for African Americans and Caucasians." *Criminology* 34: 493–518.

Federal Register (1991) Notice of FY 1991 Competitive Discretionary Grant Programs and Availability of the Office of Juvenile Justice Delinquency Prevention Program Announcement Application Kit. Washington, DC: Office of Juvenile Justice Delinquency Prevention.

Feld, B. (1987) "The Juvenile Court Meets the Principle of the Offense: Legislative Changes in Juvenile Waiver Statutes" *Journal of Criminal Law and Criminology.* 82: 156–210.

———. (1988) "'In Re Gault Revisted: A Cross-State Comparison of the Right to Counsel in Juvenile Court." *Crime and Delinquency* 34: 393–424.

———. (1989) "The Right to Counsel in Juvenile Court: An Empirical Study of When Lawyers Appear and the Difference it Makes" *Journal of Criminal Law and Criminology* 79: 1185–1346.

———. (1991) "Justice by Geography: Urban, Suburban, and Rural Variations in Juvenile Justice Administration." *Journal of Criminal Law and Criminology* 82: 156–210.

———. (1993) "Juvenile (In)Justice and the Criminal Court Alternative." *Crime and Delinquency* 39: 403–424.

———. (1995) "The Social Context of Juvenile Justice Administration: Racial Disparities in an Urban Juvenile Court." In Kempf-Leonard, K., C. E. Pope, and W. Feyerherm (eds.) *Minorities in Juvenile Justice.* Thousand Oaks, CA: Sage. Pgs. 66–97.

———. (1999) *Bad Kids: Race and the Transformation of the Juvenile Court.* New York: Oxford University Press.

Feyerherm, W. (1993) *The Status of the States: A Review of State Materials Regarding Over-Representation of Minority Youth in the Juvenile Justice System.* Portland: Portland State University.

———. (1995) "The DMC Initiative: The Convergence of Policy and Research Themes." In Kempf-Leonard, K., C. E. Pope, and W. Feyerherm (eds.) *Minorities in Juvenile Justice.* Thousand Oaks, CA: Sage. Pgs. 1–15.

———. (1996) *Disproportionate Minority Confinement: Lessons Learned from the Pilot State Experience.* Portland State University. Portland.

Fisher, G. A. and S. M. Doyle-Martin (1981) "The Effects of Ethnic Prejudice on Police Referrals to the Juvenile Court." *California Sociologist* 4: 443–453.

Fishman, M. (1978) "Crime Waves as Ideology." *Social Problems* 25: 531–543.

Flemming, R., P. Nardulli, and J. Eisenstein (1992) *The Craft of Justice: Work and Politics in Criminal Court Communities.* Philadelphia: University of Pennsylvania Press.

Foucault, M. (1965) *Madness and Civilization: A History of Insanity in the Age of Reason.* Translated from the French by Richard Howard. New York: Pantheon.

———. (1977) *Discipline and Punish: The Birth of the Prison.* Translated from the French by Alan Sheridan. New York: Pantheon.

Frank, J., S. G. Brandl, F. T. Cullen, and A. Stichman (1996) "Reassessing the Impact of Race on Citizens' Attitudes toward the Police: A Research Note." *Justice Quarterly* 13: 321–334.

Frazier, C. (1979) "Appearance, Demeanor, and Backstage Negotiations: Bases of Discretion in a First Appearance Court." *International Journal of the Sociology of Law* 7: 197–209.

Frazier, C. and D. M. Bishop (1995) "Reflections on Race Effects in Juvenile Justice." In Kempf-Leonard, K., C. E. Pope, and William Feyerherm (eds.) *Minorities in Juvenile Justice.* Thousand Oaks, CA: Sage. Pgs. 16–46.

Frazier, C., D. M. Bishop, and J. Henretta (1992) "The Social Context of Race Differentials in Juvenile Justice Dispositions." *Sociological Quarterly* 33: 447–458.

Frazier, C., P. Richards, and R. Potter (1983) "Juvenile Diversion and Net Widening: Toward a Clarification of Assessment Strategies." *Human Organization* 42: 115–121.

Gallup Report (1985) Princeton: Gallup Organization.

Gans, H. (1995). *The War Against the Poor: The Underclass and Antipoverty Policy.* New York: Basic Books.

Georges-Abeyie, D. (1990) "The Myth of A Racist Criminal Justice System?" In MacLean, B. and D. Milovanovic (eds.) *Racism, Empiricism and Criminal Justice.* Vancouver: Collective Press. Pgs. 11–14, 25–34.

Gibson, J. (1978) "Race as a Determinant of Criminal Sentences: A Methodological Critique and a Case Study." *Law and Society Review* 12: 455–478.

Gorton, J. and J. Boies (1999) "Sentencing Guidelines and Racial Disparity across Time: Pennsylvania Prison Sentences in 1977, 1983, 1992, and 1993." *Social Science Quarterly* 80: 37–54.

Gove, W., M. Hughes, and M. Geerken (1985) "Are Uniform Crime Reports a Valid Indicator of the Index Crimes? An Affirmative Answer with Minor Qualifications." *Criminology* 23: 451–501.

Grasmick, H., B. Sims Blackwell, and R. Bursik (1993) "Changes in the Sex Patterning of Perceived Threats of Sanctions." *Law and Society Review* 27: 679–705.

Griffin, P., P. Torbet, and L. Szymanski (1998) "Trying Juveniles as Adults in Criminal Court: An Analysis of State Transfer Provisions." Report to the Office of Juvenile Justice and Delinquency Prevention Pittsburgh: National Center for Juvenile Justice.

Hacker, A. (1995) *Two Nations: Black and White, Separate, Hostile, Unequal.* New York: Ballantine.

Hagan, J. (1974) "Extra-Legal Attributes and Criminal Sentencing: An Assessment of a Sociological Viewpoint." *Law and Society Review* 357–393.

———. (1977) "Criminal Justice in Urban and Rural Communities." *Social Forces* 55: 597–612.

———. (1987) "Review Essay: A Great Truth in the Study of Crime." *Criminology* 25: 421–428.

———. (1989) "Why Is There So Little Criminal Justice Theory? Neglected Macro- and Micro-Level Links between Organization and Power." *Journal of Research in Crime and Delinquency* 26: 116–1135.

Hagan, J. and C. Albonetti (1982) "Race, Class and the Perception of Criminal Injustice in America." *American Journal of Sociology* 88: 329–355.

Hagan, J. and K. Bumiller (1983) "Making Sense of Sentencing: A Review and Critique of Sentencing Research." In Blumstein, A., J. Cohen, S. Martina, and M. Tonry (eds.) *Research on Sentencing: The Search for Reform.* Vol. 2. Washington, DC: National Academy Press. Pgs. 1–54.

Hagan, J., J. D. Hewitt, and D. F. Alwin (1979) "Ceremonial Justice: Crime and Punishment in a Loosely Coupled System." *Social Forces* 58: 506–527.

Hagan, J. and B. McCarthy (1994) "Double Jeopardy: The Abuse and Punishment of Homeless Youth." In Bridges, G. and M. Myers (eds.) *Inequality, Crime, and Social Control.* Boulder: Westview Press. Pgs. 195–211.

Hagan, J. and A. Palloni (1990) "The Social Reproduction of a Criminal Class in Working-Class London circa 1950–1980." *American Journal of Sociology* 96 (2).

Hagedorn, J. M. (1994) "Homeboys, Dope Friends, Legits, and New Jacks." *Criminology* 32: 197–219.

Hamparian, D. and M. J. Leiber (1997) "Disproportionate Confinement of Minority Juveniles in Secure Facilities: 1996 National Report." Prepared for the Office of Juvenile Justice and Delinquency Prevention, Champaign, ILL, Community Research Associates.

Hamparian, D., R. Schuster, S. Dinitz, and J. Conrad. (1978) *The Violent Few: A Study of Dangerous Juvenile Offenders.* Lexington, MA: Lexington Books.

Harris, D. (1997) "Driving While Black and All Other Traffic Offenses: The Supreme Court and Pretextual Traffic Stops." *Journal of Criminal Law and Criminology* 87: 544–582.

Hasenfeld, Y., and P. Cheung (1985) "The Juvenile Court as a People-Processing Organization: A Political Economy Perspective." *American Journal of Sociology* 90: 801–824.

Hawkins, D. (1987) "Beyond Anomalies: Rethinking the Conflict Perspective on Race and Criminal Punishment." *Social Forces* 65: 719–745.

———. (1995) Ethnicity, Race, and Crime: A Review of Selected Studies. In Hawkins, D. (ed.) *Ethnicity, Race, and Crime: Perspectives across Time and Place.* Albany: State University of New York Press. Pgs. 11–45.

Hawkins, D., J. Laub, and J. Lauritsen (1998) "Race, Ethnicity, and Serious Juvenile Offending." In Loeber, R. and D. Farrington (eds.) *Serious Violent Juvenile Offenders: Risk Factors and Successful Interventions.* Beverly Hills, CA: Sage. Pgs. 30–46.

Heckman, J. (1974) "Shadow Prices, Market Wages, and Labor Supply." *Econometrica* 42: 679–694.

Heimer, K. (1995) "Gender, Race, and the Pathways to Delinquency: An Interactionist Explanation." In Hagan, J. and Ruth Peterson (eds.) *Crime and Inequality*. Stanford: Stanford University Press. Pgs. 140–173.

Hepburn, J. (1978) "Race and the Decision to Arrest: An Analysis of Warrants Issued." *Journal of Research in Crime and Delinquency* 15: 54–73.

Herrnstein, R. and C. Murray (1994) *The Bell Curve: Intelligence and Class in American Life*. New York: Free Press.

Hindelang, M. (1978) "Race and Involvement in Common Law Personal Crimes." *American Sociological Review* 43: 93–109.

Hindelang, M., T. Hirschi, and J. Weis (1981) *Measuring Delinquency*. Beverly Hills: Sage.

Hsia, H. and D. Hamparian (1998) "Disproportionate Minority Confinement: 1997 Update." Juvenile Justice Bulletin, Office of Juvenile Justice and Delinquency Prevention, September.

Huizinga, D. and D. Elliott (1987) "Juvenile Offenders: Prevalence, Offender Incidence, and Arrest Rates by Race." *Crime and Delinquency* 33: 206–223.

Humphrey, J. and T. Fogarty (1987) "Race and Plea Bargains." *Social Forces* 6: 176–182.

Humphries, D. (1999) *Crack Mothers: Pregnancy, Drugs, and the Media*. Columbus: Ohio State University.

Iowa Department of Economic Development (1990) 1990 Profile of Iowa. Iowa Department of Economic Development, Des Moines.

Iowa Juvenile Code Statute 232.29.

Irwin, J and J. Austin. (1994) *It's about Time: America's Imprisonment Binge*. Belmont, CA: Wadsworth.

Jaccard, J., R. Turrisi, and C. Wan (1990) *Interaction Effects in Multiple Regression*. Beverly Hills: Sage.

Jackson, P. (1989) *Minority Group Threat, Crime and Policing: Social Context and Social Control*. New York: Praeger.

———. (1992) "Minority Group Threat, Social Context, and Policing." In Liska, A. E. (ed.) *Social Threat and Social Control*. Albany: State University of New York Press. Pgs. 89–102.

Jackson, P. and L. Carroll (1981) "Race and the War on Crime: The Sociopolitical Determinants of Municipal Police Expenditures in 90 Non-Southern Cities." *American Sociological Review* 46: 290–305.

Jaynes, G. D. and R. M. Williams (1989) *A Common Destiny: Blacks and American Society*. Washington DC: National Academy Press.

Jencks, C. (1992) *Rethinking Social Policy: Race, Poverty, and the Underclass.* Cambridge: Harvard University Press.

Johnson, L. B. (1988) "Perspectives on Black Family Empirical Research: 1965–1978." In McAdoo, H. (ed.) *Black Families.* Newbury Park: Sage.

Jones, L. and L. Newman (1997) *Our America: Life and Death on the South Side of Chicago.* New York: Scribner.

Justice Policy Institute (2002) "Reducing Disproportionate Minority Confinement: The Multnomah County, Oregon Success Story and Its Implications." Justice Policy Institute. Washington, DC. http://www.cjcj.org/portland/portland_main.html

Juvenile Justice and Delinquency Prevention Act (1974) Section 223a(23).

———, as amended (Public Law 93–415). Section 233(a)(23).

Kempf, K. and R. Austin (1986) "Older and More Recent Evidence on Racial Discrimination in Sentencing." *Journal of Quantitative Criminology* 2: 29–47.

Kempf-Leonard, K. and H. Sontheimer (1995) "The Role of Race in Juvenile Justice in Pennsylvania." In Kempf-Leonard, K., C. E. Pope, and W. Feyerherm (eds.) *Minorities in Juvenile Justice.* Thousand Oaks, CA: Sage. Pgs. 98–127.

Kempf–Leonard, K., C. E. Pope, and W. Feyerherm (1995) *Minorities in Juvenile Justice.* Thousand Oaks, CA: Sage.

Kleck, G. (1981) "Racial Discrimination in Criminal Sentencing: A Critical Evaluation of the Evidence with Additional Evidence on the Death Penalty." *American Sociological Review* 46: 783–804.

Kluegel, J. R. and E. R. Smith (1986) *Beliefs about Equality: American's Views of What Is and What Ought to Be.* Hawthorne: Aldine de Gruyter.

Krisberg, B. (1988) Testimony before the House Subcommittee on Human Resources.

Krisberg, B., E. Currie, D. Onek, and R. G. Wiebush (1995) "Graduated Sanctions for Serious, Violent, and Chronic Juvenile Offenders." In Howell, J. C., B. Krisberg, J. D. Hawkins, and J. J. Wilson (eds.) *A Sourcebook: Serious, Violent, and Chronic Juvenile Offenders.* Thousand Oaks, CA: Sage.

Krisberg, B., I. Schwartz, G. Fishman, Z. Eisikovits, E. Guttman, and K. Joe (1987) "The Incarceration of Minority Youth." *Crime and Delinquency* 33: 173–204.

Krisberg, B., R. DeComo, and N. C. Herrera (1992) National Juvenile Custody Trends 1978–1989. Washington, DC: U.S. Department of Justice, Office of Juvenile Justice and Delinquency Prevention.

Kuker, D. (1991) "The Disproportionate Overrepresentation of Minority Youth in Secure Facilities." Paper prepared by the Department of Human Rights, Criminal and Juvenile Justice Planning Statistical Analysis Center, Des Moines.

LaFree, G. (1980) "The Effects of Sexual Stratification by Race on Official Reactions to Rape." *American Sociological Review* 45: 842–854.

———. (1985) "Official Reactions to Hispanic Defendants in the Southwest." *Journal of Research in Crime and Delinquency* 22: 213–237.

———. (1989) *Rape and Criminal Justice: The Social Construction of Sexual Assault.* Belmont, CA: Wadsworth.

Langan, P. (1985) "Racism on Trial: New Evidence to Explain the Racial Composition of Prisons in the United States." *Journal of Criminal Law and Criminology* 76: 666–683.

———. (1994) "No Racism in the Justice System." Public Interest 117: 48–51.

Leiber, M. J. (1988) "Interaction between Civil Commitment and Protective Services: A Case Study." *New England Journal on Criminal and Civil Confinement* 14: 41–64.

———. (1992a) "Juvenile Justice Decision-Making in Iowa: An Analysis of the Influences of Race on Case Processing in Three Counties: Technical Report." Des Moines: Iowa Office of Criminal and Juvenile Justice Planning.

———. (1992b) "Juvenile Justice Decision-Making in Iowa: An Analysis of the Influences of Race on Case Processing in Scott County: Technical Report." Des Moines: Iowa Office of Criminal and Juvenile Justice Planning.

———. (1992c) "Interactions between Civil Commitment and Protective Placement: An Empirical Assessment" *International Journal of Law and Psychiatry* 15: 265–281.

———. (1993) "The Disproportionate Overrepresentation of Minority Youth in Secure Facilities: A Survey of Decision-Makers and Delinquents." Prepared for the State Juvenile Advisory Group of Iowa and the Office of Criminal and Juvenile Justice Planning, Des Moines, and the Office of Juvenile Justice and Delinquency Prevention.

———. (1994) "A Comparison of Juvenile Court Outcomes for Native Americans, African Americans, and Whites." *Justice Quarterly* 11: 257–279.

———. (1995) "Toward Clarification of the Concept of 'Minority' Status and Decision Making in Juvenile Court Proceedings." *Journal of Crime and Justice* 18: 79–108.

———. (2000) "Gender, Religion, and Correctional Orientations among a Sample of Juvenile Justice Personnel." *Women and Criminal Justice* 11(2): 15–44.

———. (2002a) "Disproportionate Minority Youth Confinement (DMC): An Analysis of the Requirement and State Responses." *Crime and Delinquency.*

Leiber, M.J. and K. Mack. (2002b) "Race, Age, and Juvenile Justice Decision-Making." *Journal of Crime and Justice.* 25: 23–47.

Leiber, M. J. and A. C. Woodrick (1995) "Theoretical and Empirical Developments in the Study of Race and Juvenile Court Processing." *Social Pathology: A Journal of Reviews* 1: 149–164.

Leiber, M. J. and A. C. Woodrick (1997) "Religion, Attributional Styles, and Adherence to Correctional Orientations." *Criminal Justice and Behavior* 24: 495–511.

Leiber, M. J. and J. Stairs (1999) "Race, Contexts, and the Use of Intake Diversion." *Journal of Research in Crime and Delinquency* 36: 56–86.

Leiber, M. J. and K. Jamieson (1995) "Race and Decision-Making within Juvenile Justice: The Importance of Context." *Journal of Quantitative Criminology* 11: 363–388.

Leiber, M. J. and K. Mack (2003) "The Individual and Joint Effects of Race, Gender, and Family Status on Juvenile Justice Decision-Making." *Journal of Research in Crime and Delinquency.* 40: 34–70.

Leiber, M. J. and T. L. Mawhorr (1995) "Evaluating the Use of Social Skills Training and Employment with Delinquent Youth." *Journal of Criminal Justice* 23: 127–141.

Leiber, M. J. with K. Roth, H. Streeter, S. Federspiel, T. Engstrom, and J. Gibson (1997) "A Survey of Juvenile Justice Personnel, Parents, and Youths Concerning Services in King County, Washington, DC." Prepared for King County Department of Youth Services and Community Research Associates.

Leiber, M. J., A. C. Woodrick, and E. M. Roudebush (1995) "Religion, Discriminatory Attitudes and the Orientations of Juvenile Justice Personnel: A Research Note." *Criminology* 33: 431–449.

Leiber, M. J., E. M. Roudebush, and A. C. Woodrick (1996) "Race, Contextual Factors, and the Waiver Decision within Juvenile Court Proceedings: Preliminary Findings from a Test of The Symbolic Threat Thesis." In Lynch, M. and E. B. Patterson (eds.) *Justice with Prejudice: Race and Criminal Justice in America.* Albany: Harrow and Heston. Pgs. 49–71.

Leiber, M. J., K. Jamieson, and M. Krohn (1993) "Newspaper Reporting and the Production of Deviance: Drug Use among Professional Athletes." *Deviant Behavior* 14: 317–340.

Leiber, M. J., M. Nalla, and M. Farnworth (1998a) "Explaining Juveniles' Attitudes toward the Police." *Justice Quarterly* 15: 151–174.

Leiber, M. J., K. Sandstrom, T. Engstrom, and M. Puls. (1998b) "Crime, Drugs, Guns, and Claimsmakers: A Constructionist Analysis of Newspaper Reporting of Gang Problems in a Midwestern State." In Jensen, Eric and Jurg Gerber (eds.) *The New War on Drugs: Its Construction and Impacts on Criminal Justice Policy in North America.* Cincinnati: Anderson Publishing. Pgs. 71–90.

Leiber, M. J., K. Schwarze, K. Y. Mack, and M. Farnworth. (2002) "The Effects of Occupation and Education on Punitive Orientations among Juvenile Justice Personnel." *Journal of Criminal Justice* 30: 1–14.

Lemert, E. (1967) *Human Deviance, Social Problems, and Social Control.* Englewood Cliffs, NJ: Prentice-Hall.

Lewin, K. (1943) "Forces Behind Food Habits and Methods of Change." *Bulletin of National Resources Council* 108: 35–65.

Liazos, A. (1972) "The Poverty of Sociology of Deviance: Nuts, Sluts and Perverts." *Social Problems* 20: 103–120.

Liebow, E. (1967) *Tally's Corner: A Study of Negro Street-Corner Mom.* Boston: Little, Brown.

Liska, A. (1987) "A Critical Examination of Macro Perspectives on Crime Control." *Annual Review of Sociology* 13: 67–88.

Liska, A. (1992) *Social Threat and Social Control.* Albany: State University of New York Press.

———. (1994) "Modeling the Conflict Perspective of Social Control." In Bridges, George and Martha Myers (eds.) *Inequality, Crime, and Social Control.* Boulder: Westview Press. Pgs. 53–71.

Liska, A. and M. Chamlin (1984) "Social Structure and Crime Control among Macrosocial Units." *American Journal of Sociology* 90: 383–395.

Liska, A., M. Chamlin, and M. Reed (1985) "Testing the Economic Production and Conflict Models of Crime Control." *Social Forces* 64: 119–138.

Lizotte, A., J. Mercy, and E. Monkkonen (1982) "Crime and Police Strength in an Urban Setting: Chicago, 1947–1970." In Hagan, J. (ed.) *Quantitative Criminology: Innovations and Applications.* Beverly Hills: Sage. Pgs. 129–148.

Lugaila, T. (1998) Marital Status and Living Arrangements: March 1998 (Update). U.S. Census Bureau Current Population Survey Report P20–514. Washington DC: U.S. Government Printing Office.

Lynch, M. (1990) "Racial Bias and Criminal Justice: Definitional and Methodological Issues." In MacLean, B. and D. Milovanovic (eds.) *Racism, Empiricism and Criminal Justice.* Vancouver: Collective Press. Pgs. 35–42.

Lynch, M. and B. Groves (1989) *A Primer in Radical Criminology.* Albany: Harrow and Heston.

MacLean, B. and D. Milovanovic (1990) "The Anatomy of the No Discrimination Thesis." In MacLean, B. and D. Milovanovic (eds.) *Racism, Empiricism and Criminal Justice.* Vancouver: Collective Press. Pgs. 1–2.

Maguire, K. and A. L. Pastore (eds.) (1998) *Sourcebook of Criminal Justice Statistics 1997.* U.S. Department of Justice, Bureau of Justice Statistics. Washington DC: U.S. Government Printing Office.

Mann, C. and M. Zatz (1998) *Images of Color, Images of Crime.* Los Angeles: Roxbury Publishing Company.

Mann, C. R. (1984) "Race and Sentencing of Women Felons: A Field Study." *International Journal of Women's Studies* 7: 160–172.

———. (1989) "Minority and Female: A Critical Justice Double Bind." *Social Justice* 16: 95–114.

———. (1993) *Unequal Justice: A Question of Color.* Bloomington: Indiana University Press.

———. (1994) "A Minority View of Juvenile 'Justice'" *Washington and Lee Law Review* 51: 465–478.

Massey, D. and N. Denton (1993) *American Apartheid: Segregation and the Making of the Underclass.* Cambridge: Harvard University Press.

Matza, D. (1964) *Delinquency and Drift.* New York: Wiley.

Mauer, M. (1995) *Young Black Americans and the Criminal Justice System: Five Years Later.* Washington, DC: Sentencing Project.

Maynard, D. (1982) "Defendant Attributes in Plea Bargaining: Notes on the Modeling of Sentencing Decisions." *Social Problems* 29: 347–360.

Maynard, R. A. and E. M. Garry (1997) "Adolescent Motherhood: Implications for the Juvenile Justice System." Report of the Office of Juvenile Justice and Delinquency Prevention. Fact Sheet #50.

McCarthy, B. and B. Smith (1986) "The Conceptualization of Discrimination in the Juvenile Justice Process: The Impact of Administrative Factors and Screening Decisions of Juvenile Court Decisions." *Criminology* 24: 41–64.

McCleary, R., B. Nienstedt, and J. Erven (1982) "Uniform Crime Reports as Organizational Outcomes: Three Time Series Experiments." *Social Problems* 29(4): 361–372.

McDowall, D. and C. Loftin (1992) "Comparing the UCR and NCS Over Time." *Criminology* 30: 125–132.

McGarrel, E. (1993) "Trends in Racial Disproportionality in Juvenile Court Processing: 1985–1989." *Crime and Delinquency* 39: 29–48.

McLanahan, S. (1985) "Family Structure and the Reproduction of Poverty." *American Journal of Sociology* 90: 873–901.

McNeely, R. L. and C. E. Pope (1978) "Race and Involvement in Common Law Personal Crime: A Response to Hindelang." *Review of Black Political Economy.* 8: 405–410.

McNeely, R. L. and C. E. Pope (1981) *Race, Crime, and Criminal Justice.* Beverly Hills: Sage.

Mears, D. (1998) "The Sociology of Sentencing: Reconceptualizing Decision-Making Processes and Outcomes." *Law and Society Review* 32: 667–724.

Melossi, D. (1985) "Overcoming the Crisis in Critical *Criminology*: Toward a Grounded Labeling Theory." *Criminology* 23: 193–208.

Merlo, A. (2000) "Presidential Address-Juvenile Justice at the Crossroads." Presented to the Academy of Criminal Justice Science. Justice Quarterly 17: 639–661.

Merton, R. (1957) *Social Theory and Social Structure.* Glencoe, IL: Free Press.

Miethe, T. and C. Moore (1985) "Socioeconomic Disparities under Determinate Sentencing Systems: A Comparison of Preguideline and Postguideline Practices in Minnesota." *Criminology* 23: 337–363.

———. (1986) "Racial Differences in Criminal Processing: The Consequences of Model Selection on Conclusions about Differential Treatment." *Sociological Quarterly* 27: 217–237.

Miller, J. (1996) *Search and Destroy.* Cambridge: Cambridge University Press.

Miller, W. (1958) "Lower Class Culture as a Generating Milieu for Gang Delinquency." *Journal of Social Issues* 14(3): 5–19.

Moffitt, R. A. (1995) "The Effect of the Welfare System on Nonmarital Childbearing." In *Report to Congress on Out-of-Wedlock Childbearing.* Hyattsville, MD: U.S. Department of Health and Human Services. Pgs. 167–176.

Montgomery, I. M., P. M. Torbet, D. A. Malloy, L. P. Adamcik, M. J. Toner, and J. Andrews (1994) *What Works: Promising Interventions in Juvenile Justice.* Washington, DC: U.S. Department of Justice, Office of Juvenile Justice and Delinquency Prevention.

Molgaard, V., R. Spoth, and C. Redmond. 2000. "Competency Training Families Program: For Parents and Youth 10–14." 2000 National Report Series Juvenile Justice Bulletin. Washington, DC: U.S. Department of Justice, Office of Juvenile Justice and Delinquency Prevention.

Moon, M. M., J. L. Sundt, F. T. Cullen, and J. P. Wright (2000) "Is Child Saving Dead? Public Support for Juvenile Rehabilitation." *Crime and Delinquency* 46: 38–60.

Moore, R. and D. Kuker (1993) "A Description and Discussion of Minority Overrepresentation in Iowa's Juvenile Justice System." Paper prepared by the Division of Criminal and Juvenile Justice Planning, Des Moines.

Morton, P. (1991) *Disfigured Images: The Historical Assault on Afro-American Women.* New York: Praeger.

Moynihan, D. (1965) *The Negro Family: The Case for National Action.* Washington, DC: U.S. Department of Labor, Office of Policy Planning and Research.

Murray, C. (1984) *Losing Ground: American Social Policy, 1950–1980.* New York: Basic.

Muzzatti, S. (2003) "Labeling Theory and Cultural Criminology: The Case of Marilyn Manson." *Moral Crusades.* New York: Peter Lang Publishing.

Mydral, G. (1944) *An American Dilemma: The Negro Problem and Modern Democracy.* New York: Harper and Brothers.

Myers, M. (1979) "Offended Parties and Official Reactions: Victims and the Sentencing of Criminal Defendants." *Sociological Quarterly* 20: 529–540.

———. (1988) "Social Background and the Sentencing Behavior of Judges." *Criminology* 26: 649–675.

———. (1989) "Symbolic Policy and the Sentencing of Drug Offenders." *Law and Society* 23: 295.

Myers, M. and S. Talarico (1986a) "The Social Contexts of Racial Discrimination in Sentencing." *Social Problems* 33: 236–251.

Myers, M. and S. Talarico (1986b) "Urban Justice, Rural Injustice? Urbanization and Its Effect on Sentencing." *Criminology* 24: 367–392.

Myers, M. and S. Talarico (1987) *The Social Contexts of Criminal Sentencing.* New York: Springer-Verlag.

Nagin, D. and R. Patternoster (1991) "On the Relationship of Past and Future Participation in Delinquency" *Criminology* 29: 163–190.

Nalla, M., M. Lynch, and M. J. Leiber (1997) "Determinants of Police Growth in Phoenix, 1950–1988." *Justice Quarterly* 14: 115–143.

O'Brien, R. (1985) *Crime and Victimization Data.* Beverly Hills: Sage.

Odem, M. (1995) *Delinquent Daughters: Protecting and Policing Adolescent Female Sexuality in the United States, 1885–1920.* Chapel Hill: University of North Carolina Press.

Office of Juvenile Justice and Delinquency Prevention (OJJDP) (1998) Distribution of Formula Grants by State—FY 1998.

Omi, M. and H. Winant (1986) *Racial Formation in the United States: From the 1960s to the 1980s.* New York: Routledge & Kegan Paul.

Orlando, F. (1998) "Controlling the Front Gates: Effective Admissions Policies and Practices." Working draft. In *Pathways to Juvenile Detention Reform.* Vol. 3. Baltimore: Annie E. Casey Foundation.

Packer, H. (1968) *The Limits of the Criminal Sanction.* Palo Alto: Stanford University Press.

Paternoster, R. and L. Iovanni (1989) "The Labeling Perspective and Delinquency: An Elaboration of the Theory and Assessment of the Evidence." *Justice Quarterly* 6: 359–394.

Peeples, F. and R. Loeber (1994) "Do Individual Factors and Neighborhood Context Explain Ethnic Differences in Juvenile Delinquency?" *Journal of Quantitative Criminology* 10: 141–157.

Petersilia, J. (1980) "Criminal Career Research: A Review of Recent Evidence." *Crime and Justice: An Annual Review of Research* 2: 321–379.

———. (1983) *Racial Disparities in the Criminal Justice System.* Santa Monica: Rand.

———. (1985) "Racial Disparities in the Criminal Justice System: A Summary." *Crime and Delinquency* 31: 15–34.

Peterson, R. and J. Hagan (1984) "Changing Conceptions of Race: Towards an Account of Anomalous Findings of Sentencing Research." *American Sociological Review* 49: 56–70.

Peterson, T. (1985) A Comment on Presenting Results from Logit and Probit Models." *American Sociological Review* 50: 130–131.

Piliavin, I. and S. Briar (1964) "Police Encounters with Juveniles." *American Journal of Sociology* 70: 206–214.

Piven, F. and Cloward, R. (1971) *Regulating the Poor: The Functions of Public Welfare.* New York: Vintage Books.

Platt, A. (1969) *The Child Savers.* Chicago: University of Chicago Press.

Pope, C. E. (1976) "The Influence of Social and Legal Factors on Sentence Disposi-tions: A Preliminary Analysis of Offender Based Transaction Statistics." *Journal of Criminal Justice* 4: 203–221.

———. (1978) "Post-Arrest Release Decisions: An Empirical Examination of Social and Legal Criteria." *Journal of Research in Crime and Delinquency* 15: 35–53.

———. (1979) "Race and Crime Revisited." *Crime and Delinquency* 25: 347–357.

———. (1984) "Blacks and Juvenile Crime: A Review." In Georges–Abeyie, D. (ed.) *The Criminal Justice System and Blacks.* New York: Clark Boardman Company.

———. (1995) "Equality within the Juvenile Justice System: Directions for the Future." In Kempf-Leonard, K., C. E. Pope, and W. Feyerherm (eds.) *Minorities in Juvenile Justice.* Thousand Oaks, CA: Sage. Pgs 201–216.

Pope, C. E., R. Lovell and H. Hsia (2001) "Synthesis of Disproportionate Minority Confinement (DMC) Literature (1989–1999)." Washington, DC: U.S. Department of Justice. Office of Juvenile Justice and Delinquency Prevention.

Pope, C. E. and M. J. Leiber (2003) "Disproportionate Minority Confinement (DMC): The Federal Initiative." Darnell Hawkins and Kimberly Kempf-Leonard (eds.) *Race, Development, and Juvenile Justice.* MacArthur Foundation Research Network on Ado-lescent Development and Juvenile Justice. John T. and Catherine MacArthur Foun-dation. University of Chicago Press.

Pope, C.E. and H.N. Snyder (2003) "Race as a Factor in Juvenile Arrests." *Juvenile Jus-tice Bulletin* (April). Washington, DC: U.S. Department of Justice. Office of Juvenile Justice and Delinquency Prevention.

Pope, C. E. and W. Feyerherm (1990) "Minority Status and Juvenile Justice Processing: An Assessment of the Research Literature (Parts I and II)." *Criminal Justice Abstracts* June, 327–385; September, 527–542.

Pope, C. E. and W. Feyerherm (1992) *Minorities and the Juvenile Justice System: Full Re-port.* Rockville: U.S. Department of Justice. Office of Juvenile Justice and Delin-quency Prevention, Juvenile Justice Clearing House.

Pope, C. E. and W. Feyerherm (1993) "Minorities and the Juvenile Justice System: Research Summary." Office of Juvenile Justice and Delinquency Prevention.

Popper, K. (1968) *The Logic of Scientific Knowledge.* Chicago: University of Chicago Press.

Puritz, P. and W. Wan Long Shang (1988) "Innovative Approaches to Juvenile Indigent Defense." *Juvenile Justice Bulletin,* Office of Juvenile Justice and Delinquency Prevention, December 1998.

Quillian. L. (1996) "Group Threat and Regional Change in Attitudes toward African-Americans." *American Journal of Sociology* 102: 816–860.

Quinney, R. (1970) *The Social Reality of Crime.* Boston: Little, Brown.

Rhoden, E. (1994) "Disproportionate Minority Representation: First Steps to a Solution." *Juvenile Justice* 2: 9–14.

Rome, D. M. (1998) "Stereotyping by the Media: Murderers, Rapists, and Drug Addicts." In Mann, C. R. and M. S. Zatz (eds.) *Images of Color, Images of Crime.* Los Angeles: Roxbury. Pgs. 85–96.

Roscoe, M. and R. Morton (1994) "Disproportionate Minority Confinement." Office of Juvenile Justice and Delinquency Prevention. Fact Sheet #11.

Rubin, T. (1985) *Juvenile Justice: Policy, Practice, and Law. 2d ed.* New York: Random.

———. (2001) "A Community Imperative: Curbing Minority Overrepresentation in the Juvenile Justice System." *Juvenile Justice Update* 7(2): 1, 2, 14–16.

Sampson, R. (1986) "Effects of Socioeconomic Context on Official Reaction to Juvenile Delinquency." *American Sociological Review* 51: 876–885.

———. (1987) "Urban Black Violence: The Effect of Male Joblessness and Family Disruption." *American Journal of Sociology* 93: 348–382.

Sampson, R. and D. Bartusch (1999) "Attitudes Toward Crime, Police, and the Law: Individual and Neighborhood Differences." Summary Report to the National Institute of Justice Research Preview, June.

Sampson, R. and J. Laub (1993) "Structural Variations in Juvenile Court Processings: Inequality, the Underclass, and Social Control." *Law and Society Review* 27: 285–311.

Sampson, R. and J. Lauritsen (1997) "Racial and Ethnic Disparities in Crime and Criminal Justice in the United States." In Tonry, M. (ed.) *Ethnicity, Crime and Immigration: Comparative and Cross-National Perspectives.* Chicago: University of Chicago Press. Pgs. 311–374.

Sampson, R. and W. J. Wilson (1995) "Toward a Theory of Race, Crimes, and Urban Inequality." In Hagan, J. and R. Peterson (eds.) *Crime and Inequality.* Stanford: Stanford University Press.

Sanborn, J. B. Jr. (1996) "Factors Perceived to Affect Delinquent Dispositions in Juvenile Court: Putting the Sentencing Decision into Context." *Crime and Delinquency* 42: 99–113.

Schlossman, S. (1977) *Love and the American Delinquent: The Theory and Practice of "Progressive" Juvenile Justice.* Chicago: University of Chicago Press.

Schwartz, I. (1989) *(In)Justice for Juveniles: Rethinking the Best Interest of the Child.* Lexington: Lexington Books

Schwartz, Ira. (1986) Testimony before the House Subcommittee on Human Resources.

Sentencing Project (2000) Facts and Prisons and Prisoners. Washington, DC.

Sherman, L., D. Gottfredson, D. MacKenzie, J. Eck, P. Reuter, and S. Bushway (1997) "Preventing Crime: What Works, What Doesn't, What's Promising." Office of Justice Programs Research Report.

Sickmund, M., H. Snyder, and E. Poe-Yamagata (1997) *Juvenile Offenders and Victims: 1997 Update on Violence.* Washington, DC: Office of Juvenile Justice and Delinquency Prevention.

Singer, Simon (1997) *Recriminalizing Delinquency: Violent Juvenile Crime and Juvenile Justice Reform.* New York: Cambridge University Press.

Snyder, H. (1990) *Growth in Minority Detentions Attributed to Drug Law Violators.* Washington, DC: U.S. Department of Justice, Office of Juvenile Justice and Delinquency Prevention.

Snyder, H. and M. Sickmund (1995) *Juvenile Offenders and Victims: A National Report.* Washington, DC: Office of Juvenile Justice and Delinquency Prevention.

Snyder, H. and M. Sickmund (1999) *Juvenile Offenders and Victims: A National Report.* Washington, DC: Office of Juvenile Justice and Delinquency Prevention.

Spitzer, S. (1975) "Toward a Marxian Theory of Deviance." *Social Problems* 22: 638–651.

Spohn, C. and D. Holleran. (2000) "The Imprisonment Penalty Paid by Young, Unemployed Black and Hispanic Male Offenders." *Criminology* 38: 281–206.

Spohn, C., J. Gruhl, and S. Welsh (1980–1981) "The Effect of Race on Sentencing Disparities: A Reexamination of an Unsettled Question." *Law and Sociology Review* 16: 71–88.

Stahl, A. (1999) "Delinquency Cases Waived to Criminal Court, 1987–1996." Report to the Office of Juvenile Justice and Delinquency Prevention. Fact Sheet # 99. April.

Stapleton, V., D. Aday, and J. Ito (1982) "An Empirical Typology of American Metropolitan Juvenile Courts." *American Journal of Sociology* 88: 549–564.

Steffensmeier, D. and S. Demuth (2001) "Ethnicity and Judges' Sentencing Decisions: Hispanic-Black-White Comparisons." *Criminology* 39: 145–178.

Steffensmeier, D., J. Ulmer, and J. Kramer (1998) "The Interaction of Race, Gender, and Age in Criminal Sentencing: The Punishment Cost of Being Young, Black, and Male." *Criminology* 36: 763–798.

Stolzenberg, R. and D. Relles (1990) "Theory Testing in a World of Constrained Research Design." *Sociological Methods Research* 18: 395–415.

Sudnow, D. (1965) "Normal Crimes: Sociological Features of the Pearl Code in the Public Defender's Office." *Social Problems* 12: 255–277.

Suttles, G. (1968) *The Social Order of the Slum: Ethnicity and Territory in the Inner City.* Chicago: University of Chicago Press.

Sutton, J. (1988) *Stubborn Children: Controlling Delinquency in the United States 1640–1981.* Berkeley: University of California Press.

———. (1994) "Children in the Therapeutic State: Lessons for the Sociology of Deviance and Social Control." In Bridges, G. and M. Myers (eds.) *Inequality, Crime, and Social Control.* Boulder: Westview Press. Pgs. 227–248.

Swigert, V. and R. Farrell (1977) "Normal Homicides and the Law. *American Sociological Review* 42 (February): 16–32.

Tauke (1987) Hearing before the House Subcommittee on Human Resources.

Taylor, D. (2000) "Cultural Mistrust and Racial Divides." *Social Pathology* 6: 199–212.

Taylor, I., P. Walton, and J. Young (1973) *The New Criminology: For Social Theory of Deviance.* New York: Harper.

Thornberry, T. (1979) "Sentencing Disparities in the Juvenile Justice System." *Journal of Law and Criminology* 64: 163–171.

Thornberry, T., M. Farnworth, M. Krohn, and A. Lizotte (1999) "Measurement in the Study of Class and Delinquency: Integrating Theory and Research." *Journal of Research in Crime and Delinquency* 31: 32–61.

Tittle, C. (1980) "Labeling and Crime: An Empirical Evaluation." In Walter R. Gove (ed.), *The Labeling of Deviance. 2d ed.* Beverly Hills: Sage. Pgs. 241–263.

———. (1994) "The Theoretical Cases for Inequality in Formal Social Controls." In Bridges, G. and M. Myers (eds.) *Inequality, Crime, and Social Control.* Boulder: Westview Press. Pgs. 21–52.

Tittle, C. and D. Curran (1988) "Contingencies for Dispositional Disparities in Juvenile Justice." *Social Forces* 67: 23–58.

Tolnay, S., E. M. Beck, and J. Massey (1989) "Black Lynchings: The Power Threat Hypothesis Revisited." *Social Forces* 67: 605–623.

Tonry, M. (1995) *Malign Neglect: Race, Crime and Punishment in America.* New York: Oxford University Press.

Torbet, P. and L. Szymanski (1998) *State Legislative Responses to Violent Juvenile Crime: 1996–1997 update.* Washington, DC: Office of Juvenile Justice and Delinquency Prevention.

Triplett, R. (2000) "The Dramatization of Evil: Reacting to Juvenile Delinquency during the 1990's." In S. S. Simpson (ed.) *Of Crime and Criminality.* Thousand Oaks, CA: Pine Forge.

Turk, A. (1969) *Criminality and Legal Order.* Chicago: Rand McNally.

Ulmer, J. (1995) "The Organization and Consequences of Social Pasts in Criminal Courts." *Sociological Quarterly* 36: 587–605.

———. (1997) *Social Worlds of Sentencing: Court Communities under Sentencing Guidelines*. Albany: State University of New York Press.

Ulmer, J. and J. Kramer (1996) "Court Communities under Sentencing Guidelines: Dilemmas of Formal Rationality and Sentencing Disparity." *Criminology* 34: 383–708.

Weber, M. (1969) *Max Weber on Law in Economy and Society*. Translated by Rheinstein, M. Cambridge: Harvard University Press.

Weitzer, R. and Tuch, S. (1999) "Race, Class, and Perceptions of Discrimination by the Police." *Crime and Delinquency* 45: 494–507.

Welch, S. C. Spohn, and J. Gruhl (1985) "Convicting and Sentencing: Differences among Black, Hispanic and White Males in Six Localities." *Justice Quarterly* 2: 67–77.

Welsh, W. N., P. W. Harris, and P. H. Jenkins (1996) "Reducing Overrepresentation of Minorities in Juvenile Justice: Development of Community-Based Programs in Pennsylvania." *Crime and Delinquency* 42: 76–98.

Welsh, W. N., P. H. Jenkins, and P. W. Harris (1999) "Reducing Minority Overrepresentation in Juvenile Justice: Results of Community-Based Delinquency." *Journal of Research in Crime and Delinquency* 36: 87–110.

West, C. (1993) *Race Matters*. New York: Vintage Books.

Wilbanks, W. (1987) *The Myth of a Racist Criminal Justice System*. Monterey: Brooks/Cole Publishing Company.

———. (1990a) "The Myth of a Racist Criminal Justice System." In Maclean, B. and D. Milovanovic (eds.) *Racism, Empiricism and Criminal Justice*. Vancouver: Collective Press. Pgs. 5–10.

———. (1990b) "Response to The Critics of the Myth of a Racist Criminal Justice System." In Maclean, B. and D. Milovanovic (eds.) *Racism, Empiricism and Criminal Justice*. Vancouver: Collective Press. Pgs. 21–24.

Willie, C. F. (1991) *A New Look at Black Families*. 4th ed. New York: General Hall.

Wilson, W. (1987) *The Truly Disadvantaged: The Inner City, the Underclass, and Public Policy*. Chicago: University of Chicago Press.

———. (1996) *When Work Disappears: The World of the New Urban Poor*. New York: Knopf.

Wolfgang, M. and F. Ferracuti (1967) *The Subculture of Violence: Towards an Integrated Theory in Criminology*. Beverly Hills: Sage.

Wolfgang, M., R. Figlio, and T. Sellin (1972) *Delinquency in a Birth Cohort*. Chicago: University of Chicago Press.

Zatz, M. (1984) "Race, Ethnicity and Determinate Sentencing: A New Dimension to an Old Controversy." *Criminology* 22: 147–171.

———. (1987a) "The Changing Forms of Racial/Ethnic Biases in Sentencing." *Journal of Research in Crime and Delinquency* 24: 69–92.

———. (1987b) "Chicano Youth Gangs and Crime: The Creation of a Moral Panic." *Contemporary Crises* 11: 129–158.

———. (1990) "A Question of Assumptions." In MacLean, B. and D. Milovanovic (eds.) *Racism, Empiricism and Criminal Justice*. Vancouver: Collective Press. Pgs. 113–120.

Ziedenberg, J. (2001) *Drugs and Disparity: The Racial Impact of Illinois' Practice of Transferring Young Drug Offenders to Adult Court*. Washington, DC: Building Blocks for Youth.

Index

Index